'Parkes provides a sophisticated, theoretically grounded yet practical approach to drama pedagogy. She guides the reader through an exciting exploration of German dramatic genres and specific works, ranging from canonical to black-box pieces that can be employed across the entire curriculum. Both novices unfamiliar with German-language theatre and experts in the field will benefit from Parkes's insightful and highly original contribution.'

Professor Glenn Levine, *University of California, Irvine*

Spielraum: Teaching German through Theater

Spielraum: Teaching German through Theater is a sourcebook and guide for teaching German language and culture, as well as social, cross-cultural, and multi-ethnic tensions, through dramatic texts. This book presents a range of theoretical and practical resources for the growing number of teachers who wish to integrate drama and theater into their foreign-language curriculum. As such, it may be adopted as a flexible tool for teachers seeking ways to reinvigorate their language classrooms through drama pedagogy; to connect language study to the study of literature and culture; or to embark on full-scale theater productions.

Focusing on specific dramatic works from the rich German-speaking tradition, each chapter introduces unique approaches to a play, theme, and genre, while also taking into account practical issues of performance.

Lisa Parkes is a senior lecturer and director of the German Language Program at Harvard University.

Spielraum: Teaching German through Theater

Lisa Parkes

Routledge
Taylor & Francis Group

LONDON AND NEW YORK

First published 2022
by Routledge
2 Park Square, Milton Park, Abingdon, Oxon OX14 4RN

and by Routledge
605 Third Avenue, New York, NY 10158

Routledge is an imprint of the Taylor & Francis Group, an informa business

© 2022 Lisa Parkes

British Library Cataloguing-in-Publication Data
A catalogue record for this book is available from the British Library

Library of Congress Cataloging-in-Publication Data
Names: Parkes, Lisa, author.
Title: Spielraum : teaching German through theater / Lisa Parkes.
Description: Abingdon, Oxon ; New York : Routledge, 2022. |
Includes bibliographical references and index. |
Identifiers: LCCN 2021020277 (print) | LCCN 2021020278 (ebook) |
ISBN 9780367445478 (hardback) | ISBN 9780367445461 (paperback) |
ISBN 9781003010289 (ebook)
Subjects: LCSH: German language--Study and teaching--Foreign speakers. | Drama in education.
Classification: LCC PF3065 .P37 2022 (print) | LCC PF3065 (ebook) |
DDC 438.0071--dc23
LC record available at https://lccn.loc.gov/2021020277
LC ebook record available at https://lccn.loc.gov/2021020278

ISBN: 978-0-367-44547-8 (hbk)
ISBN: 978-0-367-44546-1 (pbk)
ISBN: 978-1-003-01028-9 (ebk)

DOI: 10.4324/9781003010289

Typeset in Times New Roman
by MPS Limited, Dehradun

Contents

Acknowledgments

If there were ever a time for reflection on estrangement and the alienating effects of mask-wearing, for making sense of social injustice, for responding to political polarities, for defamiliarizing the curriculum and rechoreographing the classroom towards critical engagement, then the global COVID-19 pandemic of 2020–21 has been it. But it has also been a time, for many of us, of social isolation; for others, of enforced family overtime; and for everyone, a time bereft of in-person teaching or performance. All of this has prompted a reappraisal of both the educational and performance institutions as we ventured on to "remote" online venues. The shift has forced everyone to consider the potential and limitations of different spaces, virtual or other, for community, interaction, and learning, and has reinforced many of the arguments presented in this book. Although written almost entirely during this period of social isolation, however, this book represents a much longer period of social and pedagogical engagement. And it is to the many individuals with whom I have collaborated – students, colleagues, friends, and family – that this book is indebted and dedicated.

I am indebted first of all to the many colleagues and friends for their support over the years: to Harvard's library staff, for finding ways to make so much material available during the pandemic; to Martin Bäumel, Ian Fleishman, Thomas Herold, Yvonne Ivory, Glenn Levine, Ursula Lindqvist, David Pister, Dominica Radulescu, Judith Ryan, Barbara Schmenk, Andrea Speltz, Tin Wegel, Christopher Wild, and Peng Xu for the ongoing exchange of ideas; to Bettina Matthias, whose inspirational theater and opera productions one can but hope to emulate; to Brenna Byrd, for giving me the initial nudge in 2004 to embark on a full production of Büchner's *Leonce und Lena*; to Pascale LaFountain, for giving me the courage to tackle Erpulat's *Verrücktes Blut*; to Robert Vilain, for putting me on to Goll's *Die Chapliniade*; to Mark Römisch, for his extremely helpful acting workshops; to Donna van Handle, for her years of dedication to the Mount Holyoke Deutsches Theaterfest; to Richard Bergin, for all the years of filming, last-minute ingenious solutions, support and heavy lifting; and to Ted Bahr and Jill Kowalik, in whose memory this book is written, for their enduring mentorship. I am also grateful to the many audience members, whose unflagging support over the years – from schlepping through the snow in Massachusetts or sitting on sodden grass after an almost-unheard-of rainfall in Los Angeles, not to mention their admirable *Sitzfleisch* – has made it all worthwhile. Of course, none of the productions would have been possible without the students at UCLA and Harvard, whose commendable talent, courage, and hard work brought so many plays to life in so many spaces – from lecture halls, theaters, museum spaces, and outdoor amphitheaters at UCLA, to the "Pool" theater at Harvard.

Last, but not least, I am indebted to my family for their long-distant but limitless support, to my siblings, Adam and Clare, for their attentiveness and encouragement over the years, and in particular to my ever-supporting parents, Margaret and David, whose own performing adventures set the scene early on; and to John Hamilton, without whose emotional, musical, and intellectual sustenance none of the lines in this book would have been possible.

Vorspiel: prelude

Einbildung and *Ausbildung*: a renewed case for integrating drama in the foreign-language classroom

When Goethe's Faust returns from a restorative Easter Morning promenade to his cramped Gothic study, he turns to the Gospel of John in search of renewed inspiration. Having despaired over the futility of his bookish existence, he has already decided to abandon his study of academic disciplines – those of philosophy, law, medicine, and, unfortunately, also theology. He longs instead for a direct experience with the sacred Word, and turns to the Bible itself, bypassing the academic intermediaries, to set about the task of interpreting the first line of the Gospel. Just like his contemporary Martin Luther, he translates it thus: "Im Anfang war das Wort!" Unlike Luther, however, Faust is dissatisfied: The word "word" strikes Faust as deficient; it cannot possibly capture the various possible connotations of the Greek *logos*: "Ich kann das Wort so hoch unmöglich schätzen, / Ich muß es anders übersetzen" (1226–7). This frustration drives Faust through a series of attempts to find a more satisfactory alternative for *das Wort*. Having dismissed "word" (*Wort*), "sense" (*Sinn*), and "power" (*Kraft*) as equally powerless in capturing the idea of divine creation, his fourth and final translation seems to hit the mark. Moving from *das Wort* to *die Tat* (or from "word" to "deed"), Faust is at once relieved of his frustration:[1] "Im Anfang war die *Tat!*"

The move in translation from word to *deed* is revealing on several levels. First, Faust's frustration with words is an expression of his desire to break with conventional wisdom: To imitate Luther's orthodox translation from Greek to German would mean to remain uncritically bound to the very tradition from which he desperately seeks to escape. Despite having gained an academic masters, and even a doctorate, Faust now stands, as before, *ein armer Tor*, none the wiser, merely dragging his students "up, down, across, and astray." He has exhausted all intellectual endeavors and yet acknowledges that we "cannot know anything." Such accumulation and storage of pre-existing knowledge transmitted through words – such as those in Luther's translation of the Bible – within the dark confines of his study has little revelatory or enlightening promise, but rather stifles critical thought and creative imagination.

DOI: 10.4324/9781003010289-101

The reason, Faust maintains, is that his desire for revelation (*Offenbarung*, 1217) remains obscured by language and that, far from penetrating the inner mysteries of the universe, he has been rummaging around what seem to have been empty words (382–3). In other words, words are just words, of which Faust has grown weary. By instead invoking "deeds," Faust articulates his desire for a direct experience of the world through action. Deeds (*Taten*) recall the ancient Dorian verb *dran*, which, according to Aristotle, gives us the word *drama*. Aristotle thus suggests that drama is praxis – a doing, an acting, a performing (*Poetics* 1, 1448b, 36–7). Until now, Faust's conception of language is one that merely *represents* deeds that precede it; until now, he has conceived of words as mere descriptions of a world that already exists. However, precisely in his struggle to translate from Greek to German, Faust would seem to be undermining such a conception of language. For, in moving from word to sense, power, and deed, he discovers that there is no necessary one-to-one equivalence between the foreign language and his own, or indeed a natural relation between language and its alleged referent. Thus, in his moment of self-questioning, Faust has hit upon a hermeneutical conundrum regarding the meaning of language: namely, the representational and the performative role of language – a question also raised by the Gospel itself. If God's Word in-deed summoned the world into existence, then the Biblical narrative also suggests a performative paradigm of language. Such a paradigm proposes that language existed *a priori*, before the beginning, and that God's word constituted the first speech act – or doing "things with words" (Austin). The performative is distinguished from the constative thus: The former, as an action, deed, performance, assumes a productive function that creates reality; the latter, as a denotation, assumes a purely representational function for a preexisting reality.

Understood as performative, language need not obfuscate; rather, language becomes dynamic and disclosive, and Faust's initial disillusionment with the word "word" may be overcome: By resituating language within a dynamic relation to deeds, the distinction between the two becomes blurred; words in action unfold over time and thus resist fixed denotation, enacting instead new meaning and experiences. Words, then, are not just words. Faust's translation of the Gospel is an illustrative case in point. He now rejects the compulsion to accept the world through pre-existing knowledge and instead challenges it, interrogates its meaning, negates it, and *imagines* something new. In this way, language discloses something to Faust about the mysteries of the universe and responds to his desire for revelation.

Most significantly, however, the disclosive moment for Faust is prompted by his encounter with a foreign language. By reinterpreting the first line of the Gospel, Faust demonstrates that a linguistic and cultural gap demands a different conception of language, one that reveals a whole range of interpretive possibilities that might otherwise not have been apparent. This encounter with the foreign language forces him to negate, critique, and reinterpret the world he now realizes he did not know at all. In this sense, the word assumes a creative force, just as God's Word in-deed summoned the world into existence. Faust is not interested in religious faith in any sense, however, but rather the negation of blind acceptance of such. Hence the appearance of Mephisto, who has been waiting restlessly in the wings, precisely at this disclosive moment. If the Word is to become flesh, as per the Gospel, then the Devil Incarnate, Mephisto, incarnates the word negatively. As the ensuing exchange with Mephisto confirms, Faust vehemently rejects blind faith and uncritical fact-finding (*Wissensaneignung*) in favor of enlightened critical interrogation. The encounter with the foreign language constitutes the moment of realization, in fact, that such self-examination and critical thought are not only possible, but desirable. His ensuing pact with Mephisto seals his allegiance to this new perspective on the world.

This moment of linguistic translation in Goethe's *Faust* constitutes a moment of critical thought and creative imagination. As we have seen, critical thought demands a negation of pre-existing knowledge of the world. Through Mephisto, the negative assumes a productive function, both on the level of Faust's striving for knowledge, and in terms of the dramatic unfolding of Goethe's play. The *Vorspiel auf dem Theater* that precedes the dramatic action anticipates precisely this tension in the discussion between the Director, the Poet, and the Comic Actor (*lustige Person*), who rehearse the same tensions between words and deeds: The Director, concerned primarily with crowd-pleasing for short-term profit, stresses the importance of action in the real world; the Poet, concerned primarily about poetic compromise in the face of crowd-pleasing, stresses the ideal of genuine poetry, not for short-term profit, but for posterity. Resolving these tensions is the *lustige Person,* who mediates between the Director's realism and the Poet's idealism by treating poetry like a love affair that develops not by adherence to poetic rules that ignore dynamism, but rather organically. In other words, the *lustige Person* wants to breathe organic life back into drama, which has been stifled by poetic rules inherited from tradition – a critical nod to the unpopular *Literaturpapst* Johann Christoph Gottsched, who banned the popular *Hanswurst* figure from the German stage in steadfast adherence to French Classical drama.[2] Upon further exchange of words, the Director then calls an end to the debate by announcing: "Der Worte sind genug gewechselt, / Laßt mich auch endlich Taten sehn!" (214–5). That is to say, only when the *word* becomes a *deed*, when words are in action, can the real play begin.

When the play does begin, the negative challenge performed by the *lustige Person* assumes a creative function, both in terms of the dramatic form of *Faust*, and in the reincarnated form of Mephisto – "der Geist, der stets verneint" (1338), the dark force that also gives birth to light ("Ein Teil der Finsternis, die sich das Licht gebar," 1350f). Hence the feeling of relief when Faust's student is instructed by Mephisto to abandon "grey theory" and the dark confines of his study to explore the natural world (2038f). Similarly, Faust is to abandon his conventional academic pursuits in his dark, cramped study (*Stubengelehrsamkeit*) and act on his desire for knowledge through experience, with the help of Mephisto's devilish magic: "Du wirst, mein Freund, für deine Sinnen / In dieser Stunde mehr gewinnen / Als in des Jahres Einerlei" (1436f). All of this is anticipated in the *Vorspiel*: When words become deeds, Faust will succeed in overcoming the tradition towards enlightenment by way of negative dialectic – a principle that also operates on the formal level of *Faust*. Without abandoning either idealism or realism, the organic form of *Faust* assumes a disclosive function, as the *lustige Person* promises: "Dann sammelt sich der Jugend schönste Blüte / Vor eurem Spiel und lauscht der *Offenbarung*" (174f).

Taken as a whole, Goethe's *Faust* reveals a number of instructive educational models both in general and for language education in particular. Following the interventions of the *lustige Person*, such a model does not discard idealism for the sake of realism or vice versa; nor it does embrace a notion of language as purely representational or purely disclosive, as purely descriptive or purely performative. Rather, Faust's model proposes a dynamic relation between idealism and realism, and between language and deeds – one that also reflects an important shift in the history of German educational thought, and that resonates with pedagogical debates of today.

In regard to German educational thought, the dynamic relation between words and deeds in *Faust* reflects a paradigm shift that took place around the end of the eighteenth century from a conception language as merely designative to consider the disclosive dimension of language. Former notions of linguistic reductionism yielded to the expressive potential of language that Johann Gottfried von Herder, for example, attributed to the disclosive capacity of language. As such, language is no longer fixed in meaning and time, but emerges as a more dynamic process, unfolding in time. According to Herder, furthermore, language and thought have their source in the experience of the body. "Our thought depends upon sensation," Herder continues, because "we have no concept of anything that lies outside the circle of our sensations" (qtd. in Sikka 188).

The reemphasis on experience and the dynamic dimension of language coincides with a correlative development in the realm of pedagogy. The term *Bildung*, which was first theorized by Wilhelm von Humboldt in the 1790s, is itself an illustrative case in both points. Indeed, the history of the German concept *Bildung* is as rich and instructive as it is elusive. By no means uniform or readily translatable, the concept of *Bildung* has negotiated vast historical, political, and theoretical terrain, from the aesthetic and ethical (for example in Schiller, Herder, and Humboldt) to critical, emancipatory, and political (for example in Nietzsche, Horkheimer, and Adorno). Crucial in all accounts is the term's etymological rootedness in ideas relating to aesthetics, in the "image" (*Bild*) and the "imagination" (*Einbildung*), which underscore the sense of *Bildung* as playing a central role in individualized creativity and *ethical* formation (*bilden*, "to create, to educate"). *Einbildungskraft* assumes a central and productive place in the concept of genius during the mid-eighteenth century, when emotional affect gains an elevated status in poetry, now unconstrained by rules of the *Vorbild*. Thus *Bildung*, in capturing the ethical and aesthetic dimension of education, tends towards inner cultivation. In contrast, and as the prefix *aus* may already suggest, *Ausbildung* ("training, apprenticeship") directs education *away from* itself, towards specific goals for a ready-made world determined more by economic or political pressures than by purely humanistic pursuits. Treating language as nomenclature that can be applied to a ready-made world enables and justifies the capacity to produce quantifiable outcomes. It is this emphasis on the accumulation of knowledge over experience that leads to the kind of complacency for which Faust's freshman student, now the proud graduate, is later mocked by Mephisto in *Faust II* (Act II, Sc. 1). Much later, in 1959, Theodor W. Adorno warns against precisely this tendency towards fact-storing, the fetishization of knowledge for the sake of social conformity, which automatically affirms, rather than opposes existing conditions: "die geistige Verdopplung dessen, was ohnehin ist, wird zu ihrem eigenen Gehalt und Rechtsausweis" (Adorno GS 8, 186). The outcome of such a complacent, non-critical attitude has recently been witnessed, Adorno argues, at Auschwitz. The only real power "gegen das Prinzip von Auschwitz wäre Autonomie" (Adorno GS 10, 679). An insistence on the values of critical *Bildung*, "die Kraft zur Reflexion, zur Selbstbestimmung, zum Nicht-Mitmachen" (Adorno GS 10, 679), in contrast, stands to teach students further possibilities and alternatives that may not necessarily rhyme with the status quo.

One famous alternative that did not rhyme with the status quo was the innovative *Waldorfschule* of Rudolf Steiner. Steiner's fascination with Goethe, and Goethe's *Faust* in particular, culminated in the building of his *Goetheanum*, a cultural center to house all the arts. His *Waldorf* educational approach, which similarly had its source in a Faustian self-cultivation through experience and imagination, was not tolerated by the Nazis, who closed the schools in Germany in the 1930s (Hardorp 135). Germany apparently had no room for an educational alternative that taught children to think for themselves rather than educate them for the state. If critical thought or the education of the individual was not tolerated under the Nazis, then it is also not yet fully accepted even today, when pedagogical models such as the Waldorf School continue to stand apart from the growing emphasis on non-humanities subjects, quantifiable outcomes, and national performance standards. And yet, as Martha Nussbaum reminds us in *Not For Profit*, silencing critical voices is unhealthy for democracy, whose wellbeing depends on precisely this kind of rigorous critical thought and imagination. As Max Horkheimer puts it, only by cultivating *Bildung* may we avoid becoming dominated by and dependent on "blinden Mächten, von scheinhaften Vorstellungen, überholten Begriffen, abgetanen Ansichten und Einbildungen" (Horlacher 142). It is hardly surprising, then, that *Bildung*, which likewise embraces inner cultivation and imagination, has commonly been invoked in critical debates about economic forces, utilitarianism, and the quantification and commodification of education – what Adorno calls *Halbbildung* (GS 8, 93–121) and what Konrad Liessmann calls *Unbildung* – that threaten to devalue humanistic education.

This continues to plague educational institutions globally today. The most recent debates in education similarly confront a utilitarian view of education, which favors highly applied skills for short-term profit. Amid this current environment, and particularly since the terrorist attacks of 9/11, an increasingly instrumentalist view of language has been nurtured that favors so-called "critical" or "strategic" languages for national defense over a constitutive view of language in relation to its cultural, literary, and historical context. The reduction of language to its referential function limits the task of foreign-language learning to linguistic decoding by uncoupling stored linguistic knowledge from critical thought and creative imagination. As we have witnessed, this results in departmental divisions between lower-level language courses and upper-division content. The increasing tendency within higher-educational institutions to "house" languages in a resource center is but one visible and logical outcome of this trend. The *MLA Report* of 2007 is another outcome of the urgency felt among foreign-language professionals to counter this trend by realigning our curricular priorities.

The *MLA Report* calls on us to "situate language study in cultural, historical, geographic, and cross-cultural frames within the context of humanistic learning"; further, we can "challenge students' imaginations," "help them consider alternative ways of seeing, feeling, and understanding," and foster "critical language awareness, interpretation and translation, historical and political consciousness, social sensibility, and aesthetic perception" (MLA 4). As Claire Kramsch has argued in *The Multilingual Subject* (2009), there is much more to language than direct reference or denotation, and, by the same token, much more to foreign-language learning beyond acquiring a linguistic code for communicative exchanges. As Mephisto, upon Faust's question about how he "names himself," remarks: "Die Frage scheint mir so klein / Für einen, der das Wort so sehr verachtet, /Der, weit entfernt von allem Schein, / Nur in der Wesen Tiefe trachtet" (1328f). Rather, as a symbolic power that constructs subjective realities "such as perceptions, emotions, attitudes, and values" (Kramsch 7), language is also an embodied experience that shapes our sense of self, and language learning "the construction of imagined identities" (Kramsch 17). "Some learners," Kramsch continues, "will start having thoughts that they never had in their mother tongue [...] The experience of the foreign always implies a reconsideration of the familiar" (Kramsch 5). Learning a foreign language involves a kind of emotional and physical transformation. And for this reason, Kramsch argues, it is as equally important to enrich a predominantly instrumental approach to foreign languages by indulging more deeply in its aesthetic and affective dimensions.

If pedagogical utilitarianism tends to view the foreign lexicon merely as a different nomenclature for an essentially identical world (and language *a posteriori*), socio-cultural contextualism insists that different worlds are shaped by different means of verbal formulation (*a priori*). An instrumentalist approach to language focuses on tasks of linguistic decoding and direct reference; any student frustrated with Faust's struggle to translate, for example, might advise him to simply "google it" and move on. In contrast, a broader approach aims to engage learners in the discursive, disclosive, and embodied dimension of language, and to join Faust in apprehending deeds from words. The divergent conceptualizations of German *Bildung* illustrate the importance of such an approach; Goethe's *Faust* offers a possible way forward. As Mephisto suggests, "Wir müssen das gescheiter machen, / Eh uns des Lebens Freude flieht!" (1818).

Through the efforts of the *lustige Person*, the perspective of Goethe's fictional director, whose concern for short-term profit directs his outward appeal to realism and action, is brought into cooperation with the Poet's concern for posterity through the poetic ideal. Taking our cue from the *lustige Person* by putting words and deeds in operation with each other, drama pedagogy in the foreign-language classroom offers one way to meet this challenge. Theater mediates between the two perceived opposites by making performance a necessary part of language, where words become deeds. Far from applying language to a ready-made world in order to justify the production of quantifiable outcomes, learners are animated in dramatic performance to incarnate different roles, to move beyond their own cultural embeddedness, and to adopt and empathize with positions that would otherwise remain unexplored. In doing so, dramatic performance enables learners to undergo the kind of transformation that may allow them to see the world not as it already is but rather as it could be. Furthermore, it can stimulate a critical awareness of the dynamic, expressive, aesthetic, and affective dimension of language.

In order to make this possible in an educational setting, I make the renewed case in the present book for integrating drama in the foreign-language classroom, for drawing us figuratively or literally out of the confines of the traditional classroom into a space where truly discursive education may take place.[3] As suggested by the term *Vorstellung* (which means not only performance, but also idea and imagination), embodied performance necessarily involves discursive, creative, and imaginative interaction with the world that may potentially resist an emphasis on *Verwissenschaftlichung*. In contrast, drama pedagogy highlights a kind of "play acting" already intrinsic to language learning – this revealing of another self, the awakening in our audience a sense of something new, a new way of seeing, re-cognizing (the moment of *Erkenntnis*), as we do in theater, and potentially also to question the old and familiar. In the process, learners find new ways of seeing literary and dramatic texts, which may be brought to life through performance: "Der Worte sind genug gewechselt, / Laßt mich auch endlich Taten sehn!" (214–15).

Spielraum

Spielraum is a sourcebook for teaching German language and culture through theater and dramatic texts. It presents a range of resources for teachers who wish to integrate German-speaking theater into their curriculum. Following in part the example set by Nicoletta Marini-Maio and Colleen Ryan-Scheutz in *Set the Stage! Teaching Italian through Theater*, I propose a series of drama-based approaches that may be used as a flexible tool for teachers seeking ways to reinvigorate their language classrooms, to connect language to the study of literature and culture or to embark on full-scale theater productions. This book differs considerably from that of Marini-Maio and Ryan-Scheutz, however, in its focus on specific dramatic works from the vast German-language tradition, and with the goal of suggesting particular and unique approaches to each play, theme, or genre. Each chapter proposes a variety of strategies to choreograph a classroom that transforms students into active agents in their learning about language, culture, history, and aesthetics. Thus, the book is intended less as a template for a particular course than as an adaptable reference or ancillary text for high school, college, and adult instruction.

As interdisciplinary, intercultural, and global competencies gain increasing significance – and as educators recognize the need to engage the imagination, critical thinking, and multiple intelligences of our students – theater and drama have much to offer foreign-language education.[4] Theater presents a unique opportunity to immerse foreign-language learners in an authentic learning context and to witness German in action; drama focuses attention on the dynamics of dramatic form and on the socio-pragmatics of communication. By embodying fictional roles and by connecting verbal to non-verbal communication, students are permitted more space (*Raum*) for the kind of creative play (*Spiel*) that supports the cognitive, social, and affective dimensions of learning that are otherwise neglected in our predominantly functional and instrumentalist language classrooms. Embodied learning synthesizes multiple resources, including linguistic, cognitive, bodily-kinesthetic, interpersonal and intrapersonal intelligence, while making space to explore emotional expression through accent, rhythm, intonation, gesture, and creative language play (*Sprachspiel*). In the process, learners develop interpersonal, interpretive, and presentational modes of communication, as recommended by ACTFL's *World-Readiness Standards for Learning Languages* (The National Standards Collaborative Board, 2015). And through greater intimacy with the text, students may engage self-reflectively and imaginatively in the creative process itself.

Thus, I make the case for more *Spielraum* (literally, room for play, or wiggle room) for creativity in the foreign-language curriculum in general. As a performance-based course may be both process- and product-oriented, this approach necessarily disturbs the customary hierarchies and rituals of the traditional classroom, animating students instead to become active agents in their own learning with a real stake in the outcome of the course. Following further recommendations of the 2007 *MLA Report*, this approach helps to cultivate critical language awareness as well as interpretive and aesthetic perception. Attention not only to the lines, but also to what lies between the lines is precisely the kind of stumbling block to interpreting a foreign-language text, where the tendency to "decode" is so often para-mount. Embodied learning, in contrast, prompts deeper reflection, a more precise, nuanced interpretation and, ultimately, critical reflection about re-presentation and spectatorship. Moreover, the study of literature – perhaps the most daunting prospect for many a foreign-language student – is transformed into a wealthy source of creative and linguistic possibilities for students to bring to life through performance. Ultimately, then, this book should also serve as a source of inspiration for overcoming such perceived obstacles as well as the bifurcation between lower-level language and upper-division literature courses.

With this in mind, I present an approach to teaching drama that remains sensitive to the process of reading in a second language and to sustained language development, and generally involves a three-step process: guided reading and discussion, interactive drama workshops, and follow-up re-flective or creative writing. Depending on the particular goals and level of the course, the teaching suggestions may be adopted wholesale, or may be selectively adapted to the teacher's needs. Similarly, drama workshops may lead to a full-fledged production, or they may be incorporated over a small number of class sessions. For this reason, nearly all of the works presented in detail have been selected from my own tried-and-tested repertoire from the past two decades and are deemed suitable for performance. This re-commendation is partly on account of the play's relative brevity (under 1½ hours of performance time) and/or the cast size, generally suitable for a class of about ten students or adaptable to various class sizes. The afterword (*Nachspiel*) also includes plays with a larger cast that I have produced at a larger institution, or that colleagues have performed elsewhere.

While theater has not gained a central place in the foreign-language curriculum, generally sidelined instead as a sub-section of literary study, the level of interest in drama integration has certainly increased, especially over the past two decades. The communicative, interpersonal, and motivational benefits associated with drama, such as such role-playing and short skits, have become an indispensable part of today's foreign-language classroom. Interest in theater is further evidenced and sustained in co-curricular theater productions, cabaret performances, and theater festivals. Such initiatives have yielded an increasing amount of pedagogical scholarship over the past two decades, from which my own pedagogy and the present book also benefits. Building on Manfred Schewe's foundational work on drama pedagogy,[5] *Fremdsprachen inszenieren* (2003), Schewe's subsequent foun-dation (in 2007) of the bi-lingual online journal *Scenario* (https://www.ucc.ie/en/scenario/) set the stage for a much more vigorous exchange among educators interested in performative teaching, learning, and research both through the journal and at associated *Scenario FORUM* conferences. Its co-editor, Susanne Even, has also contributed much to the debate in her work on teaching grammar through drama in *Drama Grammatik* (2003) and performative pedagogy (2011); further contributions to drama pedagogy in

German have appeared in *Scenario* and other teaching journals (such as *Die Unterrichtspraxis/Teaching German*) and accompany the present contribution. Other useful contributions deserve special mention here, including Spolin (1993), Huber (2003), Maley and Duff (2005), Bräuer (2002), Scheller (2004), Lutzker (2007), Butzkamm (2012), Mentz and Fleiner (2018), and Crutchfield and Schewe (2017).

Building on this previous work, the present book aims to bolster the case for integrating dramatic texts in the foreign-language curriculum. The book is thus aimed both at language instructors who have no or little experience in play direction or drama pedagogy, as well as those who have experience but still appreciate fresh ideas and approaches, particularly considering the exciting current trends in contemporary theater.

Performative learning and teaching

Particularly relevant for teachers – and teacher trainers – is Schewe's and Even's promotion of a post-methods approach to teaching, by which Even means in particular the

> participatory, performative, and democratic process of co-constructing meaning. As a post-method approach, drama grammar assumes the development of context-sensitive and culture-appropriate teaching and learning activities and transcends both the researcher–teacher divide and the teacher–student hierarchy. (Even 2011 310)

Such an approach is instructive for language teachers, especially for those who tend to over-prepare top-down lessons that leave little or no room for sensitivity to context, for unexpected insights and unplanned directions, or for an organic development of a lesson. A performative pedagogy, as Even describes it, does not prescribe every move of the lesson, but rather facilitates its unfolding, enabling learners to discover something in a new light. The instructor is therefore encouraged to cultivate an approach that liberates its recipients from the constraining control of *Frontalunterricht.* Just as language can be used productively to imagine and co-construct reality, rather than merely describe one that already exists, performative teaching allows for something new to emerge. While this might seem only feasible in more advanced-level language courses, when students are better equipped to respond and interact, the relevant principles can and should be adopted from the very beginning stages. Put simply, this includes alleviating oneself of the burden of all learning (as described in Lee and VanPatten's "Atlas Complex"): asking questions to which one already knows the answer – indeed, asking all the questions – neglecting to engage in the content of students' answers, and proceeding only through a presentation-and-practice model. A constructivist, interactive, performative approach situates learners on more equal footing with the instructor, who choreographs the lesson such that learners also ask questions and are partly responsible for the outcome of the lesson. In all these respects, a performative approach to teaching and learning involves techniques modeled on theater. This guides my approach to each lesson, to each dramatic text, and to each course that culminates in a student-led workshop or a public performance. And it is in this spirit that the present book is conceived: as an ongoing collaboration with past and future student performers in the German language.

Structure and goals of *Spielraum*

Thus, the approach in this book is motivated less by predetermined models than by the dramatic texts themselves. Each chapter takes its pedagogical cue from the dramatic texts on which it focuses. Similar to this introductory chapter, in which Faust's struggle with models of knowing sets the scene, I let each dramatic text speak for itself as I tease out the pedagogical implications. By the same token, my focus on various genres is intended not as a prescriptive means to test the validity of a text against formal conventions, but rather as a means to help students better anticipate the different ways in which texts construct and organize meaning as well as to determine their social function.

Each of the chapters is devoted to one or two primary texts and contains significant excerpts for special focus. Together, the chapters present a range of sub-genres and theories spanning the eighteenth to the twenty-first centuries and emphasize strategies for interacting with each text through reflective and creative writing, improvisation, and performance. Beginning with some key considerations, each chapter sketches a summary of information on the play's performance history, approximate performance length, cast size, level of linguistic difficulty or peculiarities (dialect, register, dialect, monologic/dialogic, archaic/modern), thematic complexity and staging practicalities, including forewarnings about potential challenges. This is intended specially to help instructors who wish to consider a text or genre for a fully fledged performance or a workshop. An introductory essay follows, detailing the themes, context, history, dramatic techniques, and pedagogical implications presented by each particular text or genre, the intention of which is to spark certain lines of inquiry that the teacher might pursue while teaching the play. Each selected text raises interpretive questions that are included in the accompanying *Leitfragen* (reading questions), suggested in order to guide students during their individual reading in preparation for in-class discussion. Rather than following the conventional question-and-answer format in the ensuing session, however, in-class drama workshops build on the *Leitfragen,* serving as an entry point to in-depth text discussion. Each chapter closes with suggested post-reading reflective or creative writing exercises, as well as a list of suggestions for further reading and available resources. Taken together, this approach aims to guide instructors in facilitating the active engagement of students before and after class discussion, synthesizing their various resources in a culminating activity.

Notes on student and teacher performance anxiety

Before turning to examples of performance and improvisation exercises, which I outline in the next chapter, the practical and very real issue of student performance anxiety merits attention. The question of performance anxiety is frequently raised by colleagues and occasionally by students themselves as they embark on a performance-based course. Moreover, as an issue that is on the rise generally and among adolescents in particular, it is gaining increasing attention in secondary and post-secondary education. This is especially pertinent to the context of foreign-language teaching, where "performance" of one's communicative ability is a central component under almost continual assessment. Hence the reticence towards certain activities, such as spontaneous role-playing, by more inhibited students. But it is even more pertinent to performance-based foreign-language courses, which would conceivably exacerbate the issue by appealing more to extroverts than introverts, and even more so with the prospect of a public performance, where the fear of language breakdown looms large.

In anticipation of these legitimate concerns – concerns that I, too, would have shared as a foreign-language student – it is advisable never to insist that students perform any role with which they are not comfortable. This principle applies not only to public performance, but also to in-class workshop activities. At the beginning of every course or project, I clarify several options for students, including on- and off-stage roles, in order to engage all student types in various aspects of a theater production. This may involve taking the lead on stage design, costume, lighting, prompting, program design and content, and even co-directing, all of which are integral to a performance, requiring equal amount of attention to the text and the final product. Similarly, in process-drama workshops that do not require a public performance, students may opt to adopt the role of "director" instead of acting.

These concerns notwithstanding, my own experience has demonstrated, without exception, that even those students who are naturally introverted, generally not prepared to volunteer or initiate social interaction, and even those prone to social anxiety, have ultimately not shied away from performance and have requested a speaking role – even in public performances. Some of these students, moreover, took on major speaking roles, which they performed with commendable poise. Key to this transformation are the process-drama activities that enable students to find their footing gradually as social interaction becomes more familiar and comfortable, and by providing the framework for more confident peers to draw out naturally more introverted participants. Such negotiated interactions not only have been proven to facilitate second-language development, as initially theorized by Long (1996), but also provide a supportive environment for peers to take risks and test hypotheses. My personal experiences are further corroborated by results yielded in studies on the role of process-drama in foreign-language instruction (Weber), on using drama techniques to lower speaking anxieties (Atas; Giebert), and the potential of unscripted, improvisational drama to help overcome public speaking among certain students (Casteleyn).

The related question of instructor apprehension, especially among those with no experience in theater, can be answered along similar lines. While I have almost no on-stage acting or directing experience – my involvement in theater is almost entirely confined to the orchestra pit – my experience teaching language through drama and theater suffices for me to extrapolate some principles common to the classroom and the stage. Besides the energy, training, and the physical and vocal ability to convey meaning clearly and with variety to an audience – itself a kind of performance – both require an environment of active, collaborative, and focused participation. *Effective* teaching, acting, and directing also require the ability, as mentioned above, to be sensitive and responsive to the context-specific situation, to create a space for learners/actors to take risks and venture something new, and to facilitate the unfolding of the lesson in such a way as to enable the learners/actors to make connections for themselves. In other words, while a lot of creative energy is required, the onus is not entirely on the teacher/director to determine the outcome of the performance. This is a balancing act that begins in elementary language courses, with their focus on peer interaction in small role-plays, and ideally continues through to the advanced level, where even literary texts may become an opportunity for productive and collaborative interaction. It is to these various levels of "dramatic" inter-action, both in the classroom and theater, that I turn in the following chapter.

Notes

1 As the Director had already announced in the *Vorspiel*, it is crucial to move from mere *words* to actual *deeds*. The progression of translations for the term *logos* – 1. Word, 2. Sense, 3. Power, and 4. Deed – correlates with the stages portrayed in the opening *Nacht* scene: 1. Faust's frustration with mere *words*; 2. The full *sense* of meaning pouring out from the macrocosm; 3. The *power* of the Earth Spirit (*Erdgeist*); and 4. The fatal *deed* of suicide.

2 Gottsched's reputation as the *Literaturpapst* adduces the figure of Luther once more, who was equally well known for his battles against all forms of "popery" (*Päpstlerei*). See Döring p. 423.

3 In this regard, Adorno's critique of 1959 is very much in tune with critical voices during the 1960s, such as that of Thomas Bernhard, who bemoaned the decline of the public sphere as a result of the rising dominance of technology. As Fatima Naqvi put it, "The open space of discussion that guarantees a democratic society is closed with the turn away from what Bernhard construes to be teaching in its true form – a discursive education that takes place in other spaces." Naqvi p. 11.

4 Seven categories of intelligence, outlined by Harvard psychologist Howard Gardner, represent the myriad learning styles among students that are best captured by a variety of instructional approaches. See Gardner (1983, 2006). Ryan-Scheutz has already shown how drama pedagogy naturally incorporates all seven intelligences (Marini-Maio and Ryan-Scheutz 2010 145–7).

5 As Schewe also notes in his introduction, his approach builds in turn on previous
  work reaching back two centuries to with Swiss education reformer Heinrich
  Pestalozzi, who rejected the authoritarian approaches of *Frontalunterricht*, encouraging children instead to learn through experience by cultivating the art of
  observation (*Anschauung*) and holistic learning (*ganzheitliche Bildung*), known as
  "Lernen mit Kopf, Herz und Hand" – to which Schewe adds "thinking on one's
  feet" (Schewe 1993 7).

References

Adorno, Theodor W. "Theorie der Halbbildung." *Gesammelte Schriften*, vol. 8:
  Soziologische Schriften 1. Frankfurt am Main: Suhrkamp, 1972, 93–121.
Adorno, Theodor W. "Erziehung nach Auschwitz." *Gesammelte Schriften*, vol. 10,
  no. 2, Frankfurt am Main: Suhrkamp, 1977, 674–690.
Aristotle, *Poetics*. Stephen Halliwell, trans. *Loeb Classical Library*, vol. 199.
  Cambridge: Harvard UP, 1995.
Atas, Mine. "The Reduction of Speaking Anxiety in EFL Learners through Drama
  Techniques." *Procedia, Social and Behavioral Sciences*, vol. 176, 2015, 961–969.
Austin, John L. *How to Do Things with Words*. 2nd ed. J.O. Urmson and Marina
  Sbisà, ed. Cambridge: Harvard UP, 1975.
Bräuer, Gerd, ed. *Body and Language. Intercultural Learning through Drama*.
  Westport, CT: Ablex, 2002.
Butzkamm, Wolfgang. *Lust zum Lehren, Lust zum Lernen: Eine neue Methodik für
  den Fremdsprachenunterricht*. Tübingen: Narr Francke Attempto, 2012.
Casteleyn, Jordi. "Playing with Improv(Isational) Theatre to Battle Public Speaking
  Stress." *Research in Drama Education*, vol. 24, no. 2, 2019, 147–154.
Crutchfield, John, and Schewe, Manfred. *Going Performative in Intercultural
  Education* (Languages for Intercultural Communication and Education), vol. 31.
  Bristol: Multilingua l Matters, 2017.
Döring, Detlef. "Die Universität Leipzig im Zeitalter der Aufklärung." *Historisches
  Jahrbuch*, vol. 122, 2002, 413–461.
Even, Susanne. *Drama Grammatik*. Munich: Iudicium, 2003.
Even, Susanne. "Moving in(to) Imaginary Worlds: Drama Pedagogy for Foreign
  Language Teaching and Learning." *Die Unterrichtspraxis/Teaching German*,
  vol. 41, no. 2, 2008, 161–170.
Even, Susanne. "Drama Grammar: Towards a Performative Postmethod
  Pedagogy." *Language Learning Journal*, vol. 39, no. 3, 2011, 299–312.
Gardner, Howard. *Frames of Mind: The Theory of Multiple Intelligences*. New York:
  Basic Books, 1983.
Gardner, Howard. *Multiple Intelligences: New Horizons*. Completely rev. and up-
  dated ed., New York: Basic Books, 2006.
Giebert, Stefanie. "Drama and Theatre in Teaching Foreign Languages for
  Professional Purposes." *Recherche Et Pratiques Pédagogiques En Langues De
  Spécialité*, vol. 33, no. 1, 2014, 138–150.
Goethe, Johann W. *Faust. Erster Teil*. In *Werke*, vol. 3: *Dramatische Dichtungen I*. Erich
  Trunz, ed. Hamburger Ausgabe. Munich: Deutscher Taschenbuch Verlag, 1996, 7–145.
Hall, Geoff, ed. *Literature in Language Education*. New York: Palgrave Macmillan, 2005.

Hardorp, Detlev: "Die deutsche Waldorfschulbewegung in der Zeit des Nationalsozialismus." In *Basiswissen Pädagogik. Reformpädagogische Schulkonzepte. Waldorf-Pädagogik*, vol. 6. Inge Hansen-Schaberg and Bruno Schonig, ed. Baltmannsweiler: Schneider, 2002, 132–141.

Huber, Ruth. *Im Haus der Sprache wohnen. Wahrnehmung und Theater im Fremdsprachenunterricht*. Tübingen: Niemeyer, 2003.

Kramsch, Claire J. *The Multilingual Subject: What Foreign Language Learners Say about Their Experience and Why It Matters*. Oxford: Oxford UP, 2009.

Lee, James F., and Van Patten, Bill. *Making Communicative Language Teaching Happen*. 2nd ed. New York: McGraw-Hill, 2003.

Liessmann, Konrad P. *Theorie der Unbildung: Die Irrtümer der Wissensgesellschaft*. Vienna: Zsolnay, 2006.

Long, Michael H. "The Role of the Linguistic Environment in Second Language Acquisition." *Handbook of Second Language Acquisition*. William C. Ritchie and Tej K. Bhatia, ed. New York: Academic Press, 1996, 413–468.

Lutzker, Peter. *The Art of Foreign Language Teaching. Improvisation and Drama in Teacher Development and Language Learning*. Tübingen: Narr Francke Attempto, 2007.

Maley, Alan, and Duff, Alan. *Drama Techniques: A Resource Book of Communication Activities for Language Teachers*. 3rd ed. Cambridge: Cambridge UP, 2005.

Marini-Maio, Nicoletta, and Ryan-Scheutz, Colleen. *Set the Stage!: Teaching Italian through Theater*. New Haven: Yale UP, 2010.

Mentz, Olivier, and Fleiner, Micha, ed. *The Arts in Language Teaching. International Perspectives: Performative – Aesthetic – Transversal*. Münster: LIT Verlag, 2018.

MLA Ad Hoc Committee on Foreign Languages. "Foreign Languages and Higher Education: New Structures for a Changed World." Retrieved from http://www.mla.org/pdf/forlang_news_pdf.pdf

National Standards Collaborative Board. *World-Readiness Standards for Learning Languages*. 4th ed. Alexandria, VA, 2015. Retrieved from http://www.actfl.org/publications/all/world-readiness-standards-learning-languages

Naqvi, Fatima. *How We Learn Where We Live: Thomas Bernhard, Architecture, and Bildung*. Evanston: Northwestern UP, 2016.

Scheller, Ingo. *Szenische Interpretation. Theorie und Praxis eines handlungs- und erfahrungsbezogenen Literaturunterrichts in Sekundarstufe I und II*. Seelze-Velber: Kallmeyersche Verlagsbuchhandlung, 2004.

Schewe, Manfred. *Fremdsprache Inszenieren. Zur Fundierung einer Dramapaedagogischen Lehr- und Lernpraxis*. Oldenburg: Zentrum für pädagogische Berufspraxis, 1993.

Sikka, Sonia. "Herder on the Relation between Language and World." *History of Philosophy Quarterly*, vol. 21, no. 2, 2004, 183–200.

Spolin, Viola. *Improvisation for the Theatre*. 3rd ed. Evanston: Northwestern UP, 1993.

Weber, Silja. "Performance for Introverts?" *Scenario*, vol. 13, no. 2, 2019, 139–156.

1 *Schauspiel*: teaching German through gestures

Introduction

Performance-based courses are generally divided into two primary groups: those in which drama workshops are integrated in order to enhance course goals, and those that culminate in a full-fledged performance. In general, the former focuses on process-drama to negotiate meaning through conflict- and problem-solving; the latter, product-orientated courses focus on the preparation towards a final public performance. Both involve a process that synthesizes multiple communicative resources, including linguistic, cognitive, bodily-kinesthetic, interpersonal, and intrapersonal intelligence, connecting the mind to the body, and individuals to the community. Furthermore, in immersing learners in the world and vocabulary of theater, acting, and dramaturgy, learners connect their language skills creatively to another discipline. Even in smaller role-plays, learners develop their potential for "playing" with different kinds of social gestures and body language, in other words, putting on a mask or a hat helps free them up to explore other identities, other versions of themselves – to experience the foreign in order to reconsider the familiar. At the same time, learners pay attention to another fundamental and yet challenging communication skill: social and cultural appropriateness, which requires sensitivity to tone, intonation, gesture, and register. As Maley and Duff point out, such process-drama activities venture beyond conventional textbook role-plays in their attention not only to physical setting and conventional structure, but also to social setting, character, status, mood and attitude (Mayley & Duff 9–12) – the foundation of authentic interaction. Whatever the primary goal of the course is, however, it is necessary to begin by establishing a cooperative working relationship among students; to help form the social bonds necessary for lowering inhibitions; to reduce anxiety and stress by providing ample space for uninhibited physical and linguistic exploration; and to coach students in verbal and non-verbal communication as well as training of clear and comprehensible speech, diction, intonation, and pronunciation. Such preparatory workshops ideally involve a combination of both pre-scripted and semi- or non-scripted improvisational exercises that target interpersonal, interpretive, and presentational modes of communication, as recommended in the *Standards*.

DOI: 10.4324/9781003010289-1

The following presents a selection of such exercises, beginning, as any performance-based course should, with pre-verbal group exercises designed to help students overcome inhibitions through mutual trust and support. These are followed by exercises that connect verbal expression to emotion by focusing on pronunciation, intonation as well as enunciation; exercises that connect non-verbal to verbal expression; exercises for improvisation and word play; and a variety of approaches to dramatic texts. There are numerous sources from which to draw inspiration and practical guidance for all kinds of process-drama exercises, from which some of these (where indicated) have also been adapted (see "Further reading and resources"). In the process, seminal texts from the German-language tradition serve to introduce innovations in drama theory and dramatic techniques (*Schauspielkunst*) from the early-eighteenth to the late-twentieth centuries. While some of these exercises may be used in any language course at various levels, as indicated in each section, they are also called upon and brought to bear on dramatic texts in the remaining chapters of the book. Most important in all exercises is their integration into a lesson: They are never intended merely to fill dead time or to lift spirits; rather, they are integral to the goals of a lesson, whether that be an entry point into a text, or a communicative goal.

Some important factors to consider

Timing: Avoid letting an exercise drag on for more than necessary! In general, the shorter the excerpt, the more productive the workshop.

Side-coaching vs. teaching: In the interest of encouraging a welcoming environment, take care to set up a relaxed atmosphere, in which everyone is welcome to coach from the side, rather than top-down correction or disapproval.

Follow-up: Always leave room for a debrief and a follow-up activity. By "follow-up," I also imply the integration of an activity into the overall goals of a lesson. Rather than let an activity dangle pointlessly, be sure to embed it within a the lesson so that it serves to further the learning goals.

Scaffolding: Warm up with physical gestures before moving towards language-based exercises with increasing complexity.

Reflection: It is preferable to have students follow up each workshop with a reflection in a theater journal. This enables participants to reflect on what was learned, what was challenging, what was enjoyable, and what needs improvement.

Vorhang auf!

Pre-verbal exercises

Even pre-verbal exercises require a certain amount of linguistic preparation: giving directions, organizing activities, sharing impressions, making suggestions, and following up with reflections and discussion, all of which call for authentic communicative strategies. Each activity therefore includes suggestions for the setup and follow-up interaction between the instructor and the class and among students.

Spiegelspiel [all levels]

As the German compound suggests, this exercise involves the playful art of trying to sidestep someone to let the other pass, with the awkward and slightly amusing result that the two people repeatedly move in each other's way – as though reflected in a mirror.[1]
Purpose: Given the role that the mirror play in psychoanalytic and developmental models of self-consciousness as it relates specifically to the body, it might seem counter-intuitive to introduce mirrors in order to help overcome one's inhibitions. However, if we adopt a Vygotskyan perspective, one that presumes that the child is not at the center of its own cognitive development, but rather in interaction with the environment, and that play "creates a zone of proximal development" (Vygotsky, *Play* 16), it is possible to understand how this exercise can sharpen the physical observation and promote a heightened sensitivity to others (Vygotsky and Cole, *Mind*). By focusing on the give and take of a dramatic situation, as initiation and response, by following the *other's* lead, and by recognizing the emotional and physical reciprocity in constructing a scene, learners might also begin to overcome *self*-consciousness. This will not occur, however, if carried out unwillingly in front of an audience; each student must be given the opportunity to rehearse unobserved if preferred. This simple activity is also a form of storytelling – the basis of theater arts – as well as social interaction, imagination, personal creativity, and self-expression. In a sense, this is drama in compact form – action and reaction, conflict and resolution, a study in character and style. It can also be used as a staging technique.
Roles: Roles can be devised by participants or provided and summarized on cards and distributed to pairs of students. Depending on one's goal, it is possible to use this exercise as a starting point for discussion of physical gesture, or as an entry point into discussing a particular character from a play. The former might be an assembly of simple, familiar routines that take place in front of the mirror, such as:

- *ein Mann/eine Frau, der/die sich auf den Arbeitstag vorbereitet.*
- *ein Mann/eine Frau, der/die sich vor dem Schlafen fertig macht.*
- *ein Clown, der seine Gesten einstudiert.*
- *ein/e SchauspielerIn, der/die sich vor einem Auftritt in einer Tragödie vorbereitet.*

For the latter, some sample roles from Dürrenmatt's *Die Physiker* are intended as a springboard to a discussion of the relation of physical appearance to character and function in the play:

- *Eine bucklige Ärztin, die sich auf einen Besuch von Inspektor Voß vorbereitet.*
- *Herbert Georg Beutler, genannt Newton, der sich aber auch für Einstein hält, zieht sein Kostüm aus dem früheren 18. Jahrhundert und seine Perücke an.*
- *Schwester Irene, die Landesmeisterin des nationalen Judoverbandes, macht sich für eine Verabredung mit Beutler fertig.*
- *Inspektor Voß steht auf und macht sich am frühen Morgen im Badezimmer fertig.*

Alternatively, one might excerpt a moment from a play that students must contextualize based on a pantomime. For example, the episode "Der junge Herr und die junge Frau" from Schnitzler's *Reigen*:

> *Dann schenkt er sich ein Glas Cognac ein und trinkt es rasch aus. Dann sieht er auf seine Uhr. Er geht im Zimmer auf und ab. – Vor dem großen Wandspiegel bleibt er eine Weile stehen, richtet mit seinem Taschenkamm das Haar und den kleinen Schnurrbart.*

Organization: Divide group into pairs and assign them roles A and B. Player A will perform the role or action described on the card; player B will perform the "mirror" action at arm's length. It is important that player A moves slowly and deliberately enough for player B to follow, and that both players maintain eye contact (rather than observing other parts of the body). Reverse the roles for A and B and repeat. Participants should rehearse until they feel there is no difference between the leader and the mirror. Most important is not to try to "trick" one's partner or to move quickly, but rather to make the movements as simple and clear as possible.
Variation: Put participants in groups of 3 or 4 and add "mirrors." Funhouse mirrors allow for some exaggerated movements.
Follow-up: Draw in those participants who prefer not to demonstrate by having them comment on the action and offer feedback. (*Beschreiben Sie die Situation! Was haben Sie gesehen? Wer hat die Führungsrolle gespielt, wer hat den Spiegel gespielt? Woran erkennt man, dass er/sie die Rolle des Spiegels gespielt hat? Was ist gut gelungen?*)
Time: 8–10 minutes (plus time for demonstration, feedback, and discussion).

Spiegelkreis [adapted from a well-known warm-up activity]

Similar to the mirror game in purpose, but especially suitable for group cohesion.
Purpose: Observation and imitation, physical awareness; building trust and lowering inhibitions.
Organization: Arrange everyone in a circle. To demonstrate, the instructor makes the first move: perform a brief gesture indicating one's current mood, or simply a gesture with a sound or remark (possibly a character from a

play), and the whole group accepts and mimics (or, if preferred, exaggerates).
Time: 5 mins.

Dirigentenspiel [all levels]

Participants stand in a circle. One begins with a brief gesture or word to imitate a character from a play, giving the *Auftakt* for each subsequent student to imitate, in chain reaction, and with increasing exaggeration.
Purpose: Warm-up, focus, observation, interaction.
Time: 5 minutes.

Marionetten und Maskenfreiheit

The following workshop takes its cue from Thomas Mann's Hans Castorp, whose social breakthrough in *Der Zauberberg* is as much linguistic as it is embodied and theatrical. During the "Walpurgis Night" carnival celebrations, Hans Castorp exploits what he calls *Maskenfreiheit* ("freedom of masks"): Carnival hats, costumes, and the French language enables the otherwise reserved Castorp to declare his love for Madame Chauchat over the course of a rambling four pages – a dramatic and linguistic transgression. Castorp shows us how to slip into a foreign mask, to revel in speaking another language, and to speak, as he puts it, *sans responsabilité.*[2]

   While the previous exercises focus on the exact mimicry of physical and especially facial expression, the present exercise draws attention away from the face as the primary source of emotional expression. In this, the goal is to rely on simple physical movements, following the reflections of Heinrich von Kleist in his essay *Über das Marionettentheater* (1810). The essay itself provides rich points of discussion for a performance-based course at the advanced level. Of particular relevance are his reflections, through the fictional dancer and the narrator, on the problem of self-consciousness in acting. Human emotion and self-consciousness hampers physically graceful movement. Such grace can only be attained by marionettes, whose movements pivot around a center of gravity, unencumbered by reflexive consciousness and nerves: "Jede Bewegung, sagte er, hätte einen Schwerpunkt; es wäre genug, diesen, in dem Innern der Figur, zu regieren; die Glieder, welche nichts als Pendel wären, folgten, ohne irgend ein Zutun, auf eine mechanische Weise von selbst" (Kleist 339). Edward Gordon Craig would develop Kleist's central idea further in calling for the replacement of actors altogether by what he calls the *Über-Marionette*: "The actor must go, and in his place comes the inanimate figure – the Über-marionette we may call him ..." (Craig 11). Following Kleist, Craig cites the Fall from Grace as the reason for the actor's physical limitations, the resulting problem of which finds its clearest articulation in his essay "The Actor and the Über-Marionette" (1908): "The actions of the actor's body, the expressions of his face, the sounds of his voice, all are at the mercy of the winds of his emotions" (Craig 4), as opposed to the *Über-Marionette*, which recuperates authenticity by avoiding mimicry. Thus, the ideal performer, both argue, is the marionette, who serves as an inspiration for acting by movement and gesture alone, seemingly free of human intervention, as well as for various avant-garde experiments with hybrid puppets, geometrical and mechanical movement and costume design (Bauhaus), as well as animation (see also ch. 5).

Marionetten [all levels]

An example of animation film can serve to introduce students to the central point of Kleist's and Craig's essays, namely: the graceful simplicity of physical movement and gesture, unencumbered by human affectation or personality, that derive from the body's center of gravity (*Schwerpunkt*). One example is Pixar's *Luxo Jr* (1986), an animation short about a typical parent-child relationship during the phase of play and exploration, told through animated architectural lamps.[3] The child (Luxo Jr) finds a ball to play with and hops about merrily until it bursts, much to the consternation of the parent (Luxo Sr). Just when Luxo Sr thinks that its child has calmed down, Luxo Jr. bounces back with another, even bigger ball.

Organization: Before showing the (2-minute-long) film, participants are primed with the following questions:

> *Wie viele Körperteile bewegen sich? Wo befindet sich der Schwerpunkt? Welche Gefühle werden ausgedrückt? Wie werden Sie ausgedrückt?*

The whole class brainstorms a list of vocabulary for the wide range emotions and expressions (such as: *neugierig, überrascht, bittend, flehend, enttäuscht, missbilligend, beschämt, reuevoll, enttäuscht, erfreut*). Participants then exchange thoughts on how these emotions are physically expressed (such as: *sich bücken; sich hinüberbeugen, hinauf- hinuntersehen, sich drehen, den Kopf drehen, den Kopf schütteln, den Kopf senken, springen, wackeln*). When juxtaposed with the number of "limbs" (four limbs, three joints) used to express this expansive range of emotions and movements, it will become clear what Kleist and Craig are suggesting in terms of simple movements. Significantly, no facial expression, no hands, and no feet are employed.

Time: 10–15 minutes (independent of readings of Kleist or Craig).

Maskenfreiheit [all levels]

If it is possible to get this much out of a faceless lamp, then it is certainly worth exploring the even greater possibilities for humans. Key is the elimination of the face as the focal point: by wearing an expressionless mask, it is possible to explore physical gesture while also lowering inhibitions.

Purpose: To build vocabulary of movement and to understand expression through physical gesture alone.

Organization: Volunteers take an expressionless mask and a card containing an emotional state, such as those listed above in German. They are asked to assume a pose or, if they wish, walk around to demonstrate the emotion, while the rest of the class guesses the emotion. If the emotion is not successfully guessed, suggest alternative physical gestures to convey the emotion. Ideally, the spontaneity of the exercise would encourage everyone eventually to join in, though this is not absolutely necessary.

Follow-up Variation [all levels; adapted from Spolin]

Purpose: To focus on controlling simple mechanical physical movement. Participants decide on a place and a simple situation involving a human and a machine, automaton, or puppet. For example: a puppeteer and its puppet (s); a mechanic fixing a robot; a child playing with a Jack-in-the-box or a mechanical toy.

Time: 10 minutes (recommended).

Walking in character [all levels]

Purpose: Character development through movement; creativity.

Organization: Pre-workshop preparation. Pick a character (from a play, if possible) and prepare to present the character (a pose, a gait, a pantomime). Then walk around the room in this character. Alternatively, have individual participants approach the front, demonstrate a gesture, gait, or pantomime that typifies their character, and possibly a line or phrase, and have participants identify the character and provide feedback.

Time: 5 minutes (if done together as a group; 10–15 minutes if allowing for individual demonstrations, feedback, and discussion).

Improvisation: from non-verbal to verbal

Regieanweisungen [all levels]

Purpose: To learn stage directions and vocabulary of physical and emotional expression, and to build vocabulary relating to a specific play. In the process, participants also learn the vocabulary of the stage, movement, and theater.

Organization: This is based on Total Physical Response: Participants respond to a series of stage directions that increase in number, combinations, and complexity as the course progresses, all of which may be derived from the plays(s) being studied. Depending on the level and ability of the class, the instructor might choose to begin with 5–10 directions on the first day, demonstrating each stage direction, introducing 2–3 at a time, and building on these each class meeting. Subsequently, participants carry out stage directions without the instructor's model, and the instructor mixes them up in a way that challenges students to focus on more than one at a time (such as: *gehen Sie gebückt nach rechts*; *kommen Sie mit leisen Schritten nach vorne*; *blicken Sie die Person links scharf an!*). While this exercise generally proceeds without any problems, it is advisable to let participants know that they need not carry anything out with which they are not comfortable. By the same token, it is advisable to avoid too much physical handling at this point.

Jetzt sind Sie dran! Useful at all levels is the practice in giving stage directions, especially given the collaborative nature of a drama-based course. Taking the list of stage directions each day, participants practice giving directions first in pairs (using the informal singular *du*-form), and subsequently in small groups (practicing the informal plural *ihr*-form). In closing, any student may volunteer to "direct" the entire group, using the informal plural form and as much creativity as desired.

Time: 10–15 minutes (recommended), depending on amount of vocabulary.

Die Straßenszene [all levels]

This exercise is based on Bertolt Brecht's short essay "Die Straßenszene: Grundmodell einer Szene des epischen Theaters" (1938) and as such, facilitates a hands-on introduction to Brecht's theory of Epic Theater. Vital to Brecht's praxis is the art of showing though theatrical gesture, that is, without trying to persuade the audience of an illusion, but rather through anti-naturalistic means. This requires a certain amount of pantomimic exaggeration.

Die Straßenszene presents an eyewitness account of an everyday occurrence: a traffic accident. The witness re-creates how the accident took place without, however, appearing natural, for which reason the exercise lends itself well to students: "Eher ist seiner Perfektion eine Grenze gesetzt … Er hat niemanden 'in seinen Bann zu ziehen.' Er soll niemanden aus dem Alltag in 'eine höhere Sphäre' locken. Er braucht nicht über besonders suggestive Fähigkeiten zu verfügen" (Brecht "Straßenszene" 92). Instead, he is to give only a picture (*ein Bild*) of how it happened, the behavior of the driver or victim, and the consequences, so that the spectators may form an opinion. And, because Brecht is drawing a connection between art and everyday life, it is possible to connect the two in this exercise.

Purpose: To convey an action through gesture alone, and to try to persuade the audience of a point of view. The audience, in turn, is supposed to respond – in agreement or disagreement – with its own gestural interpretation. Thus, by introducing students to Brecht's critical activation of the spectator and theories of acting, the exercise also lends itself well to full participation.

Organization: Taking this scene or another brief moment from any dramatic plot, a volunteer uses gestures and speech to act out what was witnessed from the perspective a certain character or from a bystander (outside the

text). The rest of the group describes what they have seen and comments on the behavior.
Time: 10 minutes.

Straßenszene-Variation [all levels]; *adapted from Brecht and Spolin*

Purpose: To apply the basic structure of Brecht's exercise to characters from a play being studied. Participants should focus on embodying characteristics (age, gender, occupation) as well as the situation.
Organization: Take two characters from plays being studied (or, alternatively, give specific details about unknown characters), and resituate them outside the text in an everyday street scene. Both characters have specific goals and/or an inner conflict. This can be a silent mime, or they can choose to introduce speech if participants are so inclined when they come into interaction.

[Any character from a play]
8:30, zur Stoßzeit. An der Bushaltestelle. Wartet auf den Bus. Auf dem Weg zur Arbeit im Restaurant. Hat nur eine Plastiktüte dabei. Hat das Handy vergessen. Will sich nicht verspäten.
Szene: eine Sitzbank, im Hintergrund ein Späti und Handyladen.

Follow-up: The rest of the class relays what, where, and whom they have just witnessed and explains which gestures expressed this. If the character (or characteristics) are not evident from the gestures, participants may offer constructive suggestions for alternative gestures, posture, and movement. Volunteers take on suggestions.
Variation I: Ask volunteers to think up a character and an age to present.
Variation II: Participants suggest additional on-the-spot conditions, such as changes in the weather, a change of mind, additional characters, and the like.
Time: From 5 minutes (part I) to 15 minutes (with variation).

Beobachtungen [all levels]

"Du, der Schauspieler / Mußt vor allen anderen Künsten / Die Kunst der Beobachtung beherrschen. //… // Eure erste Schule / Sei euer Arbeitsplatz, eure Wohnung, euer Stadtviertel. / Sei Straße, Untergrundbahn und Laden. Alle Menschen dort / Sollt ihr beobachten. Fremde, als seien es Bekannte, aber / Bekannte, als seien sie euch fremd. //… // Um zu beobachten / Muß man vergleichen lernen. Um zu vergleichen // Muß man schon beobachtet haben…." (Brecht: *Kurze Beschreibung*, 269/271).
Purpose: To sharpen observation skills and to provide the basis for discussing a situation, character, and gesture.

Organization: Based on Brecht's notes above, observe someone on the street, on public transport, or going about their business, and try to convey what has been observed in a brief pantomime.
Follow up: Group discussion of the scene: *Was haben Sie gesehen? Was ist passiert? Was für eine Person wurde gerade dargestellt? Was macht er beruflich?*
Time: 8–10 minutes (per presentation and discussion).

Sprechspiele

In order to begin connecting verbal expression to emotion, and for students preparing for a theater production, it is necessary to spend some time throughout the course on pronunciation, enunciation and intonation. Opinions on the efficacy and place of pronunciation in foreign-language instruction have long been divided, and individual student perception and uptake is equally varied: While some students will benefit marginally from direct pronunciation coaching, others will not. Nevertheless, raising consciousness about the importance of (certain) sounds for communication purposes can only support proficiency goals and, in my experience, has not had any detrimental effect on their fluency. Far from emulating the antics of Professor Henry Higgins of *My Fair Lady,* who "coaches" Eliza Doolittle into improving her accent by speaking with marbles in her mouth, the following exercises are conceived as cooperative methods to develop group cohesion while sensitizing participants to distinct sounds and a vast range of expressive possibilities.

Bühnenflüstern

Purpose: Clear enunciation of consonants, group cohesion through rhythm.
Organization: Participants practice tongue-twisters in groups, then as a whisper, clearly enunciating ("spitting out") each consonant so that it remains audible even when spoken as a group.
Variation: Participants receive a line from a play, which must be whispered in chorus on stage (or at the front of the classroom) and audible to other students at the back. This may also serve as entry points into a particular point of a scene in a play.
***Stille-Post* Variation:** Participants whisper a short phrase to a neighbor, who passes it on, and so forth, to see whether the message has been retained throughout.

Aussprachespiel [all levels]

Purpose: To help students perceive and pronounce phonemic distinctions, that is, units of sounds whose minimal difference in pronunciation alters the meaning. This is essentially an exercise in minimal pairs while working collaboratively.
Organization: To warm up, choral repetition of minimal pairs are practiced in chorus. Tongue-twisters are suitable for further reinforcement.

Participants subsequently receive minimal pairs and work in pairs: one student receives a list of underlined words to pronounce; the other receives the same list of words and must underline what is heard. Examples include:

Table 1.1 Minimal Pairs

u vs ü			
A. Lesen Sie das <u>unterstrichene</u> Wort vor!		B. <u>Unterstreichen</u> Sie das gehörte Wort!	
1. Mütter	Mutter	1. Mütter	Mutter
2. führen	fuhren	2. führen	fuhren
3. drücken	drucken	3. drücken	drucken
4. nützen	nutzen	4. nützen	nutzen
5. Brüder	Bruder	5. Brüder	Bruder
Glottal stop [Knacklaut]			
A. Lesen Sie das <u>unterstrichene</u> Wort vor!		B. <u>Unterstreichen</u> Sie das gehörte Wort!	
1. der Riegel	der Igel	1. der Riegel	der Igel
2. dein Neid	dein Eid	2. dein Neid	dein Eid
3. um Macht	um acht	3. um Macht	um acht
4. verreist	vereist	4. verreist	vereist

Follow-up: Participants exchange and check their answers with each other.
Time: 5 minutes.

Steigerung der Intensität [all levels]

Purpose: To explore and practice the intensification of emotions through a repeated utterance.
Organization: Using a brief excerpt from a play – one line or phrase per student suffices – each pair of participants engages in a "dialogue." For example: "I want it" and "You can't have it!" expressed with varying degrees of negative or positive attitude or emotion with each utterance, or varying in volume from a whisper to a (near) scream. Students are asked then to "perform" lines in any way they wish, and the group has to identify the expressed emotion or attitude before identifying characters and context from the play. Used in this way, it provides an entry point for the discussion of an entire scene.
Time: 10 minutes.

Subtext [intermediate to advanced]

This is a variation on the previous exercise. Taking lines out of context – and not necessarily from a play being studied – participants try out a range of expressive possibilities.
Purpose: To read lines out of context and explore a range of expressive possibilities through different stress and intonation; reading for subtext,

altering intonation, elaborating on context (leading to a longer exercise on script writing or improvisation).
Organization: Dividing students into pairs, each student reads an alternate line with varying intonation and expression.

> *Tut mir leid.*
> *Wirklich?*
> *Du weißt, du kannst mir vertrauen.*
> *Danke.*

Follow-up: Pairs of students volunteer to carry out their version; the rest of the group comments on what they heard and the subtext.
Time: 5–7 minutes.
Variation: This may also be used as a pre-reading or pre-viewing exercise. Participants receive a transcript of a key scene from a play or a film that contains a conflict. Participants carry out the above exercise either using their own imagination or by using character descriptions provided by the instructor. Two or three groups perform their version for discussion. The scene will be revisited during reading or viewing.
Time: 20–25 minutes.

Regeln für Schauspieler: Aussprache, Rezitation, Deklamation [advanced]

Using excerpts from Johann W. Goethe's *Regeln für Schauspieler* (1803), which were written when Goethe assumed directorship of the Weimar Hoftheater, participants prepare short passages while paying attention to these rules. It is important to contextualize these rules as guidelines specific to the culture of the court theater and as a relatively early response to the predominantly declamatory style (inherited from French theater) and improvisation (which had already been "banned" in Germany and Austria – see ch. 3). Before the appearance of Goethe's *Regeln*, there was little written guidance for actors besides Gotthold E. Lessing's translation of Francesco Riccoboni's *L'art du théâtre* (*Die Schauspielkunst*, 1750). (For further context, see Schwind.)
Purpose: To put certain "speaking rules" into practice while gaining insight into a specific concept of acting that required an education in moral decorum and grace in gesture and speech.
Time: 20–30 minutes, depending on the number of passages selected.

Stegreifspiel

This section introduces process-drama exercises that may be used in any language class as well as in preparation for a theater production. In contrast to the previous sections, these focus more on more spontaneous verbal expression and connecting to its emotions. The core of an improvisational task is a certain "problem" – or a conflict – that could range from a familiar restaurant scene (in intermediate-level courses), to marital or social conflict at more advanced stages.

Konflikt! [intermediate to advanced]

Time: This can be a challenging exercise, so ample time is needed for preparation (ca. 15 mins) and run-throughs in front of the group, followed by reflection and discussion.

Purpose: To employ communicative strategies in solving a problem (functions and vocabulary of persuasion, conviction, acquiescing, negotiating, apologizing), while paying attention to character and social context. This exercise can also be very useful as a pre- or during-reading exercise in order to identify the conflict of a drama.

Variation: Hidden Conflict. This time, the players do not know the other side of the conflict, but the audience does.

Organization: Put participants in pairs. Decide on the where, who, and what. Each player takes a suggested conflict (written on a card) without letting the other player(s) know what it is. Participants should make sure not to verbalize what the problem actually is. As soon as this happens, the scene ends. Have groups perform to each other and get constructive feedback before asking one or two groups to perform their scene to the whole group.

Example: *Wo: Die Küche. Wer: ein Ehepaar. Was: Frühstück.*

Hidden conflict: *Ehemann – Ich gehe heute nicht zur Arbeit. Ehefrau: Ich will, dass er endlich geht. Ich bekomme Besuch.*

Time: up to 10–15 minutes (including discussion).

Dramatic interactions with the text

Hot-Seating [intermediate to advanced]

This is a well-known activity (see Even 106–7), but because it is so productive, I am including it here.

Purpose: To interview a character or characters and ascertain information about an event, a character, and his or her motivations up to a specific point in the play (or any plot). This works especially well towards the end or after reading the whole text, by when students have got a good sense of the plot and the characters' various (physical and linguistic) idiosyncrasies. This exercise serves well as a review, or to ascertain moments in the texts that students do not yet understand in a fully immersive and dynamic context.

Organization: Participants are assigned (or choose) a role to prepare in advance: the character, his or her background, relations, role in the plot, motivation, and (for advanced students) idiosyncratic expression or gestures. In class, other participants "interrogate" the character. The other participants spend about 10 minutes preparing questions, to be brain-stormed before the activity begins. They may also adopt other roles from the play, perform an invented character external to the plot (for example, a police officer, a journalist), or simply play themselves. The goal is to find out as much information as possible. The interrogation might begin by simply asking for personal information, moving gradually into details relating to a specific event in the text: this might include their whereabouts, actions, re-lationships, feelings, and motivations. Alternatively, more than one parti-cipant may take the hot seat, to be interrogated by a smaller number of students. This version works well, for example, in a text such as Max Frisch's *Andorra*, in which multiple characters alternately take the stand for interrogation in the play itself. (For a sample application, see ch. 7.)

Follow-up: Discuss with the whole group what insights into the character were gained and what aspects remained unclear.

Time: 20 minutes (recommended, though this may also extend further) plus preparation time outside class, including reading the text, preparing ques-tions in class beforehand, practicing questioning techniques.

Scene-by-scene interrogations

Purpose: To turn the conventional question-and-answer discussion format upside down in order to create a livelier and more productive discussion. Instead of proceeding through questions, hoping for answers, and seeking textual evidence to substantiate a claim, participants begin with the text itself and present short excerpts as a basis for follow-up discussion. In the process of preparing short scenes for presentation, questions about the text – and what lies between the lines – naturally emerge during groupwork. Participants less eager to perform may serve as the "director" of a scene.

Organization: The instructor selects a series of key moments for close reading through performance. These scenes should be short (about half a page of text or less). Key scenes are ideally selected chronologically in such a way as to allow for certain questions and conflicts to emerge and develop. In this way, each scene adds a new perspective, a new detail, a new element of conflict, shedding new light on the previous scene and on the character or situation. The instructor organizes the appropriate number of students to prepare the text for a dramatic reading in as much detail as possible (with blocking, gestures, etc.). Allow about 10 minutes of preparation time.

Follow-up: After each individual dramatic reading, ask the observers to identify the core conflict. Some or all of the following questions prompt students to summarize what they observed; additional and specific ques-tions might emerge from the perspective of the spectators or presenters. Allow about 10–15 minutes for each discussion:

Wo spielt sich diese Szene ab?
Wer spielt in dieser Szene?
Worum handelt es sich in dieser Szene? Was passiert? Was haben Sie gesehen?
Gibt es einen Konflikt?
Was haben Sie nicht verstanden?
Beschreiben Sie die Figuren!
Beschreiben Sie das Verhältnis zwischen den Figuren? Wie gehen sie miteinander um?
Wie haben Sie das (an der Darstellung) erkannt?
Was passiert davor?
Was passiert danach? Was erfolgt daraus?

Repeat this exercise two or three times in order to reach a conclusion about an aspect of the play, or indeed the entire plot. (For a practical application of this, see ch. 2.)
Time: A full hour-long workshop (or longer).

Verfremdungsspiele [advanced]

The following exercises draw on Bertolt Brecht's theories of Epic Theater and thus also serve as an introduction to his interventions. They are described succinctly in his essay *Kurze Beschreibung einer neuen Technik der Schauspielkunst, die einen Verfremdungseffekt hervorbringt* (1940) – that is, they are designed to encourage the actor to adopt a critical distance from the character.

1. *Regieanweisungen:* Participants read a scene aloud, while one participant reads the stage directions aloud.
2. *Rollentausch*: While reading a scene aloud, participants switch roles, handing over an item representing a character. For example, a character wearing a hat hands the hat to another player, who then adopts the new role.
3. *Dritte Person*: All participants read a scene aloud, introducing their role each time with "sagte der Mann" or "sagte die Frau."
4. *Vergangenheit*: Participants read a scene aloud, but transforming lines into the past tense.
5. *Pantomime*: Exaggeration of a character's gestures.
6. *Aus der Rolle fallen/Beiseitesprechen*: Participants work in pairs to prepare a short dialogue from the play in which they step out of their roles, face the audience, and comment on their action. This may also be carried out in the context of comedy, where the same device frequently occurs (see ch. 3).

Regeln für Schauspieler

All participants read the assigned sections from Goethe's *Regeln für Schauspieler*. Pairs of participants are assigned specific sections to prepare in more detail, for example: "Stellung und Bewegung des Körpers auf der Bühne," "Haltung und Bewegung der Hände und Arme," "Gebärdenspiel," and "Stellung und Gruppierung auf der Bühne." Based on a detailed study of these sections, pairs of students prepare a short scene from a drama for presentation. Alternatively, participants prepare to direct others in carrying out Goethe's directions during the in-class workshop. For example, the following are sample excerpts from the section on "Haltung und Bewegung der Hände und Arme":

§ 35 Die Hand selbst aber muß weder eine Faust machen noch wie beim Soldaten mit ihrer ganzen Fläche am Schenkel liegen, sondern die Finger müssen teils halb gebogen, teils gerade, aber nur nicht gezwungen gehalten werden.

§ 48 Die zwei mittleren Finger sollen immer zusammenbleiben, der Daumen, Zeige- und kleine Finger etwas gebogen hängen. Auf diese Art ist die Hand in ihrer gehörigen Haltung und zu allen Bewegungen in ihrer richtigen Form.

§ 49 Die obere Hälfte der Arme soll sich immer etwas an den Leib anschließen und sich in einem viel geringeren Grade bewegen als die untere Hälfte, in welcher die größte Gelenksamkeit sein soll. [...]

§ 50 Auch sollen die Hände niemals von der Aktion in ihre ruhige Lage zurückkehren, ehe ich meine Rede nicht ganz vollendet habe, und auch dann nur nach und nach, so wie die Rede sich endigt.

Time: A 45–60-minute workshop is recommended based on two or three sections of Goethe's text.

Schauspieltheorien im Vergleich

A particularly productive exercise, one that would provide a suitable final project for a course, is to prepare an in-class staging of a scene in a specific style or two contrasting styles. For example, one might take Goethe's *Regeln für Schauspieler,* with its strict specifications for physical and verbal decorum, both on- and off-stage, and the other employing Brecht's *Verfremdungseffekte,* as outlined in his *Kleines Organon für das Theater*, and *Kurze Beschreibung einer neuen Technik der Schauspielkunst, die einen Verfremdungseffekt hervorbringt.*

Schreibaufgaben

As mentioned in the introduction, all activities are best followed up with a written exercise for further reflection, analysis, or creative writing. Besides a theater journal, this includes reflections on the comparative effects and merits of acting theories.

To give an example, one may juxtapose the theories of Brecht and Goethe for reflection:

1. *Wie soll der Schauspieler laut Goethe die Natur nachahmen? Und was hätte Brecht gegen Goethe einzuwenden? Stellen Sie Goethes und Brechts Konzepte in einer Gliederung vergleichend gegenüber.*
2. *Stellungnahme (schriftlich und mündlich): Sie sind RegisseurIn und sollen ein Theaterstück in der Art Brechts oder Goethes inszenieren. Formulieren Sie Ihren eigenen Standpunkt zu den beiden Schauspieltheorien! Bereiten Sie sich auf eine Debatte vor, in der Sie die Perspektive von Brecht oder Goethe einnehmen.*
3. *Goethe verlangt von einem Schauspieler feste und genaue Gesten und Stellungen. Inwiefern unterscheiden sich Goethe und Brecht in ihren Ansichten über die Rolle, die das Bewusstsein für einen Schauspieler spielt?*

Creative writing

Script writing: Using an excerpt from silent film or muted film: Play the film (or a scene) and have students supply a dialogue to fill the silence. Have students describe the scene, guess from context what is going on, what happened before, and what will happen next. Describe characters in detail. If using a muted film, have students compare their dialogues with the original. (Also, supply subtitles in translation and compare with film's subtitles.)

Sketch writing: Contextualize and extend a short excerpt (a few lines) from a play or a film. Turn into a script and perform to the group; compare different versions.

Story completion: Write the ending (if unseen) or re-write the ending, emulating the style of the language and remaining true to the characters of the text of film.

Missing scene: Write a missing scene (from a film, antecedent, or off-stage action).

Adaptation: Re-write antiquated language in modernized language; re-stage the play in a modern setting; transform one genre into another, such as a short story into a short play (see especially ch. 5).

Analytical task

Charakteranalyse (advanced). In the context of a theater production, it is useful to have participants analyze their assigned character(s) in writing as well as physically. The following presents a general writing task:

Für die Charakteranalyse ist Folgendes festzustellen: 1. Das Thema und die Struktur des Dramas; 2. eine Beschreibung des Charakters; 3. die Funktion des Charakters im Drama (im dramatischen Konflikt).

Um was für eine Figur handelt es sich? Ist das ein traditioneller Protagonist, ein [Anti]Held, Gegenspieler, eine Kontrastfigur, ein Bösewicht, ein Intrigant, oder ein Nebenbuhler? Oder ist das eine Nebenfigur?

Depending on the play and genre, a selection of the following questions help prompt students to look for specific details and to consider the function of their character within the structure of the whole play.

Für eine Charakteranalyse sind folgende Fragen/Punkte zu berücksichtigen. Machen Sie zuerst Notizen zu den Fragen (und notieren Sie die Szenennummern!), die Sie für wichtig halten.

1. *Wie ist das Verhältnis des Schauspielers (der Figur) zu der Rolle: Wie entstehen diese Rollen auf der Bühne? Wie werden sie dargestellt? (Denken Sie hierbei z.B. an Kleidung, Sprache, Regie, Ansprache, usw.).*
2. *Name: Hat die Figur einen Namen? Was für ein Name ist das? (z.B. Ist das ein sprechender Name?)*
3. *Biographischer Hintergrund: Wie steht es um Alter, Herkunft, Beruf, sozioökonomischen Hintergrund?*
4. *Ausdrucksweise: Wie redet die Figur und wie geht sie mit anderen um? Beschreiben Sie die Ausdrucksweise (z.B.: Ist das emotional? mechanisch?)*
5. *Welche Beziehung hat er/sie zu anderen Figuren? Treffen sie sich? Lernen sie sich kennen? Gibt es Gemeinsamkeiten mit anderen Figuren? Gibt es Aspekte, in denen sich ihre Situationen spiegeln?*
6. *Handelt die Figur beständig, konsequent, oder widerspricht sie sich? Ist sie heuchlerisch, blind, unwissend, hochmütig, unterwürfig?*
7. *Welcher Charakterzug fällt besonders auf? Hat er/sie besondere Stärken oder Schwächen, oder irgendwelche emotionellen Schwierigkeiten oder Neigungen? Wie drückt sich das aus?*
8. *(Wie) verändert sich der Charakter im ganzen Drama?*
9. *Wie soll das Publikum auf den Charakter reagieren? (Bemitleidend? Einfühlend? Mit Furcht? Hass? Soll man sich mit dem Charakter identifizieren?)*
10. *Wie wichtig ist die Figur für das Drama als Ganzes? Wie würde es sich auf den Handlungsverlauf auswirken, wenn man sie herausnähme? Was würde fehlen oder nicht eintreten?*

Production preparations

Scene visualization

Purpose: To visualize the scene and familiarize students with the vocabulary of the theater (*Requisiten, Bühne, links, rechts, vorne, hinten, hinter den Kulissen*, etc.). This is also suitable in a regular course, serving to motivate close-reading and discussion.

Organization: Students draw scene(s), to be compared with each other's visualization.

Follow-up: Participants compare their visualizations as a segue to discussing scene design and potentially to discussing potential challenges and solutions.

Director's cut

This exercise is particularly engaging and practical in the context of a course that culminates in a theater production.

Purpose: To engage participants more directly in a directorial decision-making process and to reduce a play in order to make the production more manageable. In the process, considerations of character function are pertinent: What gets lost with certain lines, passages, or even characters?

Organization: Depending on the desired amount of excision and overall length of the play, participants take an act or a scene and decide what they would cut and why. (For a sample application, see ch. 2.)

Follow-up: Decisions are justified in class, leading to further in-depth discussion and, ideally, a collaborative decision.

Notes

1 For inspiration, students might want to view a video of twin sisters who have perfected the art of the fake mirror in a public bathroom, so as to fool other customers: https://www.youtube.com/watch?v=pBzU8TD1iks
2 "Pourtant, avec toi je préfère cette langue à la mienne, car pour moi, parler français, c'est parler sans parler, en quelque manière, – sans responsabilité." Mann 462. In similar fashion, Peter Bichsel considers language acquisition an opportunity to enter new world and play a different role, to engage in a new *Spielform* – a form of play – and to "become someone else." "Ich muss in dieser Sprache nicht vor allem jemand sein, sondern ich darf etwas spielen. [...] Die Fremdsprache – und das ist ihr Wert an und für sich – befreit mich oder gibt mir zum mindesten, und das ist schon viel, die Illusion von Befreiung: ein Stück Emanzipation. Cited in Huber 328–9.
3 I acknowledge Mark Römisch, who introduced me to the Pixar film in his inspiring guest workshop on Kleist's *Marionettentheater* in my German drama course. The film is available on YouTube: https://www.youtube.com/watch?v=D4NPQ8mfKU0

Further reading and resources
On acting

Brecht, Bertolt. "Kleines Organon für das Theater." *Gesammelte Werke*, vol. 16. Frankfurt am Main: Suhrkamp, 1967, 678–685.

Brecht, Bertolt. *Kurze Beschreibung einer neuen Technik der Schauspielkunst, die einen Verfremdungseffekt hervorbringt* (1940). *Gesammelte Werke*, vol. 22, no. 2. Frankfurt am Main: Suhrkamp, 1967, 641–659.

Goethe, Johann W. *Regeln für Schauspieler*. In *Werke*, vol. 12: *Schriften zur Kunst und Literatur, Maximen und Reflexionen*. Hamburger Ausgabe. Erich Trunz, ed. Munich: Deutscher Taschenbuch, 1998, 252–261.

Kleist, Heinrich von. *Über das Marionettentheater*. In *Sämtliche Werke und Briefe*, vol. 2. Helmut Sembdner, ed. Munich: Deutscher Taschenbuch Verlag, 2001, 338–345.

On process-drama exercises in the German-language classroom

Bräuer, Gerd. *Body and Language: Intercultural Learning through Drama*. Westport: Ablex, 2002.

Even, Susanne. "Multiple Hotseating." *Scenario*, vol. 5, no. 2, 2011, 106–107.

Even, Susanne. "Moving in(to) Imaginary Worlds: Drama Pedagogy for Foreign Language Teaching and Learning." *Die Unterrichtspraxis*, vol. 41, no. 2, 2008, 161–170.

Matthias, Bettina. "'Show, Don't Tell!' Improvisational Theater and the Beginning Foreign Language Curriculum." *Scenario*, vol. 1, no. 1, 2007, 51–65.

On process-drama exercises in the language classroom

Kao, Shin-Mei, and O'Neill, Cecily. *Words into Worlds*. Westport: Ablex, 1998.

Maley, Alan, and Duff, Alan. *Drama Techniques*. Cambridge: Ca UP, 1982.

Scheller, Ingo. *Szenisches Spiel*. Berlin: Cornelsen Scriptor, 2012.

Spolin, Viola. *Improvisation for the Theater: A Handbook of Teaching and Directing Techniques*. 3rd ed. Evanston: Northwestern UP, 1999.

Thiesen, Peter. *Werkzeugkasten Kreatives Spiel*. Freiburg: Lambertus, 2012.

Tschurtschenthaler, Helga. *Drama-based Foreign Language Learning: Encounters between Self and Other*. Münster: Waxmann, 2013.

Vlcek, Radim. *Workshop Improvisationstheater. Übungs- und Spielsammlung für Theaterarbeit, Ausdrucksfindung und Gruppendynamik*. Donauwörth: Auer, 2003.

On full theater productions

Marini-Maio, Nicoletta, and Ryan-Scheutz, Colleen. *Set the Stage! Teaching Italian through Theater. Theories, Methods, and Practices*. New Haven: Yale UP, 2010.

Ryan-Scheutz, Colleen, and Colangelo, Laura M. "Full-Scale Theater Production and Foreign Language Learning." *Foreign Language Annals*, vol. 37, 2004, 374–389.

Schewe, Manfred. *Texte lesen und inszenieren. Alfred Andersch: Sansibar oder der letzte Grund*. Munich: Klett, 1995.

On German pronunciation

Hirschfeld, Ursula et al. *Phonotek intensiv: Aussprachetraining. Arbeits- und Übungsbuch.* Stuttgart: Klett, 2017. [Includes two CDs.]

References

Bräuer, Gerd. *Body and Language: Intercultural Learning through Drama.* Westport: Ablex, 2002.

Brecht, Bertolt. *Kleines Organon für das Theater. Gesammelte Werke*, vol. 16, Frankfurt am Main: Suhrkamp, 1967, 678–685.

Brecht, Bertolt. *Kurze Beschreibung einer neuen Technik der Schauspielkunst, die einen Verfremdungseffekt hervorbringt* (1940). *Gesammelte Werke*, vol. 22, no. 2. Frankfurt am Main: Suhrkamp, 1967, 641–659.

Craig, Edward Gordon. *The Actor and the Über-Marionette.* Florence: The Mask, 1908.

Hirschfeld, Ursula et al. *Phonotek intensiv: Aussprachetraining. Arbeits- und Übungsbuch.* Stuttgart: Klett, 2017.

Huber, Ruth. *Im Haus der Sprache wohnen. Wahrnehmung und Theater im Fremdsprachenunterricht.* Tübingen: Niemeyer, 2003.

Kao, Shin-Mei, and O'Neill, Cecily. *Words into Worlds.* Westport: Ablex, 1998.

Kleist, Heinrich von. *Über das Marionettentheater.* In *Sämtliche Werke und Briefe*, vol. 2. Helmut Sembdner, ed. Munich: Deutscher Taschenbuch Verlag, 2001, 338–345.

Le Bœuf, Patrick. "On the Nature of Edward Gordon Craig's *Über-Marionette.*" *New Theatre Quarterly*, vol. 26, no. 2, 2010, 102–114.

Maley, Alan, and Duff, Alan. *Drama Techniques.* Cambridge: Cambridge UP, 1982.

Mann, Thomas. *Der Zauberberg.* Berlin: Fischer, 1991.

Marini-Maio, Nicoletta, and Ryan-Scheutz, Collen. *Set the Stage! Teaching Italian through Theater. Theories, Methods, and Practices.* New Haven: Yale UP, 2010.

Ryan-Scheutz, Colleen, and Colangelo, Laura M. "Full-Scale Theater Production and Foreign Language Learning." *Foreign Language Annals*, vol. 37, 2004, 374–389.

Scheller, Ingo. *Szenisches Spiel.* Berlin: Cornelsen Scriptor, 2012.

Schewe, Manfred. *Texte lesen und inszenieren. Alfred Andersch: Sansibar oder der letzte Grund.* Munich: Klett, 1995.

Spolin, Viola. *Improvisation for the Theater: A Handbook of Teaching and Directing Techniques.* 3rd ed. Evanston: Northwestern UP, 1999.

Thiesen, Peter. *Werkzeugkasten Kreatives Spiel.* Freiburg: Lambertus, 2012.

Tschurtschenthaler, Helga. *Drama-based Foreign Language Learning: Encounters between Self and Other.* Münster: Waxmann, 2013.

Vlcek, Radim. *Workshop Improvisationstheater. Übungs- und Spielsammlung für Theaterarbeit, Ausdrucksfindung und Gruppendynamik.* Donauwörth: Auer, 2003.

Vygotsky, Lev S. "Play and Its Role in the Mental Development of the Child." *Soviet Psychology*, vol. 5, no. 3, 1967, 6–18.

Vygotsky, Lev S., and Cole, Michael. *Mind in Society: The Development of Higher Psychological Processes.* Cambridge: Harvard UP, 1978.

2   *Trauerspiel*: teaching tragedy

Key considerations

Table 2.1

Premiere	Radio broadcast, Nordwest Deutscher Rundfunk, February 13, 1947 Hamburg Kammerspiele, November 21, 1947
Performance Length	Approx. 80 minutes
Cast	16 (including non-speaking street-sweeper). Because Beckmann appears throughout, his character may be divided among participants.
Set	Seven scenes, some symbolic settings (river and dream sequence), all manageable with minimal set alterations.
Language	Generally uncomplicated, straightforward language, often short sentences, comprehensible at the intermediate-high level (B1/B2).
Topic and Complexity	War, WWII, the returning soldier, challenges of reintegration into society, estrangement, loss of faith.
Potential challenges	The length of some monologues; some cuts desirable. Managing multiple versions of Beckmann to make workload equitable. Some imaginative lighting to render symbolic level of scenes, such as the nightmare vision of the military march being played on a large xylophone made of bones.

Introduction

How does one teach or stage a play that "no theater wants to perform, and no audience wants to see"? A play, moreover, that was allegedly written in just eight days, without hope or even intention of a performance, and consequently without particular regard to formal theatrical conventions, Wolfgang Borchert's own subtitle to *Draußen vor der Tür* (1947), a play "das kein Theater spielen und kein Publikum sehen will" was no self-fulfilling prophecy, however. On the contrary, this play would become one of the most widely performed and seen of the postwar period, as the next half-century of theater history worldwide would bear out. Within a month of its premiere at the

DOI: 10.4324/9781003010289-2

Hamburg Kammerspiele on November 21, 1947, 13 theater companies had taken up the play into their repertoire (Müller-Marein). The play has since been translated into over 40 different languages and has become a staple of the German curriculum and of theaters worldwide. Its enduring success, and Borchert's posthumous rise to fame, moreover, is owed largely to the emotional directness with which the play expresses the horrors of war, giving voice to a whole generation that had been tragically silenced. As journalist and personal acquaintance Axel Eggebrechtput later recollected: "Die Wirkung war so groß, weil Borchert als Zeuge der schrecklichen Geschehnisse im Krieg sprach – ohne Mätzchen. Das wirkte so kurz nach dem Krieg unglaublich auf die Menschen" (Rehrmann). One of these silenced victims was the author himself, Wolfgang Borchert, a returning soldier who succumbed to fatal disease just one day before the play's premiere, on the occasion of which his death was formally announced.

A "tragedy of a returning soldier" (Klarmann 108), this play presents a mercilessly despairing lament of Corporal Beckmann, who recounts what he experiences as the incomprehensible indifference and complacency encountered upon his return to Germany from captivity in Siberia. Beckmann is forced to grapple with the fact that everyone else appears to have moved on: His wife has taken another; the Colonel refuses to share responsibility for the deaths of his comrades; the Cabaret Director is uninterested in his gallows humor; and his parents have committed suicide. Even the river Elbe dismisses his initial suicide attempt. Rejected or ignored at every turn, Beckman remains "outside," unable – or unwilling – to re-enter life. The play's brutally frank depiction of a soldier's experience also filled the silence of the immediate postwar theaters in search of direction at the so-called *Stunde Null* (Zero Hour) – the *tabula rasa* of German theater (Mennemaier 141) – when occupying powers re-envisioned the theater scene in their own image as part of their efforts to "re-educate" Germany. As a result of this ideological reorientation, German-language theater – along with concert halls, cinemas, newspapers, publishing houses, and media-production services[1] – would be subject to censorship and largely replaced by foreign-language cultural programs of the Western Allies. Not even Borchert would elude the scrutiny of the information control divisions of the respective occupational zones, who, much to Borchert's consternation, aggressively censored parts of the version that Borchert had rewritten for the radio. These excisions rendered the play politically and emotionally more restrained, forward-looking, and therefore "safe" for German ears by the time it was first broadcast on Hamburg's Nordwestdeutscher Rundfunk (NDWR) on February 13, 1947. Given the ongoing Nuremberg trials against war criminals (1945–6), any perceived criticism of the allied-backed institutions or overstated self-victimization – including, by implication, members of the audience itself – was to be redacted, likely in order to prevent any interference with the denazification process (Warkentin 263).[2]

Whether or not such redactions from the radio play contributed to Borchert's cynicism regarding the subsequent theatrical performance, however, remains unclear. The third version, which Borchert reluctantly revised at the request of the Hamburg Kammerspiele, was based largely on the original play (Warkentin 256–7). According to Borchert in an interview, who was by that time bed-ridden, the only reason for any theater to mount a production of his play would be for the sheer lack of anything else to do (Rühmkorf 162). But for a radio play that was not allowed to be fully heard and a stage play that supposedly nobody wanted to produce or see, *Draußen vor der Tür* immediately captured the attention of a far greater audience than anticipated, both over the soundwaves and in the theaters, and possibly for the same reasons that it provoked the censors: for its emotionally raw, heart-wrenching tone, its unremitting cynicism, its direct confrontation with questions of guilt and responsibility, and with God's apparent impotence in a world bereft of meaning and hope.

In prioritizing raw verbal expression over artistic form, and by refusing to provide any answers or closure, however, this play departs dramatically from what one would consider a conventional "tragedy." The structure and content of the play is guided instead by Beckmann's inner world – by his recollections, dreams, and hallucinations. From the opening drowning scene in the river Elbe, we witness his recollection of encounters with those he visited after the War (the Colonel, the Cabaret Director, and Frau Kramer, who now inhabits his dead parents' home); figments of Beckmann's imagination (the over-bloated figure of Death; the girl; a senile, impotent God; symbolic figures of Death; and Beckmann's own one-legged "double,*" Der Einbeinige*); as well as the company of *Der Andere*, whose insistent yeah-saying is eventually silenced by Beckmann. Beckmann's final desperate pleas for help fall on deaf ears: "Warum schweigt ihr den? ... Gibt denn keiner, keiner Antwort?" (165). The play is an open-ended lament, a *Trauerspiel*, not in the sense that the particular genre was originally conceived or subsequently developed, but rather a "play of mourning" or a "play of suffering" along the lines that Schopenhauer nihilistically viewed it – he uses the word *Trauerspiel* – as a static, resigned descent, without closure or catharsis. In its linguistic and formal terseness, the play cuts through generic conventions to lay bare the physical and psychological wreckage of Germany, including the author himself, culminating in a genuine piece of *Trümmerliteratur* ("rubble literature") or *Kahlschlagliteratur* ("clear-cutting literature") of the immediate postwar years.

Theater has frequently undergone innovation and reform in the wake of great historical tumult and crisis, of which this play is but one outcome. Innovative playwrights, in turn, have used the stage to try to lend meaning to great suffering, and as a site of moral and political education and social change. A brief overview of the place of tragedy as it develops in the German-speaking context helps us to understand what continues to draw us back to Beckmann's closing questions – "can no one, no one give me answer?" – and to probe what lies behind Borchert's *Draußen vor der Tür.*

In and outside history: *Tragödie* and *Trauerspiel*

If the development of German tragedy has played a greater role in the cultural-historical discourse, as is frequently claimed, it is largely due to the privileged status it was traditionally accorded, following Aristotle in his *Poetics*. Its superior status would especially be nurtured during the eighteenth century, when the theory of tragedy became a preoccupation of German philosophers and playwrights, who in turn sought to emancipate German-speaking theater from its dependence on inherited French models by cultivating a German national consciousness. Gotthold Ephraim Lessing's *Miß Sara Samson* (1755) was the first domestic (bourgeois) tragedy, a *bürgerliches Trauerspiel*, conceived in reaction to the domination of Louis XIV's court and its neo-classical theatrical artifice. Thus, the formal and linguistic reform of *Tragödie* and *Komödie* – the *bürgerliches Trauerspiel* and *bürgerliches Lustspiel* – coincided with a need for a specifically "German" theater and the emerging consciousness of a "German" national identity among the middle classes, who turned to theater as a means for the kind of debate formerly denied them in the public sphere.

Introduced originally by Gottlob Benjamin Pfeil in an essay *Vom bürgerlichen Trauerspiel* (1755) and subsequently by Lessing in his *Hamburgische Dramaturgie* (1769), the *bürgerliches Trauerspiel* dismantled precisely those pedantic rules – the most notable of these being an adherence to the *Ständesklausel* – previously dictated by literary critic Johann Christoph Gottsched. According to Lessing, just as the educated middle classes (*Bildungsbürger*) were morally elevated to a "high" enough standing (*Standespersonen*) to merit a tragic fall (*Fallhöhe*) in tragedy, so, too, were aristocrats deserving of ridicule in comedy. A new theater about the middle classes would also be able to morally educate the middle classes to become *Bildungsbürger*, as did a small number of bourgeois tragedies by Lessing (*Emilia Galotti*, 1772), Friedrich Schiller (*Kabale und Liebe*, 1784), and Friedrich Hebbel (*Maria Magdalena*, 1843), which mark a significant point of departure from their classical antecedents.[3]

As a specifically German genre, however, it did not have an enduring influence; in the strict sense, one might regard Hebbel's *Maria Magdalena* as marking its conclusion in 1843 (Guthke 1). Nor were many plays necessarily designated a *Trauerspiel* in order to distinguish a specifically German variety of tragedy, despite retrospective efforts, by Walter Benjamin and others, to claim a unique German literary heritage – ending, as with all historiographical theories of a German *Sonderweg*, with the tragedy of the Second World War and the Holocaust. Nevertheless, the preoccupation with tragedy and the tragic, particularly in German-speaking culture from the mid-eighteenth century onwards, is amply evident in philosophy, theory, and on the stage.

It would be an insurmountable and self-defeating task to summarize the vast number of theories of tragedy here, or indeed in the context of an undergraduate course, even one dedicated exclusively to tragedy in the German tradition. Such an overview, however, may be gleaned from Ulrich

Profitlich's very useful sourcebook, *Tragödientheorie: Texte und Kommentare vom Barock bis zur Gegenwart* (TT), which complements his *Komödientheorie* (see ch. 3). In the present context, it is more productive to carve a pathway through the vast tragic landscape that is also guided by Beckmann's own primary concern: his hopeless pursuit of existential meaning. One significant *Leitfaden* and motivation for such a sustained preoccupation with tragedy in German philosophy derives from Aristotle's distinction between the writing of poetry and the writing of history:

> The true difference [between poetry and history] is that one relates to what *has happened*, the other to what *may happen*. Poetry, therefore, is more philosophical and a higher thing than history: for poetry tends to express the universal, history the particular. By the universal, I mean how a person of a certain type will on occasion speak or act, according to the law of *probability* or *necessity*. ... (ch. 9; emphasis mine)

If history is devoid of the laws of probability or necessity, then poetry must insist upon their recuperation. Grounded in reason, the poetic universal postulates an alternative narrative to historical events, thereby lending meaning to an otherwise meaningless and seemingly irrational world (see also Aristotle ch. 6). Poetry, in other words, gives meaning and structure to otherwise seemingly senseless suffering and death. In witnessing a series of events that lead necessarily and logically (rather than irrationally or arbitrarily) to the tragic fall, the spectator is able to make sense of and even derive pleasure from the fear and pity it arouses. The resulting "tragic paradox" – the paradox of deriving pleasure from tragic pain – is an issue with which many philosophers have subsequently grappled. For Aristotle, tragedy gains its full force within the logic of probability or necessity:

> Tragedy is an imitation not only of a *complete action*, but of events inspiring fear or pity. Such an effect is best produced when the events come on us by surprise; and the effect is heightened when, at the same time, they follow as *cause* and *effect*. ... Plots constructed on these principles [and not on chance] are necessarily the best. (ch. 9, 1452a, 62–3; emphasis mine)

In other words, the *cause* provides meaning and solace in suffering and mortality. Like Beckmann, the spectator hopes for enlightenment, seeking reasonable causes for devastating effects, to penetrate the unknown. Unlike Beckmann, however, the spectator of Aristotelian tragedy witnesses formal and thematic closure – the "chief thing of all" (ch. 6, 1450a, 50–1) – and thus gains aesthetic control of the seeming irrationality of existence.

In his *Hamburgische Dramaturgie,* Lessing is the first of many German theorists to invoke a special affinity with ancient Greek thought by underscoring Aristotle's distinction between poetry and history:

> Denn der dramatische Dichter ist kein Geschichtsschreiber; ... er läßt es nochmals geschehen, nicht der bloßen historischen Wahrheit wegen, sondern in einer ganz andern und höhern Absicht; die historische Wahrheit ist nicht sein Zweck, sondern nur das Mittel zu seinem Zwecke; er will uns täuschen, und durch die Täuschung rühren. (TT 64)

The task of the poet, Lessing continues, is not in the faithful imitation of historical parts, but rather in transcending the parts to make sense of the whole:

> ... so wird es seinen guten Grund in dem ewigen unendlichen Zusammenhange aller Dinge haben. In diesem ist Weisheit und Güte, was uns in dem wenigen Gliedern, die der Dichter herausnimt, blindes Geschick und Grausamkeit scheinet. Aus diesen wenigen Gliedern sollte er ein Ganzes machen, das völlig sich rundet, wo eines aus dem andern sich völlig erkläret, wo keine Schwierigkeit aufstößt, derenwegen wir die Befriedigung nicht in seinem Plane finden, sondern sie außer ihm, in dem allgemeinen Plane der Dinge, suchen müssen; das Ganze dieses sterblichen Schöpfers sollte ein Schattenriß von dem Ganzen des ewigen Schöpfers seyn. (TT 70)

Lessing further stresses the all-important principle of necessity (*Notwendigkeit*) and probability (*Wahrscheinlichkeit*) within the plot structure (TT 65), but also raises the importance of probability through identification of the spectator with the hero, without which, pity and fear would be impossible. Most important for Lessing, however, is the aesthetic corrective to tragedy: Through emotional identification with the hero, catharsis is to purify (*re-inigen*) us of our extreme tragic passions, transforming them into virtuous dispositions: "Da ... diese *Reinigung* in nichts anders beruhet, als in der *Verwandlung der Leidenschaften* [Furcht und Mitleid] in *tugenhafte Fertigkeiten*" (TT 69; emphasis mine). And, by stressing the importance of emotion, tragedy can make us feel empathy, the most important of all social virtues: "*Der mitleidigste Mensch ist der beste Mensch*" (TT 56; emphasis in original).

With varying degrees of didactic impulse, tragedy would continue to serve a practical end in the edification and cultivation (*Bildung*) of the middle classes. The educational function of theater was further explicitly pursued by Schiller in his essay *Die Schaubühne als eine moralische Anstalt betrachtet* (1784), while also positing tragedy as a means for theodicy. Like Lessing, Schiller (in *Über die tragische Kunst*, 1792) emphasizes the principles of completeness and necessity – "dichterische Nachahmung einer zusammenhängenden Reihe von Begebenheiten (einer vollständigen Handlung)" – that also must accord with the spectator's experience. Most significant for Schiller is tragedy's poetic capacity to captivate the audience by stirring the emotions – "und dadurch wird sie der *historischen* entgegengesetzt ... Aber die Tragödie hat einen *poetischen* Zweck, d.i. sie stellt eine Handlung dar, um zu *rühren*, und durch Rührung zu *ergötzen*" (TT 94; emphasis in original). In this, Schiller emphasizes the enlightening function and of poetry and its capacity to bring sentiment and rationality into equanimous balance: "Diese hohe Gleichmüthigkeit und Freyheit des Geistes, mit Kraft und Rüstigkeit verbunden, ist die Stimmung, in der uns sein ächtes Kunstwerk entlassen soll," Schiller argues in his essay *Ueber die Ästhetische Erziehung des Menschen* (SW 20 380). It is this aesthetic freedom – the *Spieltrieb* – that brings these two drives into harmony and elevates us, as is expressed most famously in the prologue to his *Wallenstein* trilogy (1799): "Ernst ist das Leben, heiter ist die Kunst" (274).

One hears further echoes of Lessing and Schiller's primary concerns throughout the nineteenth century. What followed the late-eighteenth-century emphasis on emotionality, however, was a retreat to more restrained emotion towards the turn of the nineteenth century. Conceived as an antidote to the emotionality of *Sturm und Drang* and Weimar Classicism and the Reign of Terror in France, the ideal of restraint of Weimar Classicism was developed by Goethe and Schiller. *Edle Einfalt und stille Größe*, an ideal that Johann Winckelmann identified in Greek art, was the dictum upon which Schiller and Goethe modelled German theater in an attempt to cultivate moral sensibility, restraint and decorum not only in their audience, but also in the actor, as Goethe's *Regeln für Schauspieler* would demonstrate (see ch. 1). Goethe's appeal to the actor for restraint both on and off stage, and his prescriptions for representing nature in an idealized form, combining "truth with beauty," would yield during the nineteenth century to "realism," to depicting the real (not idealized) life of citizens, often with political ramifications. It is in this context that the development and eventual demise of conventional tragedy in the twentieth century may be understood.

One reason not to pursue one of the plays designated as tragedies, or *Trauerspiele*, in the present chapter owes to the fact that that it is the genre to whose conventions most playwrights adhered most fastidiously: most are three- or five-act plays from the pre-twentieth-century period, posing linguistic and especially logistical challenges. Realistically, such plays may only be performed with significant editing. For these reasons, shorter plays from the early twentieth century present more suitable selections, even though the conventional genre ceases to be an adequate form of expression after the turmoil of the two World Wars.

Trümmertragödie: tragedy in ruins

Borchert's play may not be considered a tragedy in the conventional Aristotelian sense: there is no closure or catharsis, no edification or pleasure to be derived from the play, no probable or necessary plot development, no elevated greatness from which to fall, no moral agency, and no moment of insight. Both Beckmann and the spectator remain "outside." In this respect,

Borchert's play continues a more general dissolution of conventional forms that had begun in the early twentieth century – albeit in continued reaction to Aristotelian aesthetics. Bertolt Brecht, for example, also does not designate any of his plays "tragedies," introducing "epic" theater instead in direct response to Aristotelian "dramatic" theater, and especially as a critique of the putative educative role of the emotions. According to Brecht, emotional involvement and empathy do not promote but rather impede learning and critical reflection. Brecht insists instead on shifting focus away from the tragic fate of the hero with whom we identify towards generalized types, whose suffering no longer derives from an individual's flaw but rather results from social contexts. These are made manifestly apparent by rendering them unfamiliar – through *Verfremdung* – so that they appear unnatural and therefore questionable. One particularly relevant defamiliarization technique is that of historical distance. In contrast to the conventional elevation of poetry over history by virtue of its capacity to present a complete and coherent narrative, Brecht constructs a series of self-contained episodes in order to demonstrate that tragic events are not always driven by necessity and probability. Rather, Brecht presents scenes in a non-causal, radically historical sequence that exposes them as unnecessary and therefore *necessarily* alterable. Brecht's *Mutter Courage und ihre Kinder,* completed in exile at the outbreak of the Second World War in 1939, and set during the Thirty Years' War (1618–48), is perhaps the most pertinent illustration. In presenting an historically distanced account of human suffering through war, and in emphasizing the (blindness to the) material conditions that cause suffering, Brecht hopes to prompt the audience to reflect critically on the interdependent problems of war and capitalism. While the solution is not presented, the conditions are set for the audience to identify the social causes of suffering and to become agents of change.

Only eight years later, shortly after World War II, however, the search for answers to human suffering would seem futile. In *Draußen vor der Tür*, the question that haunts Beckmann – and that had occupied tragedians and philosophers for centuries – remains unanswered. It is, quite literally, a tragedy in ruins. Conventional tragedy had ceased to be appropriate or conceivable after WWII, since when such designations had lost any significance and all but dissolved, as the sparsity of German-language tragedies in the postwar era indicates (TT 306).[4] Some rejected the suitability of tragedy on account of the audience's numbed capacity for critical or emotional reception – let alone a Schillerian *Spieltrieb* – and thus the possibility of changing consciousness in a positive way; others on account of the impossibility of doing justice to the enormity of mass death and suffering in war, which far exceeded art's ability to represent a plot of "a certain magnitude ... that may be easily embraced in one view" (Aristotle, *Poetics*, 7, 1450b, 54–5). Friedrich Dürrenmatt deems pure tragedy no longer conceivable on account of both the receptive and thematic challenges. Tragedy, he argues, is problematic in its proximity to its historical subject, unlike comedy, which creates the necessary distance (see ch. 3). In an interview with Artur Joseph (1966), he states:

> Sichtbar in der Kunst ist das Überschaubare. Der heutige Staat ist jedoch unüberschaubar, anonym, bürokratisch geworden ... Die echten Repräsentanten fehlen, und die tragischen Helden sind ohne Namen ... Der Staat hat seine Gestalt verloren ... Ich glaube nicht mehr, daß wir heute eine Welt haben, in der man reine Tragödien zeigen kann. (TT 315–16)

Hence Dürrenmatt's turn to comedy and mixed genres such as tragicomedy (see ch. 4). Moreover, all moral agency, a prerequisite for tragedy, has been all but lost:

> Die Tragödie setzt Schuld, Not, Maß, Übersicht, Verantwortung voraus. In der Wurstelei unseres Jahrhunderts, in diesem Kehraus der weißen Rasse, gibt es keine Schuldigen und auch keine Verantwortlichen mehr. Alle können nichts dafür und haben es nicht gewollt ... Wir sind zu kollektiv schuldig, zu kollektiv gebettet in die Sünden unserer Väter und Vorväter. (*Theaterprobleme;* TT 311)

The concept of collective guilt guided much of the public discourse and the German re-education program in the immediate postwar years, in which the theater repertoire played a central role. As a concept distinct from individual guilt, collective guilt was introduced by Karl Jaspers in his essay *Die Schuldfrage* (1946), written during the Nuremberg trials (1945–6), just one year after the Potsdam Conference (17 July–2 August 1945). At Potsdam, the United Kingdom, the United States, and the Soviet Union passed resolutions to

> convince the German people that they have suffered a total military defeat and that they cannot escape responsibility for what they have brought upon themselves, since their own ruthless warfare and the fanatical Nazi resistance have destroyed the German economy and made chaos and suffering inevitable. (Fischer-Lichte 187)

The much-reduced program of German-language plays approved by the allied powers in the same year, which were replaced largely by English-language cultural programs, was one evident outcome. Focusing particularly on plays that promoted religious tolerance and the acceptance of responsibility, the allies approved some plays previously banned during the Third Reich, such as Lessing's *Nathan der Weise* (religious tolerance), Schiller's *Wilhelm Tell* (defiance of oppressive authority), as well as productions of Sophocles' *Oedipus Rex* and *Antigone* (guilt and responsibility).[5] Moreover, it is on the occasion of receiving the Lessing-Prize that Hannah Arendt would later criticize Germany's collectively wrong-headed resolve not to confront but rather to "overcome" the past – "die Vergangenheit zu bewältigen" – at the end of the 1960s, by when the concept of collective guilt had been abandoned while economic optimism, fueled by the *Wirtschaftswunder*, took root.

In her speech, *Von der Menschlichkeit in finsteren Zeiten: Rede über Lessing*, Arendt insists on the importance of the ritualized experience of lament (*Klage*) in confronting, remembering, mourning, and understanding the atrocities of war, and that this may happen only in authentic accounts, "welche die *innere Wahrheit* des Geschehens so transparent in Erscheinung brachte, daß man sagen konnte: *Ja, so ist es gewesen*" (Arendt 33; emphasis mine). Nothing need be described,

> weniger noch erklärt und gar nichts 'bewältigt'; sein Ende sind Tränen, die der Leser mitweint, und was darüber hinaus verbleibt, ist der 'tragische Effekt' oder die 'tragische Lust,' deren Erschütterungen uns instand setzt, uns damit abzufinden, daß sich so etwas wie dieser Krieg überhaupt ereignet hat. Ich erwähne absichtlich die Form der Tragödie, weil sie mehr als andere Formen der Dichtung einen Erkennungsprozeß darstellt. Der tragische Held wird wissend, indem er das Getane noch einmal *in der Form des Erleidens* erfährt. ... (Arendt 33–4; emphasis mine)

Those who seek refuge from the world during these dark times must not ignore the reality from which they escape, Arendt continues, but instead keep it perpetually present ("in der ständigen Präsenz behalten," Arendt 37) so that the meaning is kept alive in the form of ever-recurrent narration (35).

Written in response to the intellectual climate of postwar Germany, these passages could just as well have been written about Borchert's *Draußen vor der Tür*. For this play confronts, recalls, and mourns the "inner truth" of what happened during the war "in the form of suffering," kept alive in ever-recurring narration – as a lamentation. Quite in contrast to Brecht, whose audience is discouraged from thinking "Ja, das habe ich auch schon gefühlt," but encouraged instead to think "Das hätte ich nicht gedacht" (Brecht 55), Borchert confronts his audience directly, in linguistic simplicity, without constraint or defamiliarization, so that the audience might think "Ja, so ist es gewesen." Both the immediate physical and psychological impact of the war as well as questions of guilt and responsibility form the key formal and thematic concerns of Borchert's *Draußen vor der Tür*, in which inner truths are juxtaposed with outright denial that this is "how it was." It is in this context that one can read Borchert's intimation that this is a play "that no theater wants to perform and no audience wants to see." And it is all the more fitting, therefore, that Arendt should deliver her speech on "humanity in dark times" in Hamburg, home to both Lessing's Nationaltheater and of Borchert's play, by which time the embers of Enlightenment had long been extinguished. The play would in fact be performed over and over, as a kind of ritual experience of lament and mourning of the kind that Arendt describes, and that refuses to "overcome" past atrocities.

As a ritualized staple of German theater and a hard-wearing educational tool in Germany and beyond, what, then, does Borchert's *Draußen vor der Tür* mean to us today, and how can the foreign-language learner best gain critical insight into the existential fragilities it performs?

The following outlines an approach that begins with an historical and cross-cultural contextualization, followed by drama-based explorations of the text, presented over four 90-minute class sessions. Depending on course goals and time allocated to each class session, the play may also be extended over five sessions, or indeed reduced, such that the *Vorspiel* and *Traum* are included in the introductory session.

Day 1: Introduction, pre-reading explorations, *Trümmerliteratur*

Day 2: *Vorspiel* and *Traum*

Day 3: Scenes 1–4

Day 4: Scene 5

Introduction and pre-reading explorations

Beginning with an initial exploration of students' familiarity with existing narratives of the returning soldier – from the ancient to the contemporary – it is possible to establish some basic concepts, vocabulary, and a horizon of expectations. While most students will likely be familiar with Homer's *Odyssey* or any of its adaptations, others may be familiar with more modern stories such as Rebecca West's *The Return of the Soldier* (1918), or well-known Hollywood "coming home" (or Nostos) films such as Michael Cimino's *The Deer Hunter* (1978), Ted Kotcheff's "Rambo" trilogy *First Blood* (1982–8), Rick Rosenthal's *Distant Thunder* (1988), David Jones' *Jackknife* (1989), or Oliver Stone's *Born on the Fourth of July* (1989), all dealing with Vietnam veterans; or Paul Haggis' *In the Valley of Elah* (2007), which deals with an Iraq War veteran. Common to all of these narratives are the challenges faced by soldiers attempting to reintegrate into their families and to adapt to postwar life more generally. Although these encompass a full range of perspectives, from glorified heroism to critical exposés and demoralized defeat – according to the respective ideological context in which these narratives were produced – they all share the following common tropes: tension between the returning soldier's experiences and the expectations of those he left behind; post-traumatic stress, physical impairment, disability or disfigurement; social exclusion, alienation, alcoholism, and dysfunctional, anti-social and threatening behavior, including violence.

To round off this discussion of competing ideological perspectives, it is worth reading and listening to Carl Strässer's *Tapfere kleine Soldatenfrau* (1940). A popular propaganda song of the Third Reich, it provided not only sentimental optimism for brave soldiers returning to their faithful, loving wives, but also the basis for Beckmann's highly cynical parody of the song in the fourth scene – one that reveals an experience entirely contrary to what had been promised and expected.

Because the fate of the author relates so closely to that of Beckmann, and because Borchert's play does not attempt to provide poetic sense of his suffering, Borchert's short biography merits attention before introducing the play. From the single-page biography presented succinctly in the Rowohlt *Taschenausgabe,* students can find out the answers to questions about his short life and death, his involvement in the war, the reasons for his imprisonment, and his narrow evasion of the death penalty.

Embodying the *Heimkehrer*

In contemplating a *Heimkehrerdrama* from the perspective of performance, it is worth taking into account its abandonment of formal conventions as well as its cross-media origins, even if the theater and radio versions are by no means identical. Stage directions focus almost exclusively on vocal expression and sound, rather than on physical gesture, all which must be realized by the actors as they embody characters and symbolic figures, such as the river Elbe. The challenge, however, presents an opportunity to pay special attention to precise vocal expression and its connection to appropriate emotional and physical gestures.

Walking in character: Students first explore the physicality of the returning soldier in Germany 1945. In a large space, participants walk around the room as a returning soldier, either in response to the instructor's prompts or as an embodiment of their own imagination. A variation involves dividing the class into two groups, one walking and the other observing and supplying prompts, commenting and side-coaching, and then reversing roles. This prompts a follow-up discussion about the various possible realizations of a soldier's psychological and physical trauma.

Following this brief exploration, a cross-cultural comparison of the returning soldier is facilitated by comparing photographs and images. A particularly productive pairing is provided in juxtaposed images of returning German soldiers with Alfred Eisenstaedt's famous photograph that captures a returning sailor embracing an unknown dental assistant in New York's Times Square on the Victory of Japan Day.[6] The stark contrasts between these two photographs, from the bleak return to an empty city in ruins to the warm embrace in New York, provides a suitable starting point to compare the psychological and physical impacts of war, both demoralized and heroic.

Trümmerliteratur

The images of the *Heimkehrer* finding himself amid ruins provide an introduction to the context of Germany's *Stunde Null* and to *Trümmerliteratur*, a literature whose skeletal linguistic means not only conveyed Germany's psychological and physical ruin, but also stripped itself of any associations with the language of Germany before the Zero Hour. Depending on the course goals and available time, this may be extended over a series of lessons or may be accomplished in a brief excursion in the same class session by way of a poem by Borchert, or Günter Eich's well-known "Inventur." Alternatively, students may read one of the many (over 50) short stories by Borchert, such as "Das Brot," "Nachts schlafen die Ratten doch," "Die Küchenuhr," or "Die drei dunklen Könige" – all of which have also become standard reading in the curriculum in Germany and abroad (see, for example, textbooks for intermediate German such as Wells' *Mitlesen-Mitteilen,* Teichert's *Allerlei zum Lesen*).

Draußen vor der Tür

The discussion of Borchert's play then begins as this chapter began: with a discussion of the title and subtitle. Who stands "outside the door"? What kinds of "doors," literal, figurative or symbolic, might be implied? What does one hope or hope not to find behind the door? To probe further, different frameworks – existential, religious, psychological, mythic, supernatural – may be invoked. Besides the literal meaning, doors may present an opening or closing, entry or exclusion, beginning or ending, threshold or limit, an obstacle or gateway to meaning or truth, to society or community, to new possibilities or new worlds, to reality or fantasy, the past or future, or a threshold to life or death. The door may also mark a character's activity or inactivity, defiance or passivity, courage or cowardice. In this context, reference to some other well-known narrativesm, in which doors assume a key function, will no doubt help prompt such considerations.[7] These reflections accompany the interpretation of the play as Beckmann is confronted with series of literal and symbolic doors.

The cast of characters and their appended descriptors offer preliminary insights into how to read this play and to begin interpreting the "door." Each character is associated with a different kind of door, each representing an option or an obstacle for the protagonist. Other than Beckmann, all characters are nameless, merely identified by their functions and attributes: Beckmann's wife, "who forgot him"; her new lover, a girl whose husband returned on one leg; the "humorous" Colonel and his wife, who suffers from the cold in her warm room; the Cabaret Director "who would like to be brave but prefers to be cowardly"; the Undertaker with hiccoughs; the street cleaner, "who is no street cleaner at all"; and God, "the old man, in whom nobody believes anymore." It is also worth speculating the identity of "the Other" (a figment of Beckmann's psyche), the reasons for the hiccoughs, and the symbolic function of the river Elbe (as birth or rebirth, of origins, crossings or transitions, and of the unconscious).

Predicting content: From this assembly of characters, it is already possible to begin to anticipate much of the context, symbolic mood and tone. Working in small groups, students read the opening statement preceding the prologue in order to summarize the content in their own words, beginning with the simple prompt: *Dieses Stück handelt von einem Mann, der....* The groups subsequently compare their prediction summaries as a basis for further discussion.

In drawing attention back to the opening question about the function of the door, it is important to highlight Beckmann's descriptor – "einer von denen." Beckmann is representative of the many others, "die nach Hause kommen und die dann doch nicht nach Hause kommen, weil für sie kein Zuhause mehr da ist. Und ihr Zuhause ist dann draußen vor der Tür" (8). The door, then, presents a symbolic obstacle to any returning soldier, who no longer finds a "home" but rather exclusion, "draußen, nachts im Regen, auf der Straße" (8). Beckmann, who is watching a film, finds himself unable to tell whether he is sleeping or waking, experiencing fiction or living reality: "Er muß sich bei der Vorstellung mehrmals in den Arm kneifen" (8). Moreover, he also finds that many others in the audience are experiencing the same. By invoking a cinematic audience that is unable to distinguish between reality and a "very ordinary, everyday film" about "a man who comes to Germany," Borchert implicitly suspends any clear distinction between the present audience and the stage, thereby imploring audience members likewise to "pinch themselves." Like Beckmann, the audience's capacity for aesthetic perception is numbed. From this one may infer that the audience stands, with Beckmann, outside the door and that his fate concerns everyone. The implied relation of the audience to the characters on stage relates directly to the following discussion of the play's equally significant subtitle.

Ein Stück, das kein theater spielen will, und kein Publikum sehen will

What, then, does this subtitle tell us about the situation in Germany to which Borchert returned in 1945? Considering the context and the personal circumstances in which it was written, what would a theater company probably not want to perform, and what might an utterly defeated audience not want to *see* and why? And how does this relate to the door outside which Beckmann and many others stand? The opening statement makes the claim that the audience is implicated – is "one of them" – in the story about a man returning to Germany and needs likewise to "pinch itself in the arm." Like Beckmann, everyone remains "outside" in the dark without answers; unlike Beckmann, however, nobody seems to be willing to probe further – let alone provide answers to Beckmann's closing questions.

The implications of these opening explorations are to be developed further during subsequent scene-by-scene discussions. The discussion, however, need not follow a traditional sequence of reading comprehension questions and reading aloud, but rather the reverse: Dramatic readings (or mini-presentations) are sequenced in such a way as to draw out, build, and probe the tensions as they occur throughout the text, during which students summarize and test hypotheses, interpret and reinterpret. The following outlines a drama-based approach to moments in the text designed to provoke further discussion, from which the instructor may select according to course goals and available time. For example, if time only allows for two sessions, it would be possible to incorporate the *Vorspiel* and dream-scenes into the discussion of scenes 1–4, leaving the lengthier fifth scene for the final class session. In preparation for class discussion, the following *Leitfragen* help to guide the reader.

Leitfragen: *Vorspiel* and *Traum*

1. *Wo und in welcher Stadt spielen sich diese Szenen ab? Wie wird dieser Ort beschrieben?*
2. *Der Mann auf dem Ponton hat offensichtlich etwas vor. Was vermutet der Beerdigungsunternehmer? Wie begründet er seine Vermutung? Wer scheint dieser Mann zu sein?*
3. *Warum rülpst der Beerdigungsunternehmer die ganze Zeit?*
4. *Wie wird Gott dargestellt?*
5. *Beschreiben Sie das Verhältnis zwischen dem Beerdigungsunternehmer und Gott: Welche Kritik geht aus diesem Gespräch hervor?*
6. *Was für eine Figur ist die Elbe? Wie wird sie personifiziert? Wie behandelt sie Beckmann? Wie nennt sie ihn? Unterstreichen Sie relevante Textstellen!*
7. *Worauf verweist der Vergleich mit Ophelia und wie funktioniert er in diesem Kontext?*
8. *Was wirft die Elbe Beckmann vor?*
9. *Was wissen wir über Beckmann? Warum versucht er, Selbstmord zu begehen? Beschreiben Sie ihn!*
10. *Was stellt diese Szene dar? Warum wird diese Szene an den Anfang des Stücks gesetzt?*

Workshop: *Vorspiel* and *Traum*

It is possible (though not necessary) to devote an entire 60–90-minute-long workshop to these two opening scenes, which, although they comprise only four pages, are symbolically very rich. Starting with the stage directions, students scan the text for the sound effects that will recur throughout. Moving from the water's edge (*Vorspiel*) into the river (*Der Traum*) we hear: *das Stöhnen, Wehen des Winds, Schwappen, Quasseln des Wassers, Klatschen der Wellen, Klingeln der Straßenbahn, Schnarchen,* and an onomatopoeic *Plumps* as Beckmann jumps into the river and a *Rums* of Death's Undertaker. Combined with a dramatic reading of the first scene, the sound effects help to set the play's eerie tone, its structure and content, as well as highlighting the play's mixed-media origins.

Student directors and side-coaching: In reviewing the significance of the interactions between the Undertaker and God, and between Beckmann and the Elbe, students are put into small groups, with one or two students as directors, to discuss how they would embody these characters. Of particular significance is the corpulent Undertaker, who has gorged himself on too many victims, and whose incessant boisterous belching overbears the senile, pitiable, and impotent God ("ich kann es nicht ändern," 9–10). Adopting a stance in a way that physically conveys over-bloated contentment over shrunken dejection, students either silently present a "still image" of the scene, read part of the scene dramatically, or combine both activities. Commentary and discussion follow in full class, paying close attention to the textual clues while students suggest alternative gestures through side-coaching.

Representing the river Elbe presents a particularly creative challenge, one that requires considerable attentiveness to the dynamics and symbolism of the text. Building on the preparatory questions, students either resume groupwork or volunteer instead to act out suggestions made by their peers, based on a short segment from this scene. The river may take many shapes and forms – as simple as a handy scarf or shawl, or physical gestures suggesting water – but it is important to refer to the textual clues. Details describing the embodiment of the river carry especial significance: It is by no means a romantic trope, but rather a river that stinks of fish and oil embodied not by "Ophelia mit Wasserrosen im aufgelösten Haar" with her "süßduftenden Lilienarme[n]" (11), but rather by a mother figure (*Kinderaugen, mein Sohn, Grünschnabel, Rotznase, Kleiner, mein Goldjunge, mein kleiner Menschensohn, Säugling*), yet one who remains unrelentingly indifferent, even callous towards Beckmann's suffering, ultimately rejecting his attempted suicide: "ich scheiß auf deinen Selbstmord! Du Säugling" (12). Beckmann's despair and fragility presents a stark contrast. With a fuller picture of Beckmann, the initial "walking-in-character" exercise may now be revisited and refined, incorporating the limp that will assume an audibly ominous role. In embodying this contrast between a physically and emotionally broken soldier and the coarse mother-river figure, attention should be drawn to the latter's interpretation of his attempted suicide as a cowardly retreat to the mother's refuge, "bei mir undern Rock" (12). Beckmann has been pulled downwards (into the Elbe) rather than upwards (towards Heaven, where God is forgotten), where he remains, with little hope of resurfacing ("von Hochkommen kann gar keine Rede sein," 15), despite the encouragement of others ("sehen Sie, jetzt geht es sogar aufwärts," 15). The directional adverbs that recur throughout the text should be noted during staging considerations.

Rejected by the river Elbe, Beckmann remains standing at death's door. The scene that would traditionally close a tragedy is placed at the beginning, prompting an inverted yet downward spiral of events as Beckmann revisits memories of his encounters upon his return to Germany. In the process, the reader becomes familiar with the antecedent events and witnesses Beckmann's pursuit of moral responsibility – of the cause for the tragic effects, of meaning and solace. His hopeless quest for meaning can be discerned in each scene, from his encounter with the girl who tries to help him: "Weil? Was für ein Weil? Nein, nur weil ich naß bin. Sonst gibt es kein Weil" (16), until his own cynical recreation of his biography as a five-act tragedy – enacting in brief the same inverse spiral of despair, devoid of conventional cause, a tragedy without meaning and therefore absurd (44). By placing the play's traditional closing at the beginning, the play effectively abandons any hope of poetic freedom to construct meaning from the course of events; it is overdetermined by them.

Leitfragen: Szenen 1–4

Szene 1:

1. *Welche Funktion hat Der Andere? Wie beschreibt er sich selbst? Wann erscheint er und warum?*
2. *Was lernen wir darüber hinaus in dieser Szene über Beckmann?*
3. *Wer ist der Einbeinige? Welche Funktion hat er?*

Szene 2:

1. *Warum trägt Beckmann ständig eine Gasmaskenbrille? Welche Funktion hatte diese Brille und warum trägt er sie immer noch?*
2. *Wie geht das Mädchen mit Beckmann um? Wie bezeichnet sie ihn immer wieder, und was könnte das symbolisieren?*
3. *Was erfahren wir noch über Beckmann? Wo und warum bleibt ihm eine weitere Tür verschlossen?*
4. *Warum flieht Beckmann am Ende dieser Szene? Wie fühlt er sich und warum ist das so?*

Szene 3:

1. *Wie reagiert der Oberst und dessen Familie auf Beckmann? Unterstreichen Sie relevante Textstellen!*
2. *Was meint Beckmann, wenn er sagt, dass er dem Oberst die Verantwortung zurückgeben will? Wofür?*
3. *Was erfahren wir noch über Beckmann?*

Szene 4:

1. *Warum sucht Beckmann den Kabarettdirektor auf? Was erhofft er sich?*
2. *Wie reagiert der Direktor auf Beckmann? Finden Sie die Argumente des Direktors überzeugend? Warum (nicht)?*

Workshops: *Szenen 1–4*

The ensuing class discussions may comprise one 90-minute or two hour-long class sessions, depending on class size and course schedule. By grouping these scenes together, one has the advantage of staging the discussion in such a way as to illuminate the repetitious structure that is driven by Beckmann's trauma. The following outline suggests such a sequence that both animates students to interpret the text closely, and that facilitates continued interrogation of the play's central themes and structure. In these four scenes, attention will be focused on the gasmask motif within the broader theme of confronting the past and pursuing accountability.

Scene-by-scene interrogations: Small groups of students are each assigned one brief excerpt from each scene, to be prepared carefully for dramatic presentation as a basis for the interrogation. Ideally, the number of students would correspond to the number of characters in the scene; alternatively, students may need to adopt additional or directive roles. Students should first scan the text for descriptors relating to their characters – to the frequent vocal stage directions, and to their respective physical and emotional states, statuses, current situations, and background, and consider how to convey these. Building on the preparatory reading questions, excerpts are then presented dramatically and anonymously – that is, neither the context nor the identity of the characters is announced, but rather prompts the initial interrogation of each scene's core conflict: the who, where, when, and what. This should be an entirely student-led discussion, enabling students also to clarify any misunderstandings based on the presentation or of the text itself. Once these are established, the instructor asks further questions to probe the relationship and dynamics between the characters and to invite alternative suggestions (in side-coaching) to the presentation. Finally, the excerpt needs to be situated within the play's structure: What precedes the action and what follows? Is the ensuing action a direct result? In this way, it is possible to discern the downward trajectory of the action, the relation of Beckmann's trauma to the repetitive structure and of Beckmann's own hopeless pursuit of solace and meaning to the absence of conventional cause and effect of the play. Any gaps in comprehension may subsequently be filled during discussion.

Szene 2 excerpt (two roles): Das Mädchen, Der Andere
up to Das Mädchen: *... ich glaube, Sie tragen auch innerlich auch*
                             so eine Gasmaksenbrille (17–18).

Once the context and characters are established, further questions concern the sympathetic nature of their interactions, and particularly the fascination with Beckmann's peculiar gasmask glasses, Beckmann's professed inability to cope or even see clearly without the glasses, despite others' ridicule, as well as Beckmann's ghostly appearance without them. The ensuing discussion of the presentation should probe further Beckmann's physical embodiment and vocal expression, relating with increasing detail to the textual cues: his limping, stiff leg, and the frail frame that drowns and suffocates (*ersaufen, erwürgen*) in the large coat he stole from another perished soldier; his hopelessness, exhaustion, his ghostly appearance, and his emotional dependency on the gasmask (17–18). Additional questions should review the antecedent action, what the girl finds out about Beckmann, and the connection that Beckmann's guilty conscience makes between his stolen coat and the girl's missing (probably perished) husband in Stalingrad, whose ghost now appears. This prompts Beckmann to seek others whom he may hold accountable for his own guilty conscience, visiting first the Colonel, "der sein ganzes Leben nur seine Pflicht getan, und immer nur die Pflicht! ... Eine verfluchte – fluchte – fluchte Pflicht!" (21). As the skepticism expressed by Beckmann's fivefold repetition of "duty" suggests, however, the Colonel's steadfast sense of military duty necessarily precludes and conflicts with the moral responsibility sought by Beckmann, and for the many victims that haunt Beckmann in repeated nightmares.

Szene 3 (five roles):	*Der Oberst, dessen Familie*
Excerpt 1	
MUTTER:	*Vater, sag ihm, doch, er soll die Brille abnehmen......*
SCHWIEGERSOHN:	*Ach wo, betrunken (22–3);*
Excerpt 2	
OBERST:	*... Werden Sie erstmal wieder ein Mensch, mein Lieber Junge! ...*
MUTTER:	*Ja, aber, das trockene Brot? (29–30).*

Resuming focus on the gasmask motif, it is important to note the striking contrast between the Colonel's impassive, pragmatic explanation of their specific wartime functionality and Beckmann's highly subjective version. For the Colonel, they no longer have any use and should have been discarded long ago; for Beckmann, in contrast, they ensure that he does not lose sight of the truth of war. Thus, the function of the glasses underscores the central tension of this play: between those whose indifference enables them to forget the past, and those (Beckmann) who remain traumatized by it – between those who "overcome" (*bewältigen*) and those who suffer (*erleiden*) the past. Both make claims to truth ("bei unserer guten deutschen Wahrheit," 23), yet their truths do not correspond. Beckmann's biting critique of the Colonel's version of "truth" ("Wir essen uns schön satt, Herr Oberst ... und dann halten wir die gute deutsche Wahrheit hoch, Herr Oberst," 23) is dismissed as the incoherent ramblings of a deranged or drunk person.

"Haben Sie das ganz vergessen, Herr Oberst? Den 14. Februar? Bei Gorodok?" (27), Beckmann asks the Colonel. Adopting Beckmann's question to the Colonel, students are prompted to recollect Beckmann's nightmare, in which the reason for Beckmann's demand to share responsibility is explained (26–7). Having assigned Beckmann a military duty that led to the death of many comrades, the Colonel has likewise delegated responsibility altogether, for which Beckmann now seeks acknowledgment: "Wieviel sind es bei Ihnen, Herr Oberst? ... Schlafen Sie gut, Herr Oberst?" (28). The versions of truth diverge: One enables the duty-bound Colonel to forget, and the other compels Beckmann to share the burden of moral responsibility. This excerpt highlights the inability (or refusal) of the Colonel and his family to understand Beckmann. Hence the Colonel's forced laughter in reaction to Beckmann's narration of the nightmare vision of the war, scorning Beckmann as a prankster who belongs in the theater (28–9).

The Colonel's feigned amusement fails to deflect the family from their terror in the subsequent excerpt (later in the same scene), which concludes with Beckmann once again outside the door ("Eine Tür kreischt und schlägt zu," 30). Beckmann has failed to find solace, let alone sympathy, or to "return responsibility" to the Colonel, resigning himself once more to the meaninglessness of existence (30). The second excerpt is revealing in its portrayal of a family that shudders in horror at the mere sight of Beckmann and what his presence symbolizes. Like Borchert's audience, their concern is much less for the starving, shattered Beckmann than for what Beckmann has just stolen from their dinner table – the bottle of rum and bread: "Ja, was will er denn mit dem Brot?" (30). Such blind, misdirected concern, coupled with the Colonel's deflective ridicule, portrays a crassly pragmatic turn to Germany's postwar restoration, thereby shedding further light on the play's title and subtitle.

The tensions delineated in this scene are further developed in subsequent scenes, which combine to portray the intellectual climate of postwar Germany – the tensions between the issue of guilt and responsibility, of confronting *versus* overcoming the past.

Szene 4 (two roles)
Excerpt from Scene 4:   *Übrigens bei Gesicht fällt mir ein*
KABARETTDIREKTOR: *... Positiv, positiv, mein Lieber!! (31–3).*

The question of truth (*Wahrheit*) assumes an aesthetic focus in the ensuing scene, in which Beckmann, deciding to take the Colonel at his word, seeks employment at the cabaret. The Cabaret Director introduces the concept of truth, using the exact wording of the Colonel ("die die Wahrheit hochhält"; 31) in relation to the function of art. As a play within a play, this scene rehearses Borchert's central concern with the (lost, now meaningless) function of art in postwar Germany. Drawing attention once more to the gasmask glasses, one recognizes the similarity of the Cabaret Director's reaction to that of the girl, as well as his suggestion, along similar lines to the Colonel's, that he get rid of them since the war is now long over. A dramatic reading of this scene sharpens our focus on the hypocrisy of a postwar society that refuses Beckmann's vision over and over. Beckmann's by-now mechanical explanation (*automatisch*) of the unfamiliar gasmask glasses underscores the repetitious trauma that structures the play. Upon the Colonel's suggestion that Beckmann could provide theatrical amusement, the Director responds that any laughter would likely choke most audiences (*in der Kehle stecken*), further confirming the inauthenticity of the Colonel's own laughter, which he feigns until he can laugh with conviction (*aus voller Kehle*). Once again, Beckmann appears as a frightful ghost of the underworld, and is thus rejected for postwar entertainment needs: "sich erheben, erbauen... etwas genialer, heiterer müssen wir den Leuten schon kommen. Positiv, positiv, mein Lieber!" (33).

Probing further, the Director claims that postwar Germany now needs the literary "greats": Goethe, Schiller, Heine, Grabbe (Borchert's own former role-models), lauded here for their sturdy realism and their masterful ability to confront the dark side of life unsentimentally and objectively, to grasp the world as it really is and to "uphold the truth" (31). The irony can hardly be overlooked, especially considering the Director's supplemental appeal not for anything "complete, mature and serene" but rather something courageous and emotionally raw, *ein Schrei ... ein Aufschrei ihrer Herzen* (31). This is precisely what Beckmann performs and Borchert delivers – in conscious departure from his former role-models – and yet is precisely what the audience does "not want to see." Moreover, the Director subsequently modifies his list to include some of the great entertainers such as Shirley Temple and boxer Max Schmeling – entertainment that distracts from, rather than confronts objective reality, confirmed by his own self-contradictory statement: "Mit der Wahrheit hat die Kunst doch nichts zu tun!... Mit der Wahrheit kommen Sie nicht weit" (35). Both his slippery rationale for rejecting Beckmann's audition and his impulsive repetition of the Colonel's injunction to "uphold the truth" serves to sharpen our critical focus on the collective whitewashing impulse.

One hears clear echoes of these tendencies in Beckmann's scathing parody of the song "Tapfere kleine Soldatenfrau," performed as his "audition" piece at the cabaret. When compared with the original version (see above), this parody exposes the Nazi fabrication of the soldier's happy return to a loving and loyal wife. Beckmann's bitter parody depicts his own return, which is greeted instead with derision, rejection, and abandonment. To conclude the discussion, a comparison of both versions, available on YouTube, redirects us once more to the title and to the relationship of art to truth in the immediate postwar context. Another door – an opportunity for meaningful employment – is once again closed to Beckmann.

The repetitive, static structure discerned in the preceding scenes provides a suitable segue to the fifth and final scene, in which Beckmann revisits the same encounters and reconstructs his life as a five-act *Trauerspiel*. Owing to its recapitulation of the entire sequence of events, this lengthy scene deserves a whole class session, but also enables the class to review and refine earlier interpretations. In preparation for the next session, students are assigned reflective tasks focusing on the interaction with Frau Kramer and on the function of *Der Andere* throughout. In addition – and assuming at least two days pass before the next class session – students begin to interpret the play by formulating their own questions relating to performance. By posing questions about how the various symbolic figures and personifications may be represented – audibly and visually – questions relating to literal, symbolic, mythic, and psychological interpretations of the play necessarily emerge. This approach requires a different kind of reading, one that animates students to consider practical implications of each interpretation and to think creatively with details of the text. Questions might include: How does one represent *Der Andere*? How does one visualize symbolic figures in relation to the protagonist? Are they to be heard and seen? Are they all distinct from Beckmann himself?

Szene 5

Beckmann's tragic discovery of his parents' suicide when he visits his family home is all the more shocking due to the indifference with which it is conveyed by Frau Kramer, who now resides in his parental home. By now, students will be attuned to the recurring significance of the gasmask glasses, which Frau Kramer dismisses with equal measure of indifference, even coarse dismissal (40). The crass contrast between Frau Kramer's coldness and the tragic news of his parents' death is Beckmann's last provocation. It is also the last appearance of *Der Andere*, who has remained present throughout: "Jasager, du quälst mich! Geh weg!" (56). Confronted with the details of his parents' suicide on account of their alleged association with the Nazis (41), Beckmann closes the door to his last hope of refuge.

It is instructive to review the ever-intensifying struggle between Life and Death through the recapitulation scenes that follow. Working in small groups on individual encounters (with God and the Undertaker, the Colonel, the Cabaret Director, and Frau Kramer), students can map out each character's perspective on the past/future; life/death; responsibility/denial; confrontation/overcoming; restoration/reclamation, yea-saying/naysaying. Further textual clues from the previous scenes help students to document how the text reinforces the dichotomy: loud/soft, overfed/underfed, new attire/war-time attire, warm/cold, dry/wet, hope/hopeless, inside/outside, light/dark.

These tensions are brought into focus in the fifth scene. Returning to the question about *Der Andere* from scene 1, students review how he describes himself – not with physical attributes ("du hast kein Gesicht," 13), but rather as "Der von gestern. Der von Früher. Der Andere von Immer. Der Jasager. Der Antworter... die Stimme, die jeder kennt ... der Optimist, der an den Bösen das Gute sieht und die Lampen in der finsternen Finsternis" (13). Each assigned a single scene, students work in small groups to retrace the arguments for Life offered by *Der Andere*. In full discussion, the class then writes up the arguments on the board – arguments that ultimately do not save Beckmann. To conclude, students consider these arguments together with descriptions in order to venture hypotheses about the identity and function of *Der Andere*: a positive light of hope, a force of life, a familiar voice, an omnipresent being, a projection of Beckmann's psyche, an alter ego?

Role-play: Following this activity, students stage a debate, each assuming the point of view of either *Der Andere* or Beckmann: Should Beckmann choose Life? In this way, students test the legitimacy of the arguments of *Der Andere* by reviewing each encounter and discover how each argument is directly countered by Beckmann's experiences.

Such questions play a vitally important part in the approach to the play's staging and must therefore be carefully considered. Other challenges include the length of some of the monologues: While some of the effect is lost in reducing these, it may be nevertheless advisable in some places and feasible if done with careful planning. Time permitting, it can be very productive to involve students in this process.

Director's cut: This may be carried out in two parts, which are related, or one could focus on just one part.

1. Consider the cuts made in the radio play. How do these alter the radio play? How does the radio play differ from the stage play? (Thanks to Erwin Warkentin's recent archival research, many of these cuts are available for analysis.)
2. Based on the previous discussions, read through the text and suggest cuts from certain scenes (to be identified by the instructor) and justify them in a class discussion. What gets lost? What does *not* get lost? Once all suggestions have been carefully considered and an agreement reached, the instructor may assign this task to a student who would prefer not to appear on stage.

While the play's success proved Borchert's subtitle wrong and continues to be performed and discussed today, its filmic adaptation of 1949 did not, however. Nobody wanted to see Wolfgang Liebeneiner's film *Liebe 47*, which was loosely based on the play that Liebeneiner also directed only two years earlier, and despite rave reviews in *Die Zeit* (Moeller 145–6). If the entire film is available (part of it is readily available on YouTube), an investigation into the intermedial adaptations would be a fruitful exercise, even though both are performance media. How do characters become portrayed on screen? How is the plot altered, if at all? How do the techniques proper to the new medium change the way we "read" the text? How does the greater realism and immediacy of immersion in the film (by showing scenes rather than verbally describing them) alter our perception? What is gained and what is lost? What is the effect of filmic devices, such as flashback techniques, on its reception?[8]

Reflective writing exercises

1. *Erläutern Sie die Funktion der Gasmaske für das Drama als Ganzes.*
2. *Was bedeutet der Titel und der Untertitel für das ganze Stück?*
3. *Liebe 47: Ein Film, den niemand sehen will. Vergleichen Sie Borcherts Theaterstück mit der Filmadaption. Inwiefern unterscheiden sie sich? Welche inhaltlichen und strukturellen Veränderungen wurden in der Filmadaption vorgenommen? Was könnte der Grund für den Misserfolg des Films gewesen sein?*
4. *Warum soll man das Stück heute noch spielen und sehen?*

Notes

1 This was primarily under the auspices of the US Information Control Unit (ICD) and Office of Military Governor U.S. (OMGUS).
2 On the extent and content of edits undertaken by the British Information Services Division, see Warkentin. Borchert's consternation over the allied powers' censorship gains additional significance in view of his previous narrow escape from the death penalty for allegedly attempting to evade military service, and a prison sentence for writing critical parodies of the Nazis.
3 With the coincidental publications of Lessing's *Miß Sara Samson* and Johann Joachim Winckelmann's *Gedanken über die Nachahmung der Griechischen Werke in der Malerei und Bildhauerkunst* in the same year, Fischer-Lischke identifies the same year, 1755, as the "beginning of Philhellenism and theatromania – two of the characteristic features of the German Bildungsbürgertum." See Fischer-Lischke 2.
4 Profitlich lists only a very small number of tragedies in the decades following WWII, the most significant of which are Rolf Hochhuth's controversial *Der Stellvetreter* (1963), designated a "christliche Tragödie," Günter Grass' "deutsches Trauerspiel" *Die Plebejer proben den Aufstand* (1966), Reiner Werner Fassbinder's "bürgerliches Trauerspiel" *Bremer Freiheit* (1972), and Elfriede Jelinek's "musikalische Tragödie" *Clara S.* (1982).
5 For a fuller account of postwar productions, see Fischer-Lichte, ch. 6.
6 Thanks are due here to Cori Crane for bringing my attention to this particular photograph for cross-cultural comparison.
7 For example, the many fantasy novels such as C. S. Lewis' *The Lion, the Witch and the Wardrobe* and Lewis Carroll's *Alice's Adventures in Wonderland*; the existential play by Albert Camus, *Huis clos* (*No Way Out*); Kafka's "Vor dem Gesetz"; the many time-travel and alternative or parallel reality films, such as *Being John Malkovich* and *Sliding Doors*, not to mention the many horror and fantasy films in which all sorts of doors, including basement, train, motel, tunnel, and elevator doors, are key.
8 For further considerations on intermedial adaptation, I recommend Linda Hutcheon's *A Theory of Adaptation*.

On German tragedy theory

Profitlich, Ulrich, and Alt, Peter-André. *Tragödientheorie: Texte und Kommentare vom Barock bis zur Gegenwart*. Reinbek: Rowohlt, 1999.

On German tragedy and the Trauerspiel

Guthke, Karl S. *Das deutsche bürgerliche Trauerspiel*. 6th ed. Stuttgart: J.B. Metzler, 2006.

Szondi, Peter. *Versuch über das Tragische* . 2nd ed. Frankfurt am Main: Insel, 1964.

Recordings

Borchert's adaptation of the song for the Kabarett, *Liebe 47*: https://www.youtube.com/watch?v=WzOdlraC6WI

1940 Carl Strässer's *Tapfere kleine Soldatenfrau* (1940): https://www.youtube.com/watch?v=tWyi1ofylWM

Recording of the Hörspiel (1947): https://www.youtube.com/watch?v=CsxUMj2JMSA

References

"A Postwar Tragedy." *The Stage and Television Today* (Archive: 1959–1994), December 10, 1959.

Arendt, Hannah. *Von der Menschlichkeit in finsteren Zeiten; Rede über Lessing*. Munich: Piper, 1960.

Aristotle, *Poetics*. Stephen Halliwell, trans. Loeb Classical Library. Cambridge: Harvard UP, 1995.

Bock, Christoph. "Die Stimme der Kriegskinder verstummte vor 60 Jahren." *Die Welt*, November 19, 2007.

Borchert, Wolfgang, & Heinrich Böll. *Draußen vor der Tür und ausgewählte Erzählungen.*: Hamburg: Rororo Taschenbuch Verlag, 1968.

Brecht, Bertolt, and Hecht, Werner. *Schriften zum Theater*, vol. 3. Frankfurt am Main: Suhrkamp, 1963.

Brown, Sarah A. "Introduction: Tragedy in Transition." In *Tragedy in Transition*. Sarah Annes Brown and Catherine Silverstone, ed. Oxford: Blackwell, 2007, 1–15.

Dowden, Stephen D., and Quinn, Thomas P. *Tragedy and the Tragic in German Literature, Art, and Thought*. New ed. Suffolk: Boydell & Brewer, 2014.

Fischer-Lichte, Erika. *Tragedy's Endurance: Performances of Greek Tragedies and Cultural Identity in Germany since* 1800. Oxford: Oxford UP, 2017.

Guthke, Karl S. *Das deutsche bürgerliche Trauerspiel*. 6th ed. Stuttgart: J.B. Metzler, 2006.

Hutcheon, Linda, and O'Flynn, Siobhan. *A Theory of Adaptation*. 2nd ed. London: Routledge, 2013.

Klarmann, Adolf D. "Wolfgang Borchert: The Lost Voice of a New Germany." *The Germanic Review*, vol. 27, no. 2, 1952, 108–123.

Mennemeier, Franz Norbert. *Modernes Deutsches Drama: Kritik und Interpretation*, vol 2., 3rd ed. Weidler, 2005.

Moeller, Robert G. "When Liebe Was Just a Five-Letter Word: Wolfgang Liebeneiner's Love 47." In *German Postwar Films: Life and Love in Ruins*. W. Wilms and W. Rasch, ed. New York: Palgrave Macmillan, 2008, 141–156.

Müller-Marein, Joseph. "Da reißt er sein Herz blutig." *Die Zeit*, November 27, 1947.

Profitlich, Ulrich, and Alt, Peter-André. *Tragödientheori: Texte und Kommentare Vom Barock bis zur Gegenwart*. Reinbek: Rowohlt, 1999.

Rehrmann, Marc-Oliver. "Auf den Spuren von Wolfgang Borchert." *NDR.de*. May 20, 2011.

Rühmkorf, Peter. *Wolfgang Borchert in Selbstzeugnissen und Bilddokumenten*. Reinbeck: Rowohlt, 1961.

Schiller, Friedrich. *Wallenstein*. In *Sämtliche Werke*, vol. 2: *Dramen* 2. Peter-André Alt, ed. Munich: Deutscher Taschenbuch Verlag, 2004.

Szondi, Peter. *Versuch über das Tragische* . 2nd ed. Frankfurt am Main: Insel, 1964.

Teichert, Herman, and Teichert, Lovette. *Allerlei zum Lesen*. 2nd ed. Boston: Cengage, 2004.

Warkentin, Erwin J. "War by Other Means: British Information Control and Wolfgang Borchert's *Draußen vor der Tür*." *Comparative Critical Studies*, vol. 13, no. 2, 2016, 255–271.

Wells, Larry, and Morewedge, Rosmarie. *Mitlesen-Mitteilen*. 4th ed. Boston: Cengage, 2007.

3   *Lustspiel*: teaching comedy

Key considerations

Table 3.1

Karl Valentin	*Der Theaterbesuch*
Performance Length	Ca. 10 minutes
Cast	2 major, 1 minor
Set	A single apartment room.
Language	Bavarian dialect.
Topic and Complexity	Narrow-mindedness of petit bourgeois; preparations for theater visit.
Potential challenges	Bavarian dialect and comic timing.

Table 3.2

Ödön von Horváth	*Hin und her*
Premiere	Zürich Schauspielhaus, 1934 Film adaptation, 1948
Performance Length	Approx. 75 minutes (with some cuts to the text).
Cast	16 (including 3 very minor, non-speaking smuggler roles).
Set	Written for a revolving stage, the play's action alternates between two unnamed countries, divided by a bridge. A simpler staging involves dividing the action between two sides of the stage area.
Language	Some Austrian variation and bureaucratic jargon (for effect).
Topic and Complexity	Refugee, statelessness, migration politics. Highly relevant today.
Potential challenges	Some Austrian and antiquated language; some cross-dressing; comic timing.

Introduction

Ende gut, alles gut – or so the proverb says, and so the comedy concludes. That is, if we are to accept what the proverb would have us believe. But as Johann Nestroy and others frequently remind us, the conventional conclusion

DOI: 10.4324/9781003010289-3

is often contrived, "bloß damit alles gut ausgeht–!"(Nestroy 93), and seldom renders the preceding action insignificant, pleasing, or morally justified. To be sure, the liberating effects of a light-hearted slapstick can provide amusement, blissful escape, or simply reconfirm one's place in society. But comedy can also have a more serious, moralistic, and corrective intention, and, when probing darker, more troubling dimensions of human nature, comedy can subvert, humiliate, disgust, or even enact violence. Indeed, laughter is not always the appropriate response, and comedy, traditionally upstaged in Germany by its more serious (and thus "legitimate") counterpart – tragedy – often treads a thin line between the comic and the tragic.[1]

The predominance of tragedy over comedy in German culture is all too easily explained by the widely accepted belief that Germans simply lack humor. This obviously oversimplifies the matter, since tragedy has always held the privileged place that Aristotle granted it in his *Poetics*. Nevertheless, the problematic status of comedy in Germany has long endured the ridicule of many a non-German-speaking neighbor, who considers the notion of "German comedy" an oxymoron (Kinzer; Hutchinson 16), even going so far as to cast German soldiers as the hapless butt of the "killer joke" deployed by the British in a *Monty Python* sketch. Even if laughter is provoked, it is not necessarily untroubled laughter, and to the foreign spectator, it can seem "infrequent and rather monstrous," coming from "unrefined abstract fancy, grotesque or grim, or gross..." (Magill 31).[2] Such clichés are hardly dispelled by the somewhat complex terminology and German-language definitions of humor, laughter, and comedy, as the linguistic relationship between *Komödie* (the literary form), *Komik* (comicality, humor), and *komisch* (funny, peculiar, absurd, grotesque) already suggests.[3] Nor are these commonplaces by any means lost on German writers or literary historians themselves. Johann Christoph Gottsched, reformer of German theater during the 1730s, bemoaned the relative dearth of noteworthy comedies compared with France: "Bey uns Deutschen hat es vor und nach Opitzen an Comödienschreibern zwar niehmahls gefehlt; aber nichtsdestoweniger haben wir nichts rechtes aufzuweisen, so unsrer Nation Ehre machen könnte" (KT 43). Gottsched was by no means the first or last to recognize this. Commenting with considerable self-irony on the emergence of so-called *Spaßklutur* in Germany during the mid-1990s, *Der Spiegel* wonders: "Was, so fragen sich besorgte Nachbarn im westlichen Ausland, ist eigentlich in diese Deutschen gefahren ... die jahrhundertelang den Humor entweder philosophisch erklärt oder an den Darmwind preisgegeben haben?" ("Sei Schlau" 174). *Spaßkultur*, a neologism animated in part by a flurry of romantic-comedy films in the early 1990s, describes what journalists have self-consciously ridiculed as the curious rise of a "superficial form of culture."[4] Could it be that Germany, now reunified, was finally beginning to defiantly reroute its historical and comedic *Sonderweg* ("Sei Schlau" 170)?

Similarly, German literary histories generally betray discomfort when dealing with comedy, which was long designated the *Stiefkind* of the dominant tragic genre (Hinck 5). "Warum glückt es deutschen Dichtern nur in seltensten Fällen, eine kunstvollendete Komödie zu schreiben?" asks Karl

Holl in the conclusion of his history of German comedy (343). Answers to this question tend often to invoke the "peculiarities" of the German mind and spirit (Holl 344). More generally, dramatists and critics in Germany have tended to follow Aristotle in their negative assessment of comedy's focus on "lesser characters," whose apparent failings provide plenty of fodder for caricature. For Gottsched, however, such character flaws were not merely to amuse, but rather to edify (*erbauen*) the audience. Immoral behavior was to be corrected, and comedy, like tragedy, was to raise consciousness about such middle-class virtues as physical restraint, decorum, and conformity. Thus Gottsched:

> Die Comödie ist nichts anders, als eine Nachahmung einer lasterhafften Handlung, die durch ihr lächerliches Wesen den Zuschauer belustigen, aber auch zugleich erbauen kan. [...] Die Personen, so zur Comödie gehören, sind ordentliche Bürger, oder doch Leute von mässigem Stande. (KT 44–5)

Elevated to the status of "high" art that valued only scripted texts for memorization, Gottsched's Enlightenment stage left no room for the kinds of "lazy" improvisations adopted by German wandering troupes from Italian *Commedia dell'arte* (Gottsched 342). Hence the subsequent demise in Germany of the bawdy *Hanswurst* on stage (the German-speaking counterpart to the Italian *Arlecchino*) along with the buffoonery of burlesques (*Possen*) and "vulgar" farce (*Schwank*). With the exception of a rare reappearance, such as in Goethe's farce entitled *Hanswursts Hochzeit* (1775) and Johann Ludwig Tieck's *Der gestiefelte Kater* (1791), the German *Hanswurst* was essentially erased from German literary comedy. And although Gottsched insisted on stricter adherence to the conventions of French neoclassical drama – including the three unities of time, place, and plot – a distinctly German middle-class variety was envisaged to rival its French model, just as the French loanword *Komödie* was replaced by the German *Lustspiel* – a far worthier appendage to the German *Trauerspiel.* As Georg Hensel puts it: "Seit der Vertreibung des Hanswursts und seit Lessings Komödien will man lachend nachdenken und nachdenkend, falls es möglich ist, lachen" (Georg Hensel, qtd. in Pye, 16). Indeed, ever since the Enlightenment, when the Germans began to take comedy seriously and elevated its status for a more refined, orderly bourgeois public, literary comedy in Germany was largely subject to the same aesthetic rules and class-oriented moral obligations as tragedy. And while many rejected much of Gottsched's theater reforms and ridiculed his *Hanswurst*-banishment (as did Gotthold Ephraim Lessing, most famously, in his "17. Literaturbrief" of 1759),[5] comedy's "civilizing" potential was formally established by Lessing in his *Hamburgische Dramaturgie* (1769), thus instituting the dramaturgical standards of taste and decorum for a *German* national theater. It was at the Nationaltheater Hamburg that Lessing's *Minna von Barnhelm oder das*

Soldatenglück (1767), widely considered the pinnacle of the eighteenth-century German *Lustspiel* (Guthke 49–50), was first performed. More significantly, Lessing's *Minna von Barnhelm* was the first German comedy to include nobility, thereby abandoning the long-standing *Ständeklausel* (see ch. 2) that distinguished tragedy from comedy.

The affinity of German comedy to tragedy persists well into the nineteenth century, when Romantic poets recognized the aesthetic potential of comedic irony, ambiguity and wordplay. Some contributed to the literary and theoretical debates about comedy (among them, Friedrich and August Wilhelm Schlegel, Schelling, Hegel, Heine, Schopenhauer, and Keller), and some contributed comedies, though few made their mark or survived. Besides Tieck's fairytale satires *Der gestiefelte Kater* (1797) and *Die verkehrte Welt* (1798), the comedies with the greatest influence share an ironic stance and a tragic, nihilistic undertone: Georg Büchner's *Leonce und Lena* (1836); Christian Dietrich Grabbe's *Scherz, Satire, Ironie und tiefere Bedeutung* (1827); Franz Grillparzer's *Wehe dem, der lügt* (1836); and Heinrich von Kleist's *Amphitryon* (1807) and *Der zerbrochene Krug* (1808). In each case, these comedies are considered aberrations from the authors' primary achievements as tragedians. The same can be said of the later naturalist writers, whose contributions to comedy were overshadowed by their tragedies, as is the case with Gerhard Hauptmann, whose sole comedy was *Der Biberpelz* (1893).

A survey of "German Comedy" anthologies, however, reveals that nineteenth- to early-twentieth-century comedy seems much more at home in southern Germany and Austria (see for example Arntzen, Freund, Hinck, Holl, Hutchinson). In such literary surveys, Germany often appears as the *Stiefkind* of Austria, where comedy has enjoyed a better reputation both locally and internationally. Austrian and southern German dramatists such as Brecht, Bernhard, Grillparzer, Hofmannsthal, Jelinek, Nestroy, Raimund, and Schnitzler repeatedly appear in anthologies of German comedy. Moreover, many dramatists tended not to conform to the same kinds of morally or socially edifying constraints as those established in Germany, despite the efforts of journalist Joseph von Sonnenfels – Austria's "Gottsched" – to discourage theatrical improvisation in the name of good taste. The *Hanswurst* was first introduced to Viennese folk theater (*Volksposse, Stegreifposse,* and *Zauberstück*) by Josef Anton Stranitzky, who, in 1711, became the director of Vienna's Kärntnertortheater, the first permanent German-language theater. The *Hanswurst*'s popularity would subsequently spread across German-speaking Europe, and even though eventually banned by Austria's Emperor Joseph II from the Imperial Court Theater (today, the Burgtheater), the *Hanswurst*'s various successors were able to continue wandering the suburbs, where three theaters were built to house popular folk comedies and operetta.[6] Thus, with its five permanent theaters – in comparison with Berlin's one theater at that time – Vienna dominated German-speaking theater in Europe and contributed significantly to the development of comedy. It is thus important to recognize how the Italian *commedia dell'arte,* first imported to Austria and Bavaria in the mid-sixteenth century, combined with Stranitzky's Austrian tradition in the early-eighteenth century to form the popular *Volksposse* as a valid art form (Holl 242). It survived in the various functioning suburban theaters even after the Napoleonic wars, when most German-language plays were banned, and during the severely repressive Metternich era, when theaters were heavily censored. Once in the hands of Vienna's Ferdinand Raimund and Johann Nestroy during the 1820s and 30s, this genre developed into both a highly popular form of romantic magical comedy (Raimund), as well as a device for biting satire and social critique (Nestroy).

A less formalized, less class-driven variety of comedy did develop in Germany, however, in the early part of the twentieth century and especially during the Weimar Republic, in the form of literary political cabaret (*Kabarett*) – the focus of chapter five. On account of its pointed political satire, however, *Kabarett* was subsequently censored and some of its artists imprisoned when the Nazis seized power, while other artists fled into exile. Among the literary comedians of this period, Bertolt Brecht, Marieluise Fleißer, Carl Sternheim, Ödön von Horváth, and Carl Zuckmeyer are the most notable for their use of comedy for sharp satire of political ideologies (Brecht), mechanisms of authoritarian ideology (Fleißer, Horváth), patriarchal violence and gender inequality (Fleißer), moral hypocrisy of the bourgeoisie (Sternheim) and of the petite bourgeoisie (Brecht, Horváth), and of German militarism and bureaucracy (Zuckmeyer). Brecht is preoccupied with comedy because it puts the aesthetic principles of epic theater into operation, and even though only two of his plays are formally designated as comedies (*Mann ist Mann*, 1926; *Herr Puntila und sein Knecht Matti*, 1941), many of his other plays deploy comedic techniques (see *Hans im Glück*, 1919; *Die Kleinbürgerhochzeit*, 1919; *Der aufhaltsame Aufstieg des Arturo Ui*, 1941, for example). The difference lies in the ending, which is left open to provoke the audience's critical reflection. Any such provocative comedy, however, was blacklisted as "abusive and undesirable" during the Third Reich and banned from performance by the Nazis (Grange 197). Thus, while Brecht and Zuckmeyer continued in exile to satirize the political upheavals, folk comedy's more traditional focus on simple provincial life was promoted by the Nazis to cultivate the blood-and-soil values of the *Heimat*.

In the postwar era, there was little chance for comedy to deliver on its promise of escape from the gruesome realities (Freund 295). In post-WWII Switzerland, however, Friedrich Dürrenmatt and Max Frisch emerge as the prominent writers of comedy, which they consider the only suitable form for grappling with the absurd paradox of postwar and cold-war existence – with comic distance. As Dürrenmatt puts it in his *Theaterprobleme*: "Die Komödie schafft Distanz [...] Das Komische muß uns nicht 'nahe gehen' wie das Tragische [...] das Komische wirkt auf uns, weil wir von ihm Abstand nehmen, unser Gelächter ist die Kraft, die den komischen Gegenstand von uns wegtreibt" (KT 249–67). Dürrenmatt's and Frisch's shared focus on tragic themes of death and suffering, power and corruption, both produce sharply ironic (tragic) comedies that reveal the pessimism and cynicism dominating the immediate postwar era. Among the most significant are Dürrenmatt's popular *Der Besuch der alten Dame* (1956) and *Die Physiker* (1962), and Frisch's *Biedermann und die Brandstifter* (1953), all of which are regularly performed today. In Germany, an equally biting dark tone also characterizes lesser-known comedies from this period, including Günter Grass's *Die bösen Köche* (1961), Tankred Dorst's farces *Freiheit für Clemens* (1960) and *Die Kurve* (1960), and Botho Strauß' farcical *Die Hypochonder* (1972). Most notably, the literary *Volksstück* of the 1920s (Horváth, Fleißer), which dealt with the rise of fascism, was revived in the 1970s by Rainer Werner Fassbinder, Franz Xaver Kroetz, Martin Sperr and Peter Turrini in the face of fascism's enduring influence. All of the postwar co-medies are very much indebted to Brechtian epic theater. Few of those written in Germany, however, survived the test of time, and some critics would even dispute their status as comedy at all (Pye 2). Thus, German comedy lay relatively dormant until post-reunification, when Germany's *Spaßkultur* asserted itself – less self-critically in film, but more provocatively in television, literature, and local *Kabarett* (see ch. 5). Since then, con-temporary theater's critical engagement in social-political issues – take, for example, Nurkan Erpulat (see ch. 7), Elfriede Jelinek, Dea Loher, René Pollesch, Christoph Schlingensief, Roland Schimmelpfennig (see ch. 4) – owes much to the anti-realistic aesthetics of comedy and such Brechtian devices as defamiliarization, breaking the fourth wall, interruption through direct address and song, improvisation, and metatheatrical reflection.

While this brief introduction by no means offers an exhaustive history of German-language comedy, its broader strokes do reveal the long shadow of the tragic over the comic mode, as well as the appropriation of comedy as a subversive force for critical rather than unreflective laughter. And while exceptions to this tendency have existed all along, they have remained ex-ceptions without any lasting impact on the genre. This is not to suggest that such exceptions never had any impact; on the contrary, some comedies (such as those of August von Kotzebue) were far more popular in their time than those that are widely performed today (such as Kleist's *Der zerbrochene Krug,* whose 1808 premiere was a flop). What this introduction does provide is a survey of noteworthy dramatic comedies that have weathered historical and cultural changes, made a lasting mark on the genre, are readily avail-able, and most of which (listed in the *Nachspiel*) are suitable for study and performance by advanced learners of German.

In the context of a course on "German Comedy," to which I now turn, an overview of the genre grants students a unique perspective on the distinct literary and cultural histories in German-speaking Europe. More significantly, such a course showcases comedy as a rich source of linguistic, aesthetic, psychological, and philosophical lessons from the German-language tradition, revealing it as far more sophisticated than generally anticipated. Indeed, the challenge of comedy's complexities should not be underestimated. Besides the numerous sub-genres, some of which are noted above, students are confronted with a vast range of regional dialects that distinguish the lower and lower-middle classes of a particular place, ranging from dialects of southern Germany and Austria (Fleißer, Jelinek, Nestroy, Raimund, Horváth, Valentin), to Rhenish (Zuckmeyer) and Berlin dialect (Brecht, Hauptmann), as well as ethnolect (Erpulat). Additional challenges presented by comedy include the playful exploitation of intertexts (including allusions, quotation, or parody), for which students seldom have a frame of reference (see also ch. 7); the prevalence of rhetorical devices (puns, *double entendres*, irony, and metaphor); and the variations in linguistic, social, and cultural background that determine an audience's response: What might provoke wild hilarity in one era or culture might well be met with a sardonic smirk or even glum incomprehension in another. These challenges are not alleviated by the fact that comedy eludes any overarching definition and remains relatively under-theorized compared to other genres. Indeed, comedy is full of surprises that constantly challenge our expectations. As Dürrenmatt explains in his *Theaterprobleme*: "Die Komödie ist eine Mausefalle, in die das Publikum immer wieder gerät und immer noch geraten wird" (KT 252).

To teach German-language comedy might therefore seem to run the apparent risk of sending students down a slippery course of terminological and conceptual mousetraps, particularly considering the additional linguistic obstacles that these potentially present. The remaining sections offer an approach to such challenges in the foreign-language classroom and establish the groundwork to explore comedy in the broadest sense – from theater of the eighteenth century to contemporary film. This includes theoretical principles based upon which each comedic text may be probed, questions to provoke discussion, suggestions for reflective and creative writing, as well as drama workshops to support a deeper understanding of comedy. To this end, attention is focused on two primary texts from the same period: Karl Valentin's *Der Theaterbesuch* (1934) and Ödön von Horváth's *Hin und her* (1933).

Preliminary definitions: what is funny about comedy?

Defining the *comic* in comedy is a knotty undertaking, especially when comedy finds itself entangled with elements of tragedy, as it so often does in the German tradition. Any lack of affinity for comedy, however, is compensated to some degree by an engagement in the theoretical and literary debates about comedy, and it is precisely from here that a course on "German Comedy" may be launched.

To begin, it is worth establishing students' familiarity with the genre while introducing some key terms and vocabulary. First, key vocabulary may be gathered by brainstorming all the concepts students associate with comedy or humor. It is helpful to compare students' responses with the *Duden* dictionary or the *Digitales Wörterbuch der deutschen Sprache*, both available online, which provide the most frequently associated word-groups. Second, an inquiry into what makes students laugh, including unusual, surprising instances of laughter, can be more fruitful and thought-provoking than one might imagine. An even more productive discussion will ensue if students complete this as a short reflective-writing assignment and explore key vocabulary independently before sharing their answers with the class. Answers often reveal a complex array of situations and emotions, making it difficult to deduce a clear or continuous logic behind the comic. It becomes clear that no one situation or topic is necessarily inherently comic or tragic; rather, the effect is determined by the context and treatment – comic or tragic – and the response determined by one's background. Inquiries into the moral implications of laughter complicate matters further: Is it morally reprehensible to laugh at another's misfortune, suffering, or even death (*Schadenfreude*)? As will become clear in what follows, there is no single answer to any of these questions.

Probing the scope and limits of genre categorization, the following selection of thought-provoking remarks and definitions from the German-language tradition will suffice to spark an initial discussion. These selections also serve to anticipate some of the main theoretical concepts, providing groundwork for further elucidation throughout the course. To begin, students take one or two of the following definitions – listed here in rising order of conceptual complexity – and, with the aid of a dictionary, consider their implications, preferably with a concrete example. Depending on time available and the instructor's goals, this can be done in small groups in class, or as a combination of in-class and independent preparation for the ensuing session.

1.   Otto Julius Bierbaum (1909): "Humor ist, wenn man *trotzdem* lacht." Originating in Bierbaum's *Yankeedoodle-Fahrt* (308), this has since become a well-known German proverb.
2.   Sigismund von Radecki (1964): "*Deutscher* Humor ist, wenn man trotzdem *nicht* lacht" (113).
3.   Friedrich Nietzsche (1882): "Lachen heißt: schadenfroh sein, aber mit gutem Gewissen" (*Die fröhliche Wissenschaft*, KSA 506).

     According to Nietzsche, one needs no moral compunction in laughing at another's misfortune. This introduces the theory of laughter as an expression of condescension from a superior position, of laughing *at* the target with derision rather than laughing *with* someone in sympathy, similar to Lessing's distinction between *lachen* and *verlachen* in his *Hamburgische Dramaturgie*.
4.   Gotthold Ephraim Lessing (1769): "Jede Ungereimtheit, jeder Kontrast von Mangel und Realität ist lächerlich. Aber lachen und verlachen sind weit auseinander... Die Komödie will durch Lachen bessern; aber nicht eben durch Verlachen." *Hamburgische Dramaturgie* (KT 66–7).

     Verlachen, Lessing continues, expresses disdain for the target (*verachten*); a scatterbrain (*der Zerstreute*), for example, does not deserve our disdain if he is otherwise morally sound. *Ungereimtheit* introduces the concept of incongruity common to many comedy theories.

5. Immanuel Kant (1790): "Das Lachen ist ein Affect aus der plötzlichen Verwandlung einer gespannten Erwartung in nichts" *Kritik der Urteilskraft* (332).

   This adds an element of surprise, sudden interruption, and contradiction of expectations to Lessing's incongruity theory. It is useful to remind students of the phrase known to them via Shakespeare's *Much ado about Nothing* (*Viel Lärm um Nichts*), whereby the tense expectation of misfortune or the basis of anticipation (or cause for concern) suddenly disappears and is revealed to have been based on a false assumption or misunderstanding.

6. Arthur Schopenhauer (1819): "Das Lachen entsteht jedesmal aus nichts anderm, als aus der plötzlich wahrgenommenen Inkongruenz zwischen einem Begriff und den realen Objekten, die durch ihn, in irgendeiner Beziehung, gedacht worden waren, und es ist selbst eben nur der Ausdruck dieser Inkongruenz" (Schopenhauer 36).

   Schopenhauer's definition echoes Lessing's and Kant's emphasis on incongruity between an idea and reality; and laughter is produced upon the sudden realization of this incongruity.

7. Sigmund Freud (1905): "Wir würden sagen, das Lachen entstehe, wenn ein früher zur Besetzung gewisser psychischer Wege verwendeter Betrag von psychischer Energie unverwendbar geworden ist, so daß er freie Abfuhr erfahren kann" (Freud 124–5).

   For Freud, laughter results from a release of pent-up ("unwervendbar geworden") psychic energy caused by an incongruence between expectation and reality, or in the release of something repressed.

Three of the most prevalent theories of how we respond to comedy emerge from this compilation: incongruity, superiority, and relief. Incongruity theory underlies all of the definitions above: Laughter is produced despite (*trotzdem*) or because of a subverted expectation – namely, a contradiction between the expected and actual outcome. When that expectation involves mounting tension or even fear, the resulting laughter relieves the pent-up energy. Incongruity further relates to the social and moral dimensions that underlie superiority theory – to the dynamics of empowerment and subjugation, pleasure and derision, edification and rectification. Perhaps least expected, then, is comedy's capacity not only to arouse empathy but also antipathy towards its target – responses that relate to one's understanding of the moral and social expectations. Such a range of dynamics, effects, and responses provide fertile ground for further exploration throughout the course as more theoretical texts are introduced. To begin examining some common strategies and techniques, it is helpful to review and compare the basic mechanisms of dramatic comedy.

Depending on course goals and historical scope, a second introductory lesson would facilitate a review of these key concepts in the context of a brief historical overview of comedy as it develops alongside tragedy. Highlights include a brief introduction to the late-medieval beginnings in carnival entertainment (*Fastnachtspiel*) and the German counterpart to the Italian and French Harlequin (*Hanswurst*). An overview of Gottsched's introduction of French Classical rules helps to familiarize students with the *Ständeklausel:* only those characters of high standing (*Standespersonen*) would merit a tragic fall (*Fallhöhe*) of Aristotelian tragedy, whereas those of the middle and lower classes, not sufficiently dignified for a tragic fall, were to be ridiculed in comedy. This serves in turn as an important introduction to Lessing, who subsequently redefined the rules in his *Hamburgische Dramaturgie* by introducing a specifically German bourgeois tragedy (*bürgerliches Trauerspiel*; see also ch. 2) and by making both aristocrats and the middle classes the subjects of comedy (*das Lustspiel*). "Lower" bourgeois characters were no longer merely two-dimensional, ridiculous caricatures, but rather more dignified, virtuous, and complex. At this point, it is beneficial to review and contrast what students know so far about comedy alongside an outline of Aristotle's theory of tragedy, which occupies the extant *Poetics* (see ch. 2 and Appendix A). In essence, whereas tragedy evokes fear and pity and works towards their cathartic purging, comedy operates more ambiguously on both empathy and antipathy with variable responses. The reasons for this ambiguity, which are related to the complexities of humor itself, deserve further attention throughout the course.

Two further sessions devoted to precisely these various comedic mechanisms are a necessary next step. Both Elder Olson's *The Theory of Comedy* (1968) and Henri Bergson's "The Comic in Situations" (1990; 1998) provide easily accessible theories of comedy, to be read in English. Modelling his theory on Aristotle, Olson defines comedy as "the imitation of a worthless action, complete and of a certain magnitude ... effecting a *katastasis* of concern through the absurd" (47). By "a worthless action," Olson means "one which is of no account, which comes to nothing, so that, on hindsight at least, it would be foolish to be concerned about it" (47). And by *katastasis*, Olson means "a relaxation ... of concern due to a manifest absurdity of the grounds for concern" (16); "the annihilation of concern itself ... by the conversion of the grounds of concern into absolutely nothing (25). A clear distinction may be drawn between Olson's *removal* of concern in comedy and Aristotle's *katharsis* in tragedy, to be teased out in class with examples from well-known tragic and comic plots. Besides basic generic distinctions between comedy and tragedy, Olson and Bergson describe comedic structural devices: surprise, reversal, repetition, inversion, the mechanical Jack-in-the-box,[7] the snowball effect,[8] incongruity, comic conflict, appearance and reality, and equivocal situations; concepts relating to comic character, including exaggeration, ridicule, motivation, inferiority, superiority, moral or social standing, success and failure; attitudes towards a character, such as empathy, estrangement, antipathy and antagonism; the related appropriate response, such as empathetic laughter (*lachen*) and derisive laughter (*verlachen*); and rhetorical devices such as allusion, irony, word play, metaphor, simile, and inference. Such a list of comic strategies needs to be introduced gradually and with clear illustrations. As an example, students are asked to illustrate certain structural devices and techniques with examples familiar to them from film, television or drama. From Olson's triumph of the well-intentioned fool to the inevitable failure of the ill-intentioned wit, and the removal of concern, Olson's character and plot schemas provide easily comprehensible discussion openers. Bergson, who focuses largely on physicality, provides an equally tangible starting point to discuss the structures of mechanical repetition, inversion, and equivocal situations. Thus, the introduction to a course on German comedy may span at least a week, as follows (for a more detailed summary, see Appendix A).

Day 1: Introduction and preliminary definitions

Day 2: Elder Olson: *The Theory of Comedy,* parts I and II (especially 45–65).

Day 3: Henri Bergson: "The Comic in Situations" (nine-page excerpt)
   Karl Valentin: *Der Theaterbesuch* (12 pages)

Day 3: exploring comedic mechanisms in Valentin's *Der Theaterbesuch*

As a sketch about an impromptu visit to the theater, Karl Valentin's *Der Theaterbesuch* provides a thematic and theoretical preview of the course. Its brevity (12 pages), wealth of comedic techniques, and physical slapstick provide a clear illustration of many basic theoretical concepts, enabling the transition to dramatic texts of greater complexity. Furthermore, it serves to familiarize students with the Austro-Bavarian dialect common to a number of comedies. Valentin (1882–1948) was most well known during the first decades of the twentieth century as a writer and performer of folk comedy and cabaret, which he performed as a double act with Liesl Karlstadt (Elisabeth Wellano), initially in Munich and subsequently in Berlin. Having already gained a reputation as one of the greatest stage performers, he also began producing films during the 1920s and 30s, some in collaboration with Bertolt Brecht. Like Charlie Chaplin, Valentin had considerable influence on Brecht, who was drawn to the more popular and gestural forms of entertainment, and especially to visibly grotesque and clownish performances. Valentin's use of makeup and facial prosthetics, as well as his creative and subversive use of language – used to parody and expose social realities – had much to offer Brecht in his development of epic theater.[9] Many such comedic devices are deployed in Valentin's short sketches, as they are in the present sketch that depicts a married couple's increasingly frenzied efforts to prepare for an evening at the theater – an activity to which they are evidently not accustomed.

Before setting the reading, students preview the text by scanning the first page for basic information about the setting, plot, characters, and, if necessary or desired, some distinctive features of Bavarian dialect (though reading these aloud independently will also help them understand and guess from context). To prevent unnecessary confusion, it is necessary to point out that, unlike the rest of Germany, Bavarian *dreiviertel sieben* is a quarter *to* the hour (6:45/18:45).

Leitfragen

The following preparatory questions serve to guide students in their individual reading, keeping them focused on the comedic strategies in preparation for closer scrutiny in class discussion:

1. *Der Schauplatz: Wo spielt dieser Sketch? Beschreiben Sie den Ort der Handlung. Welche Angaben über den Ort finden Sie für die soziale Umgebung oder die Persönlichkeit der Charaktere besonders passend oder bezeichnend? Und welche Angabe(n) ist (sind) für die Komik des Sketches möglicherweise entscheidend?*
2. *Die Personen: Beschreiben Sie die handelnden Personen! Was für Charaktertypen sind das? Was fällt an dem Aussehen und der Sprache der Figuren besonders auf, und welche Angaben sind für deren sozialen Stand besonders bedeutend? Unterstreichen Sie relevante Textstellen!*
3. *Die Persönlichkeiten: Wie würden Sie den Charakter der handelnden Hauptfiguren beschreiben? Wo liegen ihre Schwächen bzw. Stärken? (Zum Beispiel: sind sie gut gesinnt oder gemein, arglos oder arglistig, fröhlich oder griesgrämig, vernünftig oder unvernünftig, schlau oder schwachsinnig, engstirnig oder aufgeschlossen, engherzig oder großzügig, achtsam oder vergesslich, tüchtig oder unfähig?) Wie würden Sie ihr Verhältnis zueinander beschreiben? Erklären Sie Ihre Antwort und unterstreichen Sie relevante Textstellen!*
4. *Die Handlung und der Aufbau: Was geht auf der Bühne vor sich? Worin besteht der Konflikt? Was gibt Anlass zur Sorge? Gibt es einen unerwarteten, plötzlichen Umschlag ins Glück?*
5. *Der Ausgang der Handlung: Wie würden Sie den Schluss beschreiben? Wird der Konflikt gelöst? Oder wird der Konflikt nur scheinbar gelöst? Wird der Anlass zur Sorge aufgehoben? Wie? Ist das ein glücklicher Ausgang? (Beziehen Sie sich auf die Theorien Olsons und Bergsons!)*
6. *Glück oder Unglück? Ist das wohlverdient oder unpassend? Warum?*
7. *Welche sonstigen Merkmale des "Komischen" bzw. der "Komik" (nach Olson oder Bergson) kommen hier vor? Geben Sie von mindestens zwei der Merkmale eine knappe Beschreibung.*

Rather than merely reproduce the question-and-answer format in class, the follow-up exercises are designed to activate students' responses and provoke further discussion. Instructors can select any number of exercises appropriate to the length and focus of the lesson.

Der Schauplatz: Beginning with the setting, and if time permits (a single-hour session will be insufficient if discussing the entire text), an initial visualization exercise is highly productive. In small groups or with a partner, students should take no more than ten minutes to sketch out what they consider the most important aspects of the setting. Discussion alone among students about the selection of pertinent details will prove productive and, with the instructor's help, clarify any mystifying descriptions. The main purpose of this exercise is to appreciate the excessive details that depict the small attic room, cluttered as it is with kitschy knickknacks, old-fashioned, cheap furnishings, busy decorations, and equipment for a multitude of household chores, all of which suggests the kind of stuffy atmosphere that befits its petit-bourgeois inhabitants. While a number of details will need to be discarded in their sketches, one detail that must be highlighted is the business calendar that prominently displays an incorrect date from a time long past (Valentin 134). While all details play an essential part in the depiction of the social milieu, this last detail relates directly to the central plot's comic reversal.

Die Personen: Consistent with the setting, the characters clearly belong to the lower middle class and thus elicit ridicule. Besides basic details such as older age (*Glatze,* 134), students should perceive the comic portrayal of the male protagonist from his unkempt appearance (for example, his wide, creased trousers, the patched vest, the rubber collar, and later, the misshapen shoes and the huge black hat); the domesticity suggested by both women's aprons (134–5); and the neighbor's disheveled appearance. As will become clear, this depiction forms a comic contrast with the endlessly misplaced petty quarrelling about trivialities. Equally significant in depicting their lower social status is their Middle Bavarian dialect (of Munich and beyond). In particular, students should try to identify and read aloud distinctive dialectal features of their speech: elisions such as *g'schenkt (geschenkt), ham (haben), ham ma (haben wir), s' (sie), z'erst (zuerst), rauf (herauf), nunter (hinunter), scho (schon),* and *i (ich)*; diphthong variation such as *oa* for *ei* in *koa (kein),* and *ua/oa* for *ei* as in *Luada (Leute)* and *hoaßt (heißt)*; voicing of consonants such as *Luada (Leute).* Other generic Bavarian variations include *net (nicht), hernach (nachher), halt (eben), Stiege (Treppe),* and the all-important *dreiviertel sieben Uhr* (18:45). At this point, it is useful to show the first minute of the film version, acted by Karl Valentin and Liesl Karlstadt, and readily available on DVD (*Theaterbesuch* 00:00–00:01). Although the dialogue is not exactly the same as in the written sketch, it is close enough for students to follow and appreciate the pronunciation.

The wildly out-of-date calendar stands out in sharp relief against the couple's ongoing quarrel about the performance's exact start-time, which escalates until the comic reversal (*Umschlag*). Amid the general kerfuffle, a number of character traits and foibles become apparent. Students can assemble a list of these, noting each textual illustration and the incongruity between expected behavior and reality. For example, the gifted tickets are received by the husband not with gratitude for the kind gesture that it is, but rather reluctantly as an offensive imposition: "Da siehst doch ganz deutlich, daß die Frau irgendwas gegen uns hat, sonst tat s' doch net ausgerechnet uns die Karten schenken" (135). Her petty-minded nagging, his miserly reactions, and their shared feeblemindedness provide plenty of further illustrations of incongruity and establish the conflict that motivates the escalation of events. Examples include her mockery of his attempt to comb his bald head (136); his meticulous measuring of a sausage only in order to secure for himself the larger portion (137); and difficulty remembering their son's name (137–8), to mention just a few. Dividing students into pairs to prepare dramatic readings of such brief moments ensures active engagement of all participants: Those performing must consider how to convey the meaning through language and gesture; those observing must draw on the new vocabulary to articulate the nature of the conflict. Sequencing dramatic readings in this way also helps illustrate the mechanical repetition of situations – mishap upon mishap – and the static, inelastic quality of the characters, recalling Bergson's Jack-in-the-box (Bergson 27–30).

Die Handlung und der Aufbau: Directly related to the Jack-in-the-box-like repetition is the escalation of events. What began as a minor conflict (the time pressure to prepare for an unwelcome theater event whose start time is not quite clear) increases like Bergson's snowball (Bergson 29–30). After brainstorming a list of significant moments, students are then prompted to identify the causal effect of each, tracing the escalation to its potentially explosive end – quite literally, in this case, when the wife swallows the laxative erroneously supplied by her husband to alleviate the headaches he has caused her. Once again, timing is everything: "Prompte Wirkung binnen einer Stunde!" (143) – that is, during the performance itself, if they had the timing right in the first place. The cause for concern – the timing of the performance, exacerbated by the timing of the laxative's effect – is at once removed when the couple discovers that the performance is not to start in 45 minutes, as they had assumed, but rather at eight o'clock the following day. Just as their folly, pedantry, and antagonism exacerbates the conflict by delaying their preparations, so too does their folly inadvertently remove all cause for concern. Like Eugene Labiche's much-desired yet elusive Italian straw hat – which, finally recovered, turns out to be the very one that has been eaten (Bergson 30) – all efforts prove futile, causing us instead to come full circle. Thus, we have the *snowball* effect, *inversion* (Bergson 29–30), and a clear case of much ado about nothing – the sudden removal of concern (Olson, Kant).

Glück oder Unglück? Our response to this resolution is partly determined by factors outlined in Olson's scheme. As a plot of folly with ill-intentioned fools, the outcome (failure), which circles to the very beginning, seems perfectly fitting for these characters. It resolves nothing of the couple's shortcomings that animate the plot, setting the stage for a repeat performance the following evening. As such, they deserve little more than mildly superior laughter – possibly of the corrective kind, reconfirming one's intellectual, moral, or social place.

Questions of empathy may then be related to Lessing's distinction between *lachen* and *verlachen*. This distinction could be exploited to deliberate on our characters' shortcomings (underscored by the setting) that would justify one or the other response – failings that are frequently connoted by the prefix *ver-*. Proceeding either from a list of *ver-* prefix verbs or situations, students may be asked to identify an example of sample *ver-* verbs, as follows: *vergilbt* (the wallpaper); *vergessen, vergesslich* (calendar; son's name); *verlegen* (misplaced ticket); *verwirrt* (the time); *sich verbrennen* (the curling iron); *verkehrt* (the mirror placement); and *verwechseln* (laxatives for pain-killers), for example. Whether such shortcomings and mishaps warrant a contemptuous *verlachen*, however, is unlikely. One potentially mitigating factor is the characters' linguistic wit, albeit inadvertent, which plays a major role in the escalation – certainly a ridiculous, but not necessarily contemptible characteristic. Exploiting every possible instance of semantic ambivalence, Valentin constructs a series of misunderstandings, such as the wife's inadvertent discovery, while cursing her memory, of her son's name ("Jeßmariandjoseph – ah Joseph heißt er," 138), to the simple pun ("mach es dir warm, weil es schon kalt ist … Es ist bereits Dezember," 138), and the *double entendre* ("Um halb acht Uhr gehts los. Ich mein ja bei mir …" 143), in reference to the anticipated bowel movements.

Sonstige Merkmale der Komik: Other comedic mechanisms include physical slapstick (recurrent falls, knocks, collisions, spills) and the related comic timing, spreading havoc in all directions (Bergson) with the effect of escalating the conflict through further delay. Such moments provide a good opportunity for a drama workshop, requiring volunteers to act out or mime the action; to ensure full participation, observering participants are required to make mental note and describe exactly what they see. As a follow-up discussion, observers may be asked to explain exactly how certain aspects (such as gender, age, an emotion) are conveyed and to make suggestions for alternative postures, gestures, and movements. For further ideas about how to discuss the comic body, see Appendix B.

Drawing attention to the comedic devices establishes a pattern that is predictable enough for students to anticipate and derive a thrill from their recurrence. To reinforce this orientation, the following activity enables students to put these into practice in a carefully-scaffolded creative writing exercise. Following a brief introduction in class, this exercise can be completed independently – or indeed collaboratively – after the lesson.

Valentin's short sketch, which is typical of the vaudeville type of comedy, may easily be supplemented with any number of additional examples, either by Valentin himself, or by others such as Loriot (Vicco von Bülow; especially "Das Bild hängt schief") and *Frasier* (especially "Three Valentines").[10] All scenes are silent, waiting to be filled with language, and all operate on the same premise: The pedantic protagonist, in attempting to create the appearance of order, inadvertently causes snowballing chaos, underscored in the audible crescendo by Ravel-like *Bolero* music (*Loriot*) and Mozart's *Symphony No. 40* (*Frasier*). These five-minute scenes can be viewed in class, providing a scaffold for a creative writing assignment. After identifying the who, the where, and the what, students assemble a vocabulary list and outline a beginning (conflict), middle (escalation) and an end (reversal) in class before reconstructing the narrative in German. Further vocabulary building may be additionally advantageous for less advanced or less creative students, reinforcing the connection between language and plot structure, from temporal connectors (*da, danach, sobald, nachdem, bevor,* etc.), to typical verbs expressing falling and tripping (*fallen, umfallen, hinfallen, abfallen, umkippen, stürzen, stolpern, ausrutschen*) or inadvertent occurrences (*aus Versehen, versehentlich; durch Zufall, zufällig, zufälligerweise,* etc.).

Involving students in the creative construction of a text heightens their awareness of the comedic structures and mechanisms at play. It also enables students to work on their writing skills and test out their understanding of the concepts before reading and analyzing increasingly "sophisticated" comedies. This approach is consistent with genre-based approaches to second-language pedagogy that promote extensive reading by sensitizing learners to texts through its generic features as well as related tasks. For further creative and analytical writing tasks, see Appendix C. Another related advantage of this writing exercise is the attention to physical slapstick – to appearance, expression, gestures, and posture as depictions of social class, gender, age, and dramatic function. These, in turn, begin to establish the essential terminology for drama workshops: Because comedy highlights character flaws through exaggeration and repetition, comic types lend themselves especially well to the kinds of improvisational workshops described at the end of the chapter (Appendix B).

Interlude

In sum, this introduction to comedy, which may be extended over three to four days, helps to prepare students linguistically and cognitively for the more demanding dramatic readings and the accompanying theoretical texts in German.[11] The reading strategies introduced previously may be reinforced throughout, and as the course unfolds, questions proceed from the declarative (character, setting, theme, plot) to interpretive reading habits on a progressively sophisticated level. Combining dramatic readings with close textual attention encourages students to advance beyond surface linguistic problems in order to appreciate what the language reveals about the deeper meaning of the text. In the process, vocabulary is further expanded and refined to include discussions of sub-genres and styles such as *Stegreifkomödie, Schwank, Posse, Satire,* and *Zauber-Lustspiel* as we traverse the comic landscape. The comic mechanism of repetition is built into the course, and with each repetition comes a certain assurance through familiarity, as well an advanced organizer that encourages students to become good readers by venturing predictions and testing hypotheses. Furthermore, far from becoming monotonous, each repetition assumes the kind of comic snowball effect, both reinforcing and challenging our expectations with each new comic surprise. The following section, which focuses on Horváth's *Hin und her*, shows how to advance to an understanding of literary comedy on a more sophisticated level – one that not only considers comedic structure, but also its use in biting social critique.

Approaching Ödön von Horváth's *Hin und her*

In many respects, Valentin serves as an apt introduction to Horváth not only in terms of a common focus on the comedy of *Kleinbürger*, but also in their shared gift for linguistic dexterity, or *Sprachwitz*. Unlike Valentin, however, Horváth exploits not only the comedy of semantic ambiguities and what language reveals about the various layers of society, but also what language can conceal, manipulate, and even abuse, granting insight into the minds and mindlessness of his characters. Against the background of rising fascism, his critique of language assumes a special place in his "unmasking of consciousness," revealing the impoverished jargon used by those in power and the pseudo-learned jargon of the dangerously small-minded petit-bourgeoisie. In a relatively short period of time – from 1922 until his untimely death in 1938 – Horváth produced a remarkable number of stage plays to great acclaim, earning him the Kleist Prize for *Geschichten aus dem Wienerwald* in 1931 along with high praise from contemporary writers and critics. Today, Horváth counts among the most popular playwrights in German-speaking theaters and is now making his mark abroad (NYT).[12]

Perhaps equally remarkable, therefore, was Horváth's relative obscurity for many years, especially outside German-speaking Europe, for reasons that remain somewhat unclear (Rosenberg; Malone). Despite early acclaim and the enduring popularity of his *Geschichten aus dem Wienerwald* (1931), which has been adapted many times for film, as well as *Jugend ohne Gott* (1937) and *Ein Kind unserer Zeit* (1938), to name but a few, Horváth was left waiting in the wings of non-German-speaking theaters until the late 1970s, when four of his plays were translated into English, and when *Tales of the Vienna Woods* was finally performed in London (1977). Moreover, his early tragedy *Niemand* (1924) had gone missing until 2015 (*Spiegel* "Niemand"), and *Hin und her* (1934) went all but unnoticed – that is, until very recently, and for reasons that may be more easily explained. *Hin und her* was initially rejected for the same reason that it later gained popularity: Horváth wrote this play while under investigation for his overtly political play *Italienische Nacht* (1931), which was met with outraged condemnation for its criticism of the Nazi party.[13] His subsequent plays were banned (and reportedly burned) in Germany as soon as the Nazis came into power in 1933. Horváth left Berlin for Austria and, subsequently, Hungary in order to renew his passport before its imminent expiration, without which he would also lose his Hungarian citizenship, and married a Jewish singer so that she could obtain Austrian citizenship and escape the Nazis. These events presumably inspired *Hin und her,* which he wrote before returning briefly to Berlin. Renewed persecution by the Nazis forced him into permanent exile, however, leaving Berlin for Zurich, where *Hin und her* also premiered in 1934. The play's unsuccessful opening, due either to an overcautious downplaying of its serious theme, or because of the Swiss' own disinclination towards refugees, prompted its closure, however, after just two performances (Malone 60–1). Thus, the play marks Horváth's ultimate banishment from the German stage along with much of his German-speaking audience. This in turn prompted his departure from drama and comedy to novels that, due to their unsparing criticism of the Nazi dictatorship, were likewise banned in Germany (*Jugend ohne Gott*, 1937; and *Ein Kind unserer Zeit*, 1938). Second, the play's focus on deportation, border politics, and statelessness, which closely reflect the absurd personal and political circumstances in which it was written, have become highly relevant today, especially amid the current global crisis concerning migration and refugees. It is such personal tragedies wrought by hostile immigration politics that Horváth subjects to sardonic critical scrutiny in *Hin und her – Posse in zwei Teilen.*

Ödön von Horváth is, as his name suggests, of mixed heritage. Born in Fiume, in what was then part of the Austro-Hungarian Empire (now Rijeka in Croatia), he grew up in Belgrade, Budapest, Munich, and Pressburg (Bratislava), and beginning in 1919, he studied in Munich, switching languages four times in the process. His multilingual upbringing underscores the sense of rootlessness that characterizes both his life and this particular play, which is set between two nameless states, and undoubtedly motivated his high level of attention to linguistic variation in depicting various members of society. Certain characters are endowed with uncharacteristically high linguistic registers only in order to unmask their inauthenticity, exposing the inanity of inflated bureaucratic language adopted by inept officials, as well as the corrosion of vernacular speech through pseudo-learned jargon (*Bildungsjargon*) among the *Kleinbürger* who struggle to control it. In emphasizing the artificiality of expression, Horváths' stated aim is to confront the audience with a *Demaskierung des Bewußtseins* (Krischke 52), revealing depraved and often violent instincts lurking behind the linguistic façade. In his critical portrayal of the *Kleinbürger*, Horváth consciously breaks with and reinvents the *Volksstück* tradition, as stated in his directions (*Gebrauchsanweisungen*):

> Der Bildungsjargon (und seine Ursachen) fordern aber natürlich zur Kritik heraus – und so entsteht der Dialog des neuen Volksstücks, und damit der Mensch, und damit erst die dramatische Handlung – eine Synthese aus Ernst und Ironie. Mit vollem Bewußtsein zerstöre ich nun das alte Volksstück, formal und ethisch.... (Krischke 54)

Formally, the traditional genre is turned against itself: Just as language is exposed as inauthentic, so too are generic conventions (the idyllic provincial setting, love and romance, mistaken identities, political intrigue and a happy ending) invoked in order to reveal them as anachronistic tropes with little relation to modern society.[14] Ethically, the plays no longer invite self-satisfied amusement, but rather demand self-critical scrutiny of the power structures (the *Ursachen*) underlying the injustices of modern society. The resulting "battle between consciousness and unconsciousness" that animates all his plays is to be realized, Horváth insists, linguistically and audibly:

> Es darf kein Wort Dialekt gesprochen werden! Jedes Wort muß hochdeutsch gesprochen werden, allerdings so, wie jemand, der sonst nur Dialekt spricht und sich nun zwingt, hochdeutsch zu reden. Sehr wichtig!... Vergessen Sie nicht, daß die Stücke mit dem Dialog stehen und fallen! (Krischke 51–5)

It is partly the non-naturalistic approach – the discernable gap between authentic and inauthentic expression, between a character's dialect and pseudo-learned High German – that makes this play especially suitable for non-native and non-professional performance. In effect, *Hin und her* resembles the kind of play-within-a-play structure characteristic of many other comedies, which create ample space between the actor and performed role for students to inhabit (as is also the case, for example, in Büchner's *Leonce und Lena*, Tieck's *Der gestiefelte Kater,* and, as discussed in ch. 7, Erpulat's *Verrücktes Blut*). Furthermore, by foregrounding language, the plays amplify the significant role of language in negotiating power and social identity and in "unmasking consciousness"; by attending to these moments, students further develop critical language awareness, social sensibility, and aesthetic interpretation (MLA

4). Finally, *Hin und her* is quite simply compelling for its thematic relevance and, with its balance of dark humor, frivolous hilarity, and ironic sentimentality, is immensely gratifying to read, rehearse and perform. Taken together, these factors help to explain why this particular play has recently gained recognition and popularity not only in German-speaking Europe but also worldwide, with an increasing number of foreign-language productions ever since migration reached a critical stage in the first part of this decade.[15]

Demaskierung des Unbewusstseins: Hin und her

Horváth stated that all of his plays are essentially tragedies, and *Hin und her* is no exception: The play has often been referred to as a *Grenz-Groteske* and its author "A Dark Playwright for Dark Times" (NYT 2019). Set on a bridge that both connects and divides two nameless states, *Hin und her* follows the experiences of Ferdinand Havlicek, a pharmacy owner who, after 50 years of residing and working abroad, is being deported due to bankruptcy. The state seizes this as an opportunity to "unburden" itself financially from a penniless non-citizen, forcing Havlicek to seek reentry into the country of his birth (Horváth 81–2). Anyone familiar with Horváth's biography, outlined in brief above, will recognize some parallel experiences. Unlike Horváth himself, however, Havlicek is *not* granted entry into his home country. Due to a bureaucratic maneuver two years prior requiring consular registration of all citizens living abroad, Havlicek's citizenship of his birth nation has also been revoked. And thus begins Havlicek's absurd vagabond existence on the bridge, moving back and forth *ad absurdum* between his former homeland (on the right bank) and his former host country (on the left). In the process, Havlicek becomes increasingly entangled in the lives and affairs of the respective border guards, Konstantin and Szamek, effectively serving as a messenger between the two enemy states. Amid a snowball of mishaps and mistaken identities involving disguised smugglers and political intrigants, Havlicek emerges as the accidental hero, miraculously regaining reentry to the country of his birth, complete with financial and romantic rewards. The spectacular absurdity of this "happy end" is underscored by a conciliatory song, in keeping with the tradition of the *Posse*, albeit with a tongue-in-cheek nod to the unresolved political conflict.

Teaching this play requires special attention to the tension between form and content, and learning how to reconcile the apparently frivolous treatment of such a serious topic is not without its challenges. Performing the play poses the additional risk of potentially sacrificing or downplaying its critical satirical intent in favor of sheer comedic effect. The following aims to offer a balanced approach to the text with these challenges in mind, and with an eye to embodied interventions.

Hin und her is a *Posse,* a sub-genre of the Viennese *Volksstück,* with its origins in Italian *commedia dell'arte* and the *Stegreif*-tradition of Strankitzky – the

Wiener Haupt- und Staatsaktionen – in early eighteenth century, lasting, in varied manifestations, until the late twentieth century. In its partially pre-textual form, the *Volksstück* began as an improvisation (*Stegreiftheater*) on a simple plot featuring local dialect, an idealized rural setting, and songs and dance, and originally deployed a *lustige Person* (*Hanswurst, Kasper, Harlekin*) as a means to poke fun at aspects of local folk-life. As a literary piece from the early nineteenth century, the *Posse* is generally categorized as a farce, a "derbkomisches, volkstümliches Bühnenstück" (*Duden*), and a "heiteres Bühnenstück im kleinbürgerlichen Milieu; sie handelt— teils verklärend, teils kritisch— vom Alltagsleben der Stadt, in der sie spielt und deren Sprache sie verlauten läßt" (Klotz 89). With these definitions in place, it is possible to appreciate Horváth's reinvention of the genre as a critical *Volkstück*.

Beginning with the title, *Hin und her* immediately draws attention to the centrality of physical movement in this play and invites speculation about its setting. As a pre-reading warm-up exercise, and to illustrate the endless back-and-forth movement that propels the plot, students consider possible emotional or situational triggers for this particular bodily movement, making suggestions as they pace back and forth (nerves, apprehension, indecision, anger, disorientation, amorous relationships, friendships, or endless bureaucratic runarounds being the most likely examples). As each student calls out a possible situation, other students assume an appropriate physical gesture and gait. This may be varied as much as possible, adding as much additional information about gender, age, profession, or indeed a character type from the plays, as desired. As an alternative, volunteers think of and act out such a scenario, to be identified and described exactly by the observers, with some additional side-coaching by the students. In this way, all participants are engaged in an exploration of physical possibilities and constraints.

It is on the tension between physical liberty and constraint, movement and stasis that *Hin und her* turns, thereby complicating the title. Therein lies one of the play's central ironies, illustrated by the inverted mirroring of Havlicek by the two border guards: While Havlicek, whose "freedom" is now restricted to the bridge ("'Freiheit' ist gut" 96) because he is no longer "zuständig" (here, Austrian for *bodenständig*, or "entitled to live"), the guards who prohibit his entry either side are themselves prohibited from the bridge. Indeed, it is precisely their restricted movement that forces Havlicek from one end of the bridge to the other. The tension between freedom and restriction is both audibly and visually captured in the play's very first word ("Halt!") and its countless repetitions, as well as in the modest wooden bridge that delimits the entire play's setting. The paradox that the bridge represents, both connecting and dividing two states, can be anticipated in a pre-reading discussion, while also establishing basic concepts: *Wozu dienen Brücken? Was symbolisieren sie? Was symbolisieren die Brücken der Euro-Scheine?* Further to this initial discussion, it is useful to frame the ensuing discussion by having students visualize and sketch the setting (*Schauplatz*, 76), complete with border guards firmly standing their ground on opposite riverbanks. We, the reader and audience, join Havlicek in determining the borders that delimit and structure the play, which never leaves the confines of the bridge. The bridge frames the play's episodic repetition and escalation of events. Indeed, this visually static setting makes Havlicek's endless physical and metaphoric back and forth appear all the more absurd.

Leitfragen: Teil I

Assuming that a pre-reading orientation has already taken place, questions about the physical setting may be further developed in relation to the play's theme and figuratively to aspects of character and plot. The following questions focus attention on structural devices of comedy, setting, character, language, the central conflict, and the sub-plots:

1. *Schauplatz: Skizzieren Sie die beiden Flussufer, die Grenzbeamten links und rechts und deren jeweiligen Angehörigen. Welchen Eindruck macht die Beschreibung der Szene (S. 77)?*
2. *Die Personen: Vergleichen Sie die beiden Grenzorgane, Szamek und Konstantin. Wie beschreiben sie sich selbst? Was sagen andere über sie? Unterstreichen Sie relevante Textstellen! Und wie ist ihr Verhältnis zueinander? Inwiefern gleichen, inwiefern unterscheiden sich die feindlichen Beamten?*
3. *Sprachlicher Ausdruck: Was fällt an der Sprache der Grenzer und Havliceks auf (Dialekt, bestimmte Wörter oder Ausdrücke, Wiederholungen)? Welche Wirkung haben diese Wiederholungen Ihrer Meinung nach auf den Leser bzw. Zuschauer? Unterstreichen Sie relevante Textstellen!*
4. *Worin besteht der Hauptkonflikt? Was gibt Anlass zur Sorge? Fassen Sie den Hauptkonflikt in max. 4 Sätzen zusammen! Wodurch wird der Konflikt verschärft?*
5. *Beschreiben Sie die jeweiligen Gesetze, die zu Havliceks Ausweisung aus beiden Ländern führen.*
6. *Welche Vorurteile hat Szemek gegenüber den anderen "da drüben" und insbesondere gegen Konstantin?*
7. *Wer ist Frau Hanusch und was hat sie auf dem Herzen? (Szenen 9, 19, 20, 22–25).*
8. *Warum sind beide Grenzer im Moment besonders wachsam? Wen wollen sie unbedingt ergreifen und was erhoffen sie sich?*
9. *Komik: Welche strukturellen Merkmale des Komischen erkennen Sie? Wie zeigen sich diese Merkmale? Geben Sie von mindestens drei der im folgenden genannten Merkmale eine knappe Beschreibung: Inkongruenz (z.B., Sein und Schein, Ideal/Selbstbild und Wirklichkeit, Aufwand und Ergebnis); Schneeballeffekt; Wiederholung; Inversion; Übertreibung; Ironie; Doppeldeutigkeiten; Wortspiel.*

10. *Inwiefern lässt sich der Titel "Hin und her" auf die Struktur und/oder auf den Inhalt weiter interpretieren? Und wie funktioniert die Brücke im ersten Teil?*

Schauplatz: To complete the important discussion of the setting, participants begin by plotting the characters either on the board, or by embodying them, on the left and right riverbanks, respectively. This helps to visualize all the familial, antagonistic, and (secretly) amorous relationships as well as the intermediary place of Havlicek set against the idyllic background ("idyllisch," 77). Second, the peaceful and idyllic setting, evocative of the traditional *Volksstück,* is abruptly disturbed by the first border guard's hostile obstruction of an innocent fisherwoman (*Halt!*; 77), thereby throwing the anachronistic conventions of the *Volksstück* into relief. It is important at this juncture to sensitize students to the critical difference between the traditional *Volksstück* and Horváth's critique of its anachronism: Not even the supposedly idyllic corners of the world are spared the dark shadow of Fascism. By highlighting the incongruity between form (traditionally light entertainment) and its seriously dark content (exile, border politics), readers are alerted to the play's all-important critical potential. Taken together, the setting establishes one of the play's many comedic incongruences.

Having visualized the setting and the relationships, it is possible to discuss the function of the bridge in Part I. With the visualization in place, students can summarize the main conflict and its escalation through sub-plots: Havlicek is removed from his host country, his birthplace, his livelihood, and any hope of personal relationships; Eva is forbidden to visit her lover, Konstantin; and Frau Hanusch, recently bereaved of her husband, now stands to lose her hotel business. The bridge serves both to connect and separate the characters and thus exacerbates the conflicts already in place, highlighting the personal turmoil wrought by border politics.

Die Personen: Awareness of the play's critical potential is especially relevant for understanding the characters. In considering empathetic questions of character, students should be encouraged to conceive of dramatic characters as linguistic constructs that are endowed with varying levels of linguistic facility, and to consider how certain linguistic choices are facilitative or empowering, and which fail or undermine a character. Having underlined passages relating to how Szamek and Konstantin express themselves, how they speak about themselves, and how others talk about them, students should begin to note the border guards' egotistical lack of self-awareness. For example, Szamek's over-inflated self-image as a guard ("treu und bieder, ehrbar und unbestechlich ... ein Exemplar von einem Grenzorgan, auf den sich die Grenz verlassen kann, ein Prachtexemplar –," 78), while not entirely invalid – no one takes his border control more seriously than he! – does not extend to his person, which, as the coarse handling of his daughter Eva demonstrates (78–9), is far from exemplary. Szamek's outright hatred for everything that Konstantin allegedly represents "da drüben" prompts him to prohibit his daughter's relationship with Konstantin. Szamek's prejudices in general include unfounded accusations of dishonesty, deviousness, and insincerity (78), and, in the particular case of Konstantin, poverty (95). His own depravity, brutality, and misogyny – especially when goaded by his co-worker, Mrschiktzka – coupled with his asinine behavior epitomizes the type of ill-intention fool doomed to failure.

Indeed, as we will see in the second part of the play, it is those very inflated virtues (loyalty, honesty, incorruptibility, and reliability as a guard) that one may expect to be punctured, contributing to his inevitable failure. And while his counterpart (*Gegenstück*), Konstantin, invites more sympathy initially ("er macht einen freundlichen Eindruck," 84), he nevertheless mirrors many of Szemak's faults: Both are emotionally and physically immovable, recalling the inelastic quality of Bergson's Jack-in-the-box. Konstantin resembles Szamek especially in his rigid adherence to border control over compassion or indeed common sense: "Gesetz ist Gesetz," even though the laws are inhuman ("Im allgemeinen Staatengetriebe wird gar oft ein persönliches Schicksal zerrieben,") and utterly absurd (84–5). The comic contrast between the guards, who remain rooted to the ground, and the now-rootless Havlicek, could not be more pronounced: Havlicek, "ein ruhiges Subjekt" (81), is the unassuming, emotionally and physically adroit, well-intentioned wit. Given the comic contrast arranged by these three characters, students are now primed to speculate the possible resolution to the play's central conflict.

All of these characteristics and contradictions can be teased out either in a discussion, or by way of dramatic readings. By carefully selecting brief interactions involving Szamek and Konstantin, it is possible for students to prepare these for brief dramatic presentation, prompting observing students to respond to what they have seen and to draw comparisons in the process. In presenting these interactions, students need not announce their characters' identities; rather, observing students are encouraged to identify the who, where, and the what and how this relates to the central conflict, which ensures active participation. The following selected passages are especially pertinent to the ironic contrast between characters' words and actions, underscoring the injustice and inhumanity lurking behind bureaucratic rhetoric.

1. Szene 2–3 (78–9): Szamek, asserting his virtues as a border guard, interrupts himself in order to scold his daughter Eva for not serving enough coffee, and for being too distracted by her feelings for Konstantin. Ironically, it will be precisely his own fuzzy head (brought about primarily by generous alcoholic complements to his coffee) that will contribute to his own failure as a guard. An example of Bergon's inversion, it is his hypocrisy and arrogant overestimation of his border-

guarding competence that will (in Part II) lead to his mistaken arrest of his own Head of State, thereby enabling the smugglers to outwit him.

2. Szene 6 (82): "Aber meine Herrschaften ... Zu-stän-dig!"
3. Szene 8 (84–5): "Hm. Und nun wollen Sie hier ... Schicksal zerrieben. Schad."
4. Szene 9 (87–8): "Wer ist denn dieser Herr? ... Werds ausrichten – – *Ab.*"
5. Szene 13 (90–1): "Was?! Schon wieder?! ... in Gottes Namen! Marsch-marsch!"
6. Szene 14 (93): "*Plötzlich zu Eva, die so nebenbei fort möcht*: Wohin? ... Merkt man ihr an."
7. Szene 14 (95): "Immer derselbe, Fräulein Eva! ... der dich gezeugt hat – –"
8. Szene 15 (96–7): "Was seh ich?! Schon wieder?! ... Als der eigene Erzeuger?! Na servus!"
9. Szene 18 (101): "Schauns, es dämmert ... Sie wären ein Engel." Here, we hear Eva talk about Konstantin.
10. Szene 26 (106–7): "... und macht sofort 'Hände-hoch!' ... Schnaps. Und Rum. Schon wieder!" Here, we witness the extent of Konstantin's heartlessness as a border guard, as well as his lack of self-awareness in a crass ironic twist: "Aber für Sie bin ich nur das Grenzorgan und kein Mensch ... man ist doch schließlich auch nur ein Mensch!" (106).

Sprachlicher Ausdruck: Regarding verbal expression, second-language readers will no doubt wish for explanation of some of Horváth's unusual expressions, especially those that recur frequently. The most prominent of these are the repeated "*zuständig* ist man dort, wo man geboren ist" (82, 90) – Austrian dialect for or "domiciled" or "right of residence" – as well as *penetrant* (annoying, irritating), used by both states' Heads of Government. Named simply X and Y and appearing incognito, the government heads are indistinguishable from one another both physically and linguistically, and amplify officialese to the point of meaningless absurdity, forming in effect a comically exaggerated doubling of the border guards. In stark contrast, Havlicek's almost resigned, mild-mannered retorts demonstrate considerable wit and serve to puncture their inflated jargon. This can be best appreciated by having students read passages in juxtaposition, including:

1. The direct mirroring of the border guard's language *Per Schub* by Szamek and Konstantin (81, 84).
2. Konstantin's occasionally friendly or polite exchanges with Frau Hanusch ("Küß die Hand!" 86) form a stark contrast with his behavior.
3. Konstantin's long-winded officialese (*Beamtendeutsch*) has the effect of a linguistic barrage, reinforcing his border with absurdly overcomplicated syntactic structures that he struggles to sustain. Examples of his attempt to effect an authoritative status include the overlong sentences containing endless subordinate and relative clauses (84–6). These stand

in stark contrast to the warm pleasantries exchanged with Frau Hanusch, for example ("A das ist aber lieb, Frau Hanusch" 86), or the private confessions to Eva that undermine his public role: "Zu was haben wir die blöde Grenz?" (107).

4. Similarly, the guards' callous, dehumanizing language is further demonstrated in the tendency to replace humans with concepts: Havlicek is variously reduced to an "Ausgewiesener" (81), an "Ausländer" (84), "Niemand. Ein amtlicher Fall" (87) – likewise mirrored in the designation of the government heads X and Y.

5. X and Y take bureaucratic language to the extreme with their repetition of the word *penetrant* (throughout scenes 30, 31, and 33) as well as the circuitous expression of a simple fact ("—so muß und darf und soll und will und kann ich nur betonen, daß diese Grenzen eine Plage sind," 114), and the nonsensical effect of attempted formal syntax ("hier können wir .... alle Strittigkeiten, die unsere beiden Länder berühren, berühren" 113). X's prevarications are constantly undercut by Havlicek's often literal and sometimes ironic interpretations: [X]: "Sie stehen so herrlich über den Dingen! [Havlicek] Ich steh nur zwischen den Grenzen." (114). Havlicek, who becomes incensed by X's impenetrable waffle that borders on insanity (*Irrengespräche*; 115), concludes that X must be anyone but a figure of authority, and inadvertently unmasks the incognito X for the Head of Government that he is: "...freu dich lieber, daß du kein Regierungschef bist, sonst könntst jetzt was erleben von mir, verstanden?!" (116).

The entirety of scenes 31 and 32 provides extended examples of an "equivocal situation" (*zweideutige Situation, Doppelbödigkeit*) and "inversion" described by Bergson. X's own border regulations ensure his self-entrapment (inversion) as he falls under suspicion of the watchful Konstantin precisely because he attempts to pass incognito: "Ich muß mich leider demaskieren," admits X in order to prevent possible arrest (112). X is forced once again to unmask himself in the ensuing scene, in which X mistakes Havlicek for his own counterpart, Y, talking at cross-purposes throughout. X's inability to grasp Havlicek's ironic or literal responses leads to X's inadvertent disclosure of his identity and of what he believes (incorrectly) to be the irreparable damage caused by inadvertently revealing a top-secret political scheme – to relax border control. X's "grand" political scheming is constantly undercut by the realism of Havlicek's responses, which, in extended dramatic irony, leads to his severely exaggerated physical reaction (he vomits) followed by his immediate resignation (116).

In drawing attention to the linguistic manifestation of these incongruences, it is also worth noting that such roles (as Konstantin and Szamek in particular) lend themselves particularly well to student performers, who will naturally appreciate the struggle to deliver convoluted officialese. Students should be reminded that they *should* sound as though they are trying hard to speak a kind of officialese that is beyond their current level. By maintaining the gap between their control of the language and the impossibly convoluted language, students realize Horváth's insistence on the audible incongruity between vernacular speech and forced, inauthentic expression (as per the *Gebrauchsanweisung*), thereby highlighting the intended "unmasking of consciousness."

In order to round off the discussion of Part I of *Hin und her*, it is worth determining the students' *Erwartungshorizont* for Part II. First, the instructor asks the full group to recall what they know about the main characters and their role in the play and map out the central conflicts on the board: Havlicek, Eva and Konstantin, Eva and Szamek, Szamek and Konstantin, X and Y, Frau Hanusch, individual and state. This may be carried out in a brief full-class review, or, time permitting, in a "Hot Seating" exercise (see ch. 1) in which key characters are interrogated (by a character outside the text) about their current situation and motivation. Second, students work in pairs or small groups and are assigned one character (Frau Hanusch, Havlicek) or a pair of characters (Konstantin and Eva, X and Y), recalling what they know about the character (including strengths and foibles). They then present their descriptions of each character to the rest of the class, who in turn identifies each character described. Using what they already know about the character types (ill-intentioned fool, well-intentioned wit, etc.) and about the comic techniques identified in this play (incongruity, inversion, exaggeration, equivocation, irony, wordplay, mistaken identities) students then work in pairs to speculate about possible outcomes. In doing so, it is useful to bear in mind each key figure's character traits and how these may or may not contribute to the outcome: *Was müsste passieren, damit das Drama gut ausgeht? Ist es überhaupt noch möglich, dass die Situation in Glück umschlägt?? Wie wird der Anlass zur Sorge beseitigt? Wer müsste letztendlich Glück haben und wer gerade nicht?* The discussion should clarify the central role that money plays in each conflict: The state unburdens itself financially of the impoverished Havlicek; both Havlicek and Frau Hanusch are jobless and penniless; Szamek's loathing of Konstantin is mainly on account of the latter's poverty; Konstantin and Szemek both want money out of sheer greed. Second, all conflicts relate to the divisive function of the bridge – the conflict between individual and state – so that all solutions hinge either on a dramatic shift in border policies or on their circumvention. Whether or not the materialization of money would solve this more fundamental issue remains to be seen. Given the border guards' "inelastic" quality, dramatic shifts will likely not occur due to a change of heart, but rather by chance, accident, or, as Havlicek himself suggests early on, "ein Wunder" (87).

Leitfragen: Teil II

Students can test their hypotheses with some additional guidance from the following reading questions:

1. *Wen glauben Szamek und Mrschitzka gefesselt und entlarvt zu haben? Wie beschreiben sie ihre vermeintliche Heldentat?*
2. *Was ist überhaupt passiert und warum? Was ist die große Ironie dieser Situation?*
3. *Welche Umstände erlauben es den Schmugglern, über die Brücke zu gelangen?*
4. *Wie überwinden die Schmuggler die Grenzer Szamek und Mrschitzka?*
5. *Welche anderen Personenverwechslungen und Missverständnisse tauchen im 2. Teil auf und was sind die Folgen?*
6. *Welche Rolle spielt Havlicek bei der Fesselung der Schmuggler und der Entlarvung der beiden Regierungschefs? Wie ist er zum "Helden" geworden?*
7. *Eva denkt, dass Konstantin das Gesetz über alles stellt (101), denn "Gesetz ist Gesetz." Wie ist Konstantins Umgang mit Szamek und Mrschitzka (Sz. 18 und 19) Ihrer Meinung nach einzuschätzen? Hat sich Konstantins Charakter geändert? Warum (nicht)?*
8. *Wie reagieren die jeweiligen Regierungschefs auf ihre Fesselung und Entlarvung?*
9. *Wie beurteilen Sie den Schluss? Wird der Anlass zur Hauptsorge aufgehoben? Welche Konflikte werden gelöst und wie? Welche Konflikte werden nur scheinbar gelöst oder bleiben ungelöst?*
10. *Welche Rolle spielt die Gerechtigkeit bei den Entscheidungen? (ab Sz. 18)*
11. *Welche Rolle spielt das Lied am Ende?*

Throughout Part I, the absurdity of border politics is compounded by the perplexing legal and political jargon and inflated self-regard that is far removed from reality. X's and Y's inadvertent self-exposure in Havlicek's presence illustrate this to the point of absurdity, anticipating and precipitating the comic reversals of fortune (inversions) in store in Part II. The most striking of these, of course, is the spectacle of mistaken entities that ensues on account of Szamek's and Mrschitzka's unreliability, corruptibility, and gullibility – in direct contradiction to their earlier self-praise. In blind (and by now drunken) pursuit of the financial reward promised by the smugglers' capture, Szamek and Mrschitzka mistake their own Head of Government, Y, for the smugglers – despite the clear visibility provided by the timely reappearance of the brightly shining moon (119). Thus, the anticipated and spectacular failure of the border guards coincides with one of the primary comic reversals that precipitates the play's ultimate happy ending. With both Heads of State now absent, the scene is set for the denouement.

A key player in the escalation of conflicts is the linguistic marking of incongruences – between expression and character, language and content, often (with Havlicek) in dramatic irony – and this is nowhere more significant than in Part II, and in the denouement in particular. To highlight this, students work in pairs to prepare short dialogues for a dramatic reading, following which they (and their fellow students) should comment on the kind of language and how – at least in their retrospective reading – these conflict with reality:

1. Szamek and Mrschitzka's deluded jubilation for having supposedly captured the smugglers (Sc. 1, 120).
2. Schmugglitschinski and Frau Leda as they approach and outwit Szamek and Mrschitzka, still blinded by egotism (Sc. 15, 134–5).
3. Konstantin's outwitting the drunkenly slumbering Szamek and Mrschitzka, whose "blindness" extends to the inability to distinguish reality from a dream, a *persönliche Fata morgana*, or a drunken *trelirium demens* (Sc. 16, 138–9).
4. Konstantin's (and Havlicek's) exploitation of legalese for word-play, whether intended or not, which Szamek chooses either to ignore (Sc. 16: "[Konstantin] Wenn ich jetzt hier die Grenz nicht verletzt hätt, wären Sie jetzt vielleicht bereits über einer anderen Grenz... [Havlicek] Versteh kein Wort!" 140), or, if it works to his own advantage, to accept ("Pflichtlich wart Ihr doch vorschriftlich! ... denn pflichtlich seid Ihr im Recht!" Sc. 18).

What seems to motivate Konstantin's apparently gracious exoneration of Szamek, however, would seem to derive less from a change of heart (and character) than from his rigid adherence to the language of *Gesetz*, a linguistic trap that appears to ensnare him. By the same token, *Wahrheit und Gerechtigkeit* oblige him to relinquish half of the financial reward to Havlicek, who saved them all (145). And thus, with various key inversions having taken place, the many relational and financial parts are set for a happy ending, complete with two weddings: Eva, previously the daughter-victim, now scolds Szamek (*Ruhe, Szamek*; 140); Szamek and Mirschitzka justifiably lose their reward for capturing their own Head of State; Szamek, now apparently satisfied with Konstantin's newfound wealth, is prepared to give his blessing for his marriage to Eva; Havlicek's forthright benevolence earns him a financial reward along with Frau Hanusch's affection; and, finally (146), the border is declared open – at least, for Havlicek. But what of the fundamental cause for concern (*Anlass zur Sorge*) – the key conditions for a genuinely happy ending?

Ende gut, alles gut?

With two happy unions, financial rewards, and an open border for Havlicek, the spectator is easily tempted to accept this as the kind of happy ending typical of the *Volksposse*. A discussion of the ending should center on the removal of concern (Olson). Focusing on the final three short scenes (Sc. 20–3), students review the conditions under which the happy ending has been achieved: *Wie, wann, für wen, und warum wird die Grenze geöffnet?*

Answers to these questions reveal the contrived nature of the happy ending. Appearing suddenly in the form a telegram delivered by Frau Hanusch, the miraculous news of the border opening is greeted with elation, but entry is granted as an exception only to *dem heimatlosen Ferdinand Havlicek* (146) – X's final decree before his resignation (146, 148). In other words, X's resignation from office is the precondition for Havlicek's freedom, and with his resignation, any promise of political compromise dissolves. In the absence of a genuine political solution, the *deus ex machina* conclusion – *Abrakadabra!* (149) – offers only a temporary and restricted reprieve.

Upon closer consideration, and while consistent with comedic convention, the play's conclusion appears self-consciously contrived for the sake of dramatic convention, very much in the tradition of Nestroy, "bloß damit alles gut ausgeht–!" (Nestroy 93). It is appropriate at this stage to ask students to revisit all the happy reunions, whether they had anticipated them, what they thought about them, and to notice each characters' reactions. The final scenes of general elation are exaggerated to such a degree that draws attention to their contrivance: Havlicek's benevolence gets the better of him, relinquishing half of his reward to border guard Szamek ("Jetzt werd aber auch gleich edel werden! Gerecht und wahr!" 146); the quarreling couple on the bridge is joyfully reconciled over their sudden and improbable fishing success (148); and Szamek finally agrees to give his daughter, Eva, and Konstantin his blessing. Frau Hanusch, who is miraculously restored to financial and emotional wellbeing by Havlicek, is justifiably jubilant: *Ende gut, alles gut!* (149). And, as Havlicek remarks, it all appears to be so simple: "wie leicht daß man so unmenschliche Gesetz menschlich außer Kraft setzen kann" (148). Havlicek's remark, however, only serves to draw attention to the fact that fundamental conflicts remain unresolved. Despite the ease with which an inhumane law can be abolished by a simple human gesture, the alleviation of political tensions is nevertheless as short-lived as Szamek's blessing; his antipathy endures to the end: "Ich habs ja immer schon gewußt, daß die Leut dort drüben einen falschen Charakter haben!.," Szamek concludes (149). Any outward magnanimity on the part of Szamek is financially conditioned and ultimately inauthentic. Indeed, just as the language of border guards and officials is largely ineffectual and meaningless, so too is the final decree – a written *letter* from a now-resigned official – ultimately a void linguistic gesture. The brief resolution remains a mere linguistic maneuver within the constraints of comedy; all the generic, idyllic tropes are distorted to reveal the fairytale-like implausibility of the ending. Horváth, like Brecht, invites the audience to cast a critical eye on the enduring political and social tensions, whose temporary solution is subsequently rescinded in the *Finale mit Gesang* – a highly ironic song of praise of borders: "Grenzen muß es geben! / Denn von die Grenzen tun wir leben. / Ich seh schon ein, daß es muß geben / Gar manche Grenz, damit wir leben (152–3).

Horváth's own deportation from Germany shortly after the Zurich premiere of *Hin und her,* as well his ultimate escape to Paris four years later, when Germany accessed Austria, adds additional ironic heft to the play's ending. Given these impending real-life circumstances, the implausibility of the play's conclusion could not have been timelier, and the scrutiny of insidious power structures at work that Horváth's *Posse* demands could not be more urgent. This important point might easily escape attention if we only take our cue from the central figure, Havlicek, whose light-hearted dealings with the guards inure himself and the spectator to the appalling situation. For this reason, special attention is directed to the border guards and politicians throughout – to their exaggerated self-regard, aggressively heartless tactics, linguistic bombard, and, ultimately, spectacular incompetence – without which, the spectator is tempted to view it simply as comic. But there is nothing comical about Y's closing threat to lock away all his opponents, and with them any chance of an open border. Havlicek's freedom ultimately occurs at the expense of everyone else's imprisonment.

Lessons of comedy

In teaching language through drama, comedy is particularly well poised to maintain a balance of emotional and intellectual engagement. It affords students the opportunity to enjoy the healthy benefits of laughter itself through the ability, as Lessing suggested, "das Lächerliche zu bemerken" (KT 67), while engaging intellectually and critically in the play's themes. For comedy also teaches us that the "happy end" is not necessarily a solution of the conflict, and that one should continue to learn from its social-critical message. As a final activity, and to situate the play in a broader context, it is worth discussing the questions raised in the final song about borders more generally: What are the reasons for and relative advantages or disadvantages of political borders? What are examples – political, cultural, or linguistic – of phenomena that transcend borders and why or how do these exist?

Aus dem Stegreif

Throughout such a course on comedy, it is especially valuable to pay careful attention on physical and verbal expression. From the simple back-and-forth movement in *Hin und her* to the significance of standing (upright, slouched), falling (fainting, stumbling, collapsing), entering and exiting, interruptions, or even a physical tick, a whole repertoire of physical gestures provide much of the comic material and additional insight not inferred from dialogue alone. The brief exercises provide a lively, playful starting point for further discussion, reinforce the vocabulary of physical and verbal expression, and animate students to explore the relation between the two. In the original spirit of the *Posse,* it is productive to preview any discussion with an improvisational warm-up exercise.[16] All the exercises (except viii, which requires more time) may be combined into a single workshop or used individually as warm-up exercises with any suitable texts that follow Appendix B.

Notes

1 An earlier version of this chapter appeared in *Die Unterrichtspraxis*, vol. 45, no. 2 (2012), 145–56.
2 The mocking tone of an English poet and critic, George Meredith, in his "Essay on comedy and the uses of the comic spirit," is cited in Hutchinson (16).
3 For a useful discussion of these complexities, see Pye (2–17).
4 "Durch Oberflächlichkeit gekennzeichnete und für die Spaßgesellschaft typische Form der Kultur." Cited in Herberg et al. 321.
5 "er ließ den Harlekin feierlich vom Theater vertreiben, welches selbst die größte Harlekinade war, die jemals gespielt worden...." See the '*Literaturbriefe, 17. Brief* in *Gesammelte Werke*, vol. 2, 623.
6 These were the Theater in der Leopoldstadt (founded 1781), the Freihaustheater auf der Wieden (1787), where Mozart's *Die Zauberflöte* was first performed, and the Theater in der Leopoldstadt (1788).
7 Bergson describes the Jack-in-a-box as "the little man who springs out of his box. You squeeze him flat, he jumps up again. Push him lower, and he shoots up still higher. Crush him down beneath the lid, and often he will send everything flying ... It is a struggle between two stubborn elements, one of which, being simply mechanical, generally ends by giving in to the other, which treats it as a plaything .... But imagine these two feelings as *inelastic* and unvarying elements in a really living man, make him oscillate from one to the other... then you will get the image we have so far found in all laughable objects, *something mechanical in the living*; in fact, something comic (Bergson 26–8).
8 The snowball effect, as described by Bergson, involves an event that repeats itself to "suggest the same abstract vision, that of an effect which grows by arithmetical progression, so that the cause, trifling at the outset, culminates by a necessary evolution in a result as significant as it is unexpected. [...]." Rather like the hat that always vanishes just when you think you have caught it, the event "runs through the entire play picking up more serious, more and more unexpected incidents on its way" (29).
9 The most widely cited evidence of such influence is contained in the anecdote, recounted by Brecht in his *Dialoge aus dem Messingkauf*, in which Valentin directly or indirectly helped Brecht to solve a theatrical quandary that resulted in Brecht's bold move to apply white chalk to the solders' faces in his first production of Marlowe's *Edward II*. For example, see Thompson and Sachs, *The Cambridge Companion to Brecht* (40–62).
10 Loriot, who sees one picture hanging askew, tries to correct this but ends up knocking everything down in the room, leaving it in utter chaos (see *Loriot*). And Niles, who wants to iron a crease out of his trousers to make a good impression on a date who will arrive shortly, ends up setting the entire apartment on fire and, now only half-dressed, blacks out, whereupon his date arrives (see *Frasier*). No doubt, there are many more current-day examples to draw from.
11 These texts were selected from Profitlich's very useful compilation of comedy theories (KT).
12 Horváth's novel *Jugend ohne Gott* was recently adapted for the stage and directed by Nurkan Erpulat, whose *Verrücktes Blut* is the focus of ch. 8. It also was performed in translation, *Youth without God*, in New York in 2019.
13 "Ödön von Horváth besaß die Frechheit, die Nazionalsozialisten anzupöbeln. Seine Italienische Nacht zeichnet uns als Feiglinge, die durch ein einziges Schimpfwort seitens einer Frau in die Flucht geschlagen werden. Wird sich der Ödön noch wundern! (*Völkischer Beobachter*, February 14, 1933, cited in *Materialien zu Ödön von Horváth* (67).

14 In this, Horváth paves the way for the critical *Neues Volkstück* of Franz Xaver Kroetz, Martin Sperr, and Peter Turrini in the 1960s and 70s.

15 Productions of *Hin und her* by foreign-language theater groups in the Czech Republic and Holland are still available on YouTube. Horváth made his first appearance in New York in 2019, when Nurkan Erpulat directed *Youth without God.*

16 While the following are my own creations gathered from years of teaching drama and theater, a wealth of guides is available for further reference, including, among others Maley and Duff, Schewe, and Spolin (see also ch. 1).

Further resources and reading

On comedy theory in German

Profitlich, Ulrich, ed. *Komödientheorie. Texte und Kommentare vom Barock bis zur Gegenwart.* Berlin: Rohwolt, 1998.

Freund, Winfried. *Deutsche Komödien vom Barock bis zur Gegenwart.* Paderborn: Fink, 1988.

Bergson, Henri. "The Comic in Situations." In *Modern Theories of Drama: A Selection of Writings on Drama and Theatre from the Middle of the Nineteenth to the Latter Part of the Twentieth Century.* George W. Brandt, ed. New York: Oxford UP, 1998, 25–34.

Olson, Elder. *The Theory of Comedy.* Bloomington: Indiana UP, 1968.

On Ödön von Horváth

Krishcke, Traugott, ed. *Materialien zu Ödön von Horváth.* Frankfurt am Main: Suhrkamp, 1970.

On Karl Valentin

Valentin, Karl. *Alles von Karl Valentin: Monologe und Geschichten, Jugendstreiche, Couplets, Dialoge, Szenen und Stücke, Lichtbildreklamen.* M. Schulte, ed. Munich: Piper, 1978.

Valentin, Karl. "Der Theaterbesuch." *Die Kurzfilme,* created and performed by Karl Valentin and Liesl Karlstadt, Bayerischer Rundfunk, 2002, disc 1.

On Loriot

Hamann, Evelyn Warner Home Video. *Loriot: Gesammelte Werke aus Film und Fernsehen.* Sonderausgabe. Hamburg: Warner Home Video, 2005.

2018 *"Loriot,* Das Bild hängt schief," uploaded to *YouTube* by movie mag, February 16, 2018, https://www.youtube.com/watch?v=a6WQaIIZ248.

References

Arntzen, Helmut. *Die ernste Komödie: das deutsche Lustspiel von Lessing bis Kleist.* Munich: Nymphenburger Verlagshandlung, 1968.

Bergson, Henri. "The Comic in Situations." In *Modern Theories of Drama: A Selection of Writings on Drama and Theatre from the Middle of the Nineteenth to the Latter Part of the Twentieth Century.* George W. Brandt, ed. New York: Oxford UP, 1998, 25–34.

Bierbaum, Otto J. *Die Yankeedoodle-Fahrt und andere Reisegeschichten: Neue Beiträge zur Kunst des Reisens.* Munich: Georg Müller, 1910.

Cardullo, Bert, trans. and ed. *German-language Comedy: A Critical Anthology.* Selinsgrove: Susquehanna UP, 1992.

Double, Oliver, et al. "Brecht and Cabaret." *The Cambridge Companion to Brecht.* 2nd ed. Cambridge: Cambridge UP, 2006, 40–62.

"Frasier, Niles causes Fire," from *Three Valentines,* Season 6, episode 14, uploaded to *YouTube* by Shaun Parker, March 6, 2012, https://www.youtube.com/watch?v=EpImet3Xwgw

Freud, Sigmund. *Der Witz und seine Beziehung zum Unbewussten* (1905). In *Gesammelte Werke,* vol. 6. Frankfurt am Main: Fischer, 1999.

Freund, Winfried. *Deutsche Komödien: Vom Barock bis zur Gegenwart.* Paderborn: Fink, 1988.

Fröhlich, Stefanie, and Gegenbauer, Christina. "Hin und Her – Grenz-Groteske von Ödön von Horváth." *Wienviertlerin.* July 27, 2017. https://www.weinviertlerin.at/hin-und-her-grenz-groteske-von-oedoen-von-horvath/

Goldman, A. J. "A Dark Playwright for Dark Times." *New York Times,* April 12, 2019.

Gottsched, Johann Christoph. *Versuch Einer Critischen Dichtkunst. Variantenverzeichnis.* Joachim Birke and Brigitte Birke, ed. Berlin: de Gruyter, 1973.

Grange, William. "Rules, Regulations, and the Reich: Comedy under the Auspices of the Propaganda Ministry." In *Essays on Twentieth Century German Drama and Theater: An American Reception, 1977-1999,* Helmut H. Rennert ed. New German-American Studies, v. 19. New York: P. Lang, 2004, , 196-201.

Greiner, Bernard. *Die Komödie: eine theatralische Sendung: Grundlagen und Interpretationen.* Tübingen: Francke, 1992.

Guthke, Karl S. *Gotthold Ephraim Lessing.* Stuttgart: Metzler, 1979.

Herberg, Dieter, Kinne, Michael, Steffens, Doris, Tellenbach, Elke, and Al-Wadi, Doris. *Neuer Wortschatz: Neologismen der 90er Jahre im Deutschen .* Schriften des Instituts für Deutsche Sprache, vol. 11. Berlin: de Gruyter, 2004.

Hinck, Walther. *Die deutsche Komödie. Vom Mittelalter bis zur Gegenwart.* Düsseldorf: August Bagel, 1977.

Holl, Karl. *Gechichte des deutschen Lustspiels.* Leipzig: J.J. Webe, 1923.

Horváth, Ödön von. *Eine Unbekannte aus der Seine und andere Stücke.* 1st. ed., Frankfurt am Main: Suhrkamp, 1988.

Hutchinson, Peter, ed. *Landmarks in German Comedy.* Oxford: P. Lang, 2006.

Jarka, Horst. "Sprachliche Strukturelemente in Ödön von Horváths Volksstücken." *Colloquia Germanica,* vol. 7, 1973, 317–339.

Kant, Immanuel. *Immanuel Kant: Gesammelte Schriften.* Akademie-Ausgabe, vol. 1-23, Berlin: de Gruyter, 1900–2004.

Kegler, Lydia. "Fascism and the Inability to Love in the 20th-Century Volksstück: Marieluise Fleisser, Martin Sperr and Franz Xaver Kroetz." Electronic Thesis or Dissertation. Ohio State U, 1992. *OhioLINK Electronic Theses and Dissertations Center.* Retrieved July 23, 2020.

Kinzer, Steven. "The German comedy, an oxymoron no more." *New York Times*, 1996, June 23, 1996.

Klotz, Volker. *Bürgerliches Lachtheater: Komödie, Posse, Schwank, Operette.* 4th ed., *Beiträge Zur Neueren Literaturgeschichte,* 3rd Series, vol. 239. Heidelberg: Winter, 2007.

Krischke, Traugott. *Materialien zu Ödön von Horváth.* Frankfurt am Main: Suhrkamp, 1970.

Lessing, Gotthold Ephraim. *Briefe, die neueste Literatur betreffend, 17er Brief* (16 February 1759). In *Werke,* 3 vol. H. G. Göpfert, ed. Munich: Hanser, 2003, vol. 2.

"Loriot, Das Bild hängt schief," uploaded to *YouTube* by movie mag, February 16, 2018, https://www.youtube.com/watch?v=a6WQaIIZ248.

Magill, Charles P. "Austrian Comedy." *German Life and Letters,* vol. 4, no. 1, 1950, 31–41.

Maley, Alan, and Alan Duff. *Drama Techniques in Language Learning. A Resource Book of Communication Activities for Language Teachers.* New York: Cambridge UP, 1982.

Malone, Paul M. "Ödön Von Horváth's Back and Forth: Teetering between Exile and Return." *Modern Drama,* vol. 46, no. 1, 2003, 55.

MLA Ad Hoc Committee on Foreign Languages. Foreign Languages and Higher Education: New Structures for a Changed World. Retrieved from http://www.mla.org/pdf/forlang_news_pdf.pdf

Nestroy, Johann N. *Der Zerrissene. Posse mit Gesang in drei Akten.* Stuttgart: Reclam, 2000.

Nietzsche, Friedrich. *Sämtliche Werke. Kritische Studienausgabe,* vol. 3. Munich: Deutscher Taschenbuch Verlag, 1988.

"Ödön von Horváths 'Niemand' am Deutschen Theater." *Der Spiegel,* March 26, 2017.

Olson, Elder. *The Theory of Comedy.* Bloomington: Indiana UP, 1968.

Profitlich, Ulrich, ed. *Komödientheorie. Texte und Kommentare vom Barock bis zur Gegenwart.* Berlin: Rohwolt, 1998.

Pye, Gillian. *Approaches to Comedy in German Drama.* Lewiston, New York: E. Mellen, 2002.

Radecki, Sigismund von. *Als ob das immer so weiterginge…* Freiburg: Herder, 1964.

Rosenberg, James. "Checklist No. 2: Ödön von Horváth." *New Theater Quarterly,* 1986, 376–384.

Sandford, John. *Encyclopedia of Contemporary German Culture.* London and New York: Routledge, 1999.

Schewe, Manfred P., ed. *Towards Drama as a Method in the Foreign Language Classroom.* Frankfurt am Main: P. Lang, 1993.

Schopenhauer, Arthur. *Die Welt Als Wille Und Vorstellung.* Heinrich Schmidt, ed. Leipzig: A. Kröner, 1911.

1996 "Sei schlau, hab Spaß," *Der Spiegel,* February 19, 1996.

Spolin, Viola. *Improvisation for the Theater. A Handbook for Teaching and Directing Techniques,* 3rd ed. Evanston: Northwestern UP, 1999.

Thomson, Peter, and Sacks, Glendyr. *The Cambridge Companion to Brecht.* Cambridge: Cambridge UP, 2006.

Valentin, Karl. *Alles von Karl Valentin: Monologe und Geschichten, Jugendstreiche, Couplets, Dialoge, Szenen und Stücke, Lichtbildreklamen.* M. Schulte, ed. Munich: Piper, 1978.

Valentin, Karl et al. "Der Theaterbesuch." *Die Kurzfilme*, created and performed by Karl Valentin and Liesl Karlstadt, Bayerischer Rundfunk, 2002.

Williams, Simon, and Hamburger, Maike, ed. *A History of German Theater.* Cambridge: Cambridge UP, 2008.

Appendix A.

Table 3.3 (Appendix A)

Day	Reading assignments	Pre-discussion tasks	Class lecture, discussion, topics, concepts
2	Elder Olson, *The Theory of Comedy,* parts I-II especially pp. 45–65Aristotle: *Poetics* (optional) Excerpts: II, IV-VII, X-X1II, XIII-XV, XVIII)	Bring an example (from theater or television) of a plot or character type described by Elder Olson.	1. *Was ist eine Komödie?* 2. *Was ist das Verhältnis der Komödie zur Tragödie? Und das Verhältnis der Komödie zur Komik?* • *Tragödie: Furcht, Mitleid, Katharsis, Umschlag vom Glück ins Unglück* • *Komödie: Umschlag ins Glück; "Katastasis" (Entspannung, Beseitigung des Anlasses zur Sorge)* 3. *Charaktertypen und Handlungsarten (nach Olson)* 4. *Katharsis (Aristoteles) vs. Katastasis (Olson). Die Komödie; die Komik; das Komische; das Lachen; das Lächerliche.* 5. *Struktur einer Komödie.* 6. *Die Komödie in Deutschland,*

(*Continued*)

Table 3.3 (Continued)

Day	Reading assignments	Pre-discussion tasks	Class lecture, discussion, topics, concepts
			Österreich, und in der Schweiz. Das Verhältnis des Komischen zur gesellschaftlichen Stellung.
3	*Henri Bergson: The Comic in Situations (9 pp.) Karl Valentin: Der Theaterbesuch (12 pp.) Karl Valentin: Der Theaterbesuch (12 pp.)*	*Reading questions for Valentin to be completed in note form in preparation for discussion.*	*Discussion based on Valentin's "Der Theaterbesuch" Komischer Kontrast und Konflikt; Wiederholung und Übertreibung; Steigerung der Situation, Schneeball-Effekt und Kettenreaktion (Bergson); Überraschung, Unterbrechung, Umschlag vom Unglück ins Glück (Olson, Aristotle); Katastasis, Anlass zur Sorge (Olson) Komischer Kontrast und Konflikt; Wiederholung und Übertreibung; Steigerung der Situation, Schneeball-Effekt und Kettenreaktion (Bergson); Überraschung, Unterbrechung, Umschlag ins Glück (Olson, Aristotle); Katastasis, Anlass zur Sorge (Olson)*
		Wer ist die Zielscheibe des Spotts? Beschreiben Sie seine äußerlichen und innerlichen Merkmale.Inwiefern	*2. Comic character: Übertreibung eines Fehlers; lächerlich; Verhältnis der Charakterdarstellung zur gesellschaftlichen*

(Continued)

Table 3.3 (Continued)

Day	Reading assignments	Pre-discussion tasks	Class lecture, discussion, topics, concepts
		sind die Figuren "komisch"? Welcher Fehler wird übertrieben und/oder wiederholt?	*Stellung (Sprache, Dialekt, Aussehen); Witz; Witzfiguren; scheitern/gelingen; belohnen/bestrafen; lachen/verlachen.*

Appendix B. Drama workshops

Pre-workshop assignment: Students review Bergson's "The Comic in Situations" and are assigned a certain character from one of the comedies. Students should identify a particular phrase or sentence that they think best illustrates the character, noting the exact moment(s), page, and line numbers where the phrase occurs or recurs. Attention should also be paid to issues of class and gender. In addition, students could rehearse a pantomime version of a characteristic gesture, facial expression, or posture to be combined with their selected characteristic phrase. Justifying their choice of phrase and gesture encourages everyone to interact intellectually and physically with the text, and ultimately provides the setting for lively discussion. The following series of exercises culminate in an improvisation exercise, designed to establish the core conflict of the play:

   i. Each student enters "on stage," declares the selected line, and takes a bow as the whole class applauds.
   ii. Each student reappears on stage this time with a pantomime gesture or facial expression that they think best illustrates the character and the line. A bow and another round of applause.
   iii. *Dirigentenspiel* (optional follow-on exercise): Everyone stands in a circle and one student performs the above, giving the *Auftakt* for each subsequent student to imitate, in chain reaction, and with increasing exaggeration. This exercise serves to visualize the snowball effect outlined by Bergson that drives many comedies. As such, it provides a useful starting point for understanding the comedic mechanisms at play.
   iv. Follow-on discussion: The other students must identify the character and, if possible, the significance of the line, and comment on the appropriateness of the gesture. If the phrase recurs, each instance can be elucidated in context. By sensitizing students to close, contextualized readings, mechanisms of word play, double entendre, and especially irony can be teased out.

v. Alternative pantomimes, including gestures that contradict a statement, social status, or gender, are explored in pairs or small groups and demonstrated, in preparation for a discussion about issues of decorum, class, and dialect.

vi. *Aus der Rolle fallen*: A common comic device in Austrian satire, and one that Brecht deploys for the purpose of *Verfremdung*, this is best illustrated in dramatic readings. Students work in pairs to prepare a short dialogue from a play in which they step out of their roles, face the audience, and comment on their action. (This is useful for discussing this particular comic device frequently found in Nestroy's comedies, often in the form of a song. It also plays an important role in comparing the Viennese distancing technique with similar techniques used by Brecht.)

vii. *Aussprache*: Discussion of the place of dialect in German vs. Austrian comedy and some pronunciation practice involving Austrian dialectal features. In the case of a *Posse* or a *Volksstück*, such distinctions play an important role in social cohesion of a particular group in a particular place.

viii. *Aus dem Stegreif*: Time permitting (at least 15 minutes for preparation and 5 minutes per performance) this impromptu exercise is based on basic situation derived from the text and transposed into another, possibly modern, setting.

ix. *Archetypal situation: Vater, Tochter, deren Geliebter. Situation: Ein junges Liebespaar will heiraten. Der eher strenge und konservative Vater billigt die Eheschließung nicht. Der junge und weniger begüterte Mann versucht einen guten Eindruck auf denb Vater zu machen. Der Vater bleibt stur und weigert sich, ihnen seinen Segen zu geben.* (This is a useful way to establish the main conflict of so many comedies and to anticipate possible outcomes, either in discussion or in a creative writing exercise.)

Appendix C.

Sample creative and analytical writing assignments
1. Creative Task: *Nacherzählung von Valentins Kurzfilm Die lustigen Vagabunden Sehen Sie sich Valentins "Die Lustigen Vagabunden" an und schreiben Sie eine Nacherzählung in ca. 300 (max. 350) Wörtern. Bei der Nacherzählung ist Folgendes zu beachten:*
Inhalt:

i. *Schildern Sie die Handlung so, dass das Wesentliche nacherzählt wird, und dass unbedeutende Einzelheiten wegfallen. Das gilt auch für die bildhafte aber knappe Schilderung von Personen, Ort und Zeit;*
ii. *Schreiben Sie den Text in der dritten Person und im Präteritum.*

Aufbau: Die Geschichte besteht aus drei Hauptteilen, wie folgt:

  i. *Kurze Einleitung (Exposition): Personen, Ort, Zeit; Konflikt?*
 ii. *Hauptteil: Haupterzählschritte, die zu einem Höhepunkt (Wendepunkt? Umschlag?) führen;*
iii. *Schluss: den Ausgang (den Umschlag) der Handlung knapp darstellen.*

Weitere Merkmale: Zur erzählerischen Knappheit und Bildhaftigkeit gehören

  i. *aktive Verben, wie z.B. die Variation der Verben des Gehens, Sprechens, Sehens;*
 ii. *Lautmalerei;*
iii. *lebendige aber kurze Dialoge: denken Sie sich passende Dialoge aus und versuchen Sie, wenn möglich, die Dialoge auch mit bayerischem Dialekt zu variieren.*

2. Analytical Task: *Charakteranalyse (see ch. 1)*
3. Creative Task: *Modernisierung des Dramas*
    Sie schreiben ein Drehbuch für einen Film. Versetzen Sie eine Szene aus einem Drama (oder bei einem kurzen Stück, das ganze Drama) an einen anderen, moderneren Handlungsort, indem Sie den Dialog modernisieren (und auf das Wesentliche reduzieren), ohne dabei jedoch den Hauptkonflikt zu verlieren.
4. *Innerer Monolog*
5. Analytical Task: Analysis of comedy (8–10 pp.) *"Seit der Vertreibung des Hanswursts und seit Lessings Komödien will man lachend nachdenken und nachdenkend, falls es möglich ist, lachen" (Georg Hensel, 1990). Diskutieren Sie diese Behauptung anhand von zwei der gelesenen Komödien.*

4 *Zwischenspiel:* teaching tragicomedy

Table 4.1

Author	Roland Schimmelpfennig
Titel	*Der goldene Drache*
Premiere	Vienna, Akademietheater, September 5, 2009
Pages	64
Performance Length	Ca. 90 mins in full; cuts are possible for the sake of brevity. Hungarian composer Peter Eötvös, who was commissioned to write an operatic version (2014), selected just 21 of the 48 scenes.
Cast	Five actors (two women and three men) are stipulated, each cast among 3–4 roles for a total of 17 roles. These may be spread among a higher number of participants in larger groups. Little "acting" required, as much is narrated and actors remain partly transparent in their roles. The paucity of descriptions and fluidity of casting enables students to co-construct these roles.
Set	A single building, housing all the characters. Due to the short-cut episodic nature of the play, scenes from each floor of the building need to be realized horizontally on stage. The lack of stage directions and emphasis on "demonstration," however, invites minimalist (and thus manageable) set design.
Language	Short, simple phrases and sentences, primarily short monologues, and third-person narration. Much repetition. Some language not suitable for younger adults or children.
Topic and Complexity	Migration and illegal workers in the era of globalization is highly relevant.
Potential challenges	Frequent role-switching and cross-dressing can present a challenge for groups of only five (as suggested in the original casting). For larger groups, however, these roles may be divided among more participants. Complexity of scene changes needs careful consideration in order to avoid confusion.

Introduction

How does one deal with the darker side of the globalized world? How can one tell stories about the fate of illegal immigrants – about greed,

DOI: 10.4324/9781003010289-4

exploitation, human trafficking, and the lack of human rights for those who must remain unseen, even when they need urgent medical attention or police protection from abusive pimps? To what extent can we remain detached from the shadowy aspects of our contemporary society? And are we perhaps more implicated that we might care to admit? The tragic fate of some anonymous Asian kitchen worker would seem to have nothing to do with us – until one of his teeth lands in our soup….

Thus begins the introductory program notes for my recent student production of Roland Schimmelpfennig's *Der goldene Drache* (2008). Questions of this sort are at the forefront of many dramatists' minds amid the current social, economic, and political upheavals, and no less so in 2010, when this play was voted "play of the year" by *Theater heute*, awarded the *Dramatikerpreis* at the *Mühlheimer Theatertage*, and featured at the Berliner *Theatertreffen*. A glance at both the Mühlheim and Berlin theater festivals in 2010 reveals the extent to which dramatists were engaging, and continue to engage, in these global upheavals. Among those shortlisted, four offer their take on global financial crises: The post-sub-prime financial crisis is treated as comedy in Elfriede Jelinek's *Die Kontrakte des Kaufmanns: Eine Wirtschaftskomödie* and as tragicomedy in Christoph Marthaler and Anna Viebrock's *Riesenbutzbach: Eine Dauerkolonie*; the Wall Street crash of 1929 forms the setting of both Ödön von Horváth's *Kasimir und Karoline* and Hans Falladas's novel, *Kleiner Mann – was nun?*, both written in 1932 and revived and adapted respectively in 2010. Another, Dirk Laucke's *Für alle reicht es nicht* (2009), offers an account of life in Germany since reunification and of migration within the borders of Fortress Europe. According to the jury discussion at the *Berliner Theatertreffen* in 2010, the selected dramas indicated a *Politisierung der neuen Dramatik* that tended towards an increasingly critical stance towards *Das Ganze der Globalisierung* (Peter). One example is Schimmelpfennig's *Der goldene Drache,* which has continued to achieve recognition not only in German-speaking Europe, but also in translation worldwide, including Asia (Seoul, 2013; Hong Kong, 2016), and North America, and in operatic adaptation by Hungarian composer Péter Eötvös (2014). Such a focus on global crises has intensified during the ensuing years, a development that was also anticipated by Schimmelpfennig in an interview with Franz Wille in 2010, years before the mass refugee migration in 2015: "Die zunehmende Globalisierung und die Vernetzung der Welt wird das Theater in Zukunft noch oft mit dieser Aufgabe konfrontieren" (Wille 115).

If the subject matter has tended in a unified direction, the same cannot be said about the dramatic approach, and answers to Schimmelpfennig's question, "Wie kann man als deutscher Theatermacher diesem Thema gerecht werden?" vary greatly (Wille 115). Perhaps the most radical and sensational of these is Christoph Schlingensief's container project, *Ausländer raus!* (2000), a weeklong *Aktion* (political performance), broadcast in *Big-Brother* style from a compound installed outside the Vienna State Opera. Inside Vienna's theaters, Elfriede Jelinek adopts ancient Greek drama, Aeschylus's *The Suppliants,* as a pre- and intertext for *Die Schutzbefohlenen,* a post-dramatic *Textfläche* that dispenses with conventional roles and dialogue, engaging instead a chorus (often comprising refugees) to present a monologic tirade on the plight of refugees ever since antiquity. Monologues addressing the audience are common in documentary theater, but in dealing with the migration crisis, migrants who are directly affected have frequently been granted an authentic voice to narrate their own stories, as is the case in Feridun Zaimoglu and Günter Senkel's *Schwarze Jungfrauen* (2006) and *Schattenstimmen* (2008), Michael Ruf's widely performed *Asyl-Monologe* (2013), and in the Berlin Refugee Club Impulse project *Letters Home* between 2014–16 (Sieg *Refugees*). This approach seeks to counteract the traditionally more common practice of black- or yellow-facing that has provoked so much controversy in recent years, as it did for example in Dea Loher's more traditionally dialogic *Unschuld* (2012, discussed in ch. 7), and for the ill-fated casting in Peter Eötvös' operatic version of *Der goldene Drache* (Gayle).[1] A similarly dialogic and more conventionally realistic approach is taken in Dirk Laucke's *Für alle reicht es nicht* (2009) and *Bambule im Herbst* (2017). The merits and pitfalls of each approach have been discussed elsewhere (see Sieg, *Refugees*; Sieg, *Race*; Obermüller; Gayle).

While the documentary play emerges as the more prevalent genre for responding to the global migration crisis, Schimmelpfennig's *Der goldene Drache* presents a distinct exception, a point on which he elaborates in the same interview with Wille: "Mir ging es nie um Dokumentation. Das können Film und Fernsehen besser. Mir ging es um Verdichtung" (Wille 116). Contrasting starkly with the realism of Laucke and the monologic documentary approach of Ruf, Senkel, and Zaimolglu, Schimmelpfennig's *Der goldene Drache* presents a unique blend of realism and magic realism, drama and epic, dialogue and monologue, theatrical and filmic technique, the mundane and the grotesque, and, most significantly, the tragic and the comic. Such a distinctive dialogue across genres, techniques, and modes extends to the specificity with which Schimmelpfennig assigns and reassigns roles across the traditional binaries of gender, age, ethnicity, and species. It is, in every sense, a *Zwischenspiel* – a whimsical and nuanced play on hybridity, but also more specifically in the sense that Hans Mayer suggested when he identified a greater presence of the tragic in Georg Büchner's only comedy, *Leonce und Lena* – a "romantisch-ironisches Zwischenspiel" (H. Mayer 294).

Critics may not be able to agree on the play's generic placement – and Schimmelpfennig, like most contemporary dramatists, refrains from any specific designation – but their range of responses to this *Zwischenspiel* is united in ambivalence, couched in appropriately hybrid terminology. The play has been variously characterized as a tragedy written as a farce (Isherwood), a tragicomedy (Affenzeller), a comedy of horrors (Dössel), an exotic fairytale (Fischer), an evil fairytale (N. Mayer), a parable (Weinzierl), a parable of apathy (Blaser), a mosaic (Marks), and a *Gesellschaftsgaukelspiel* or *Komödie mit blutigem Untergrund*, provoking the kind of laughter normally heard at a *Schauerpossenmärchen* (Stadelmaier). Such a complex array of conflicting emotions, at once tragic and comic – the "identification of opposites" (Guthke 46) – is the fundamental characteristic of tragicomedy. Why, then, does Schimmelpfennig deploy the comic mode in presenting the tragedy of an illegal immigrant, and how does this mode manifest itself?

Der goldene Drache as *Zwischenspiel*

Behind the scenes of *Der goldene Drache*, the eponymous bustling fast-food Thai/Chinese/Vietnamese-fusion restaurant, a grisly tale unfolds in its cramped, sweaty kitchen, where five illegal Asian workers are preparing a broad assortment of Asian-style dishes. One of the workers, a young Chinese man, is tormented by an excruciating toothache, but his status as an illegal immigrant prevents his visit to the dentist for fear of deportation. When the pain becomes intolerable, his co-workers are compelled to perform an emergency extraction using a handy wrench. Amid a series of chaotic mishaps, the offending tooth ends up in a cook's wok, then in the Thai soup and into the mouth of a stewardess, one of the restaurant's regulars.

Other regulars, all of whom reside or work in the building that houses the restaurant, include a young couple quarreling over an unexpected pregnancy; a married couple's break-up upon the discovery of the wife's infidelity; and the alcoholic owner of the adjacent convenience store. What would it be like, each of them ponders, if I could be something completely different? ("Wenn ich etwas ganz anderes sein könnte, als ich bin"). Throughout, an Aesop-inspired fable of an industrious ant and a cricket (the latter doubling as an illegal immigrant and prostitute) interrupts the plot, taking a gruesome turn that underscores the play's message. When winter comes and the Asian cricket has to beg for food from the ant who has taken her in, the ant, having already banked its provisions, pimps the cricket out as a sex worker to other ants, who violently take out their sexual frustrations and appetites on her – as do the grandfather, the jilted husband, and the pregnant girl's boyfriend, with tragic consequences. When the young Chinese man bleeds to death after the botched tooth extraction, he is wrapped up in the large dragon carpet that adorned the restaurant wall and is thrown into the river. From there, he finally floats home, thousands of miles, back to China.

In responding to this play, the audience is often conflicted about the mix of laughter and empathetic tears, or, as Guthke puts it, simultaneously laughing "with one eye weeping" (Guthke 82). The audience may well be troubled by its own laughter during the horrific tooth extraction, during the tooth's magical flight high into the air and into the stewardess's soup, and at the stewardess's grotesque curiosity about the taste of the tooth – a running gag that also makes the audience gag. Such ambivalence, however, is precisely what distinguishes tragicomedy from comedy or tragedy. As Guthke has pointed out, the tragicomic writer "tends to leave his audience ... in a more profound and disturbing disorientation to the human condition" (Guthke 70), a point on which the audience will reflect. Guthke draws on George Bernard Shaw's 1921 essay on Tolstoy, who, in turn, describes Ibsen's tragicomedies as

> a much deeper and grimmer entertainment than tragedy. His heroes *dying without hope or honor, his dead, forgotten*, superseded men walking and talking with the ghosts of the past, are all heroes of comedy: their existence and their downfall are not soul-purifying convulsions of pity and horror, but *reproaches, challenges, criticisms addressed to society* and to the spectator as a voting constituent of society." (Guthke 71; emphasis mine)

In *Der goldene Drache*, such discomfort or disorientation is further compounded by the dizzying short-cut montage of brief scenes, the continual role-switching and cross-dressing, moments of magic realism, third-person announcements, narrative interludes, self-interrupting stage directions (*kurze Pause*), and even the anticipated lines and doubling of another character. In direct contrast with the many documentary plays that depend on the "authentic" identity of actor and role, of actor and the outside world, Schimmelpfennig insists on the artificiality of representation, stipulated in the fluidity of role assignments: No actor is limited to one role, but rather plays multiple different roles. Rather than grant actors their "own voice," the actors mostly narrate the events in the third person, occasionally interspersed with first-person dialogue, but rarely in direct dialogue with one another. In this way, Schimmelpfennig asserts, theater shows "dass es Theater ist und nichts anderes – in gewisser Weise ist das das Ende der Illusion" (Wille 117). Reminiscent of Bertolt Brecht's rehearsal techniques designed to preclude the identification of the actors with their roles and thereby encourage a critical attitude, these techniques are among many that accentuate the theatricality of the play – techniques that are also characteristic of comedy (see ch. 3). Comic techniques also extend to the use of frequent repetition (here, of numbered food orders, situations, words, expressions, and whole passages) and parallel vignettes, interspersed in such a way as to throw the essentially tragic plot into comic relief (particularly the scenes involving the *Barbiefucker* and the stewardess).

Furthermore, the patchwork of these seemingly disparate vignettes, all of which ultimately revolve around the Asian worker's tooth, work as a doubling mechanism to reveal the common underlying consumerist malaise. All relationships are essentially economically interdependent and stripped of genuine humanity: "Jeder hängt mit jedem zusammen, die einen sind die Kunden der anderen; man lebt letztendlich voneinander – gemeinsam unter einem Dach" (Wille 116). The very notion of a "fusion" restaurant bespeaks the monocultural ambitions of corporatism – precisely the kind of unified, homogenized ideal that promises total understanding, and thus an apt setting for demonstrating where such understanding falters under the pressure of human foibles. The parable of the ant and the cricket, recast in the context of (migrant) human trafficking, greed, and exploitation, underscores the tragedy of the cricket's/Asian migrant's brother who perishes in the kitchen; exploitation and sexual abuse is paralleled by other inhabitants of the same building. From the grandfather, the grocer, the depressed "man in the striped shirt," and the newly married husband who agonizes about the financial implications of his wife's pregnancy, to the blonde stewardess and the *Barbiefucker* – all are ultimately as dispensable as the Asian worker's tooth, which, once it has lost its bloody flavor, is discarded by the stewardess. In the end, both the tooth and its owner end up in the river, beneath the surface, as though the Asian worker had never existed – "als ob er nie da gewesen wäre" – much like Ibsen's tragicomic heroes who die, "without hope or honor … forgotten." Indeed, if Erpulat and Hillje's *Verrücktes Blut* (ch. 7) is about *how* migrants are seen, then Schimmelpfennig's *Der goldene Drache* is how migrants are *not* seen.

Rather than severing the audience's empathetic bond with the characters on stage, however, Schimmelpfennig calls not only for critical reflection but also for "Nähe. Identifikation. Es geht darum zu ermöglichen, dass das Publikum den Figuren so nah wie nur irgend möglich kommt" (Wille 116). Unlike Brechtian (and most traditional) theater, which presumes an incompatibility of comic perception with emotional participation, Schimmelpfennig's play seeks to work both ways: Aesthetic or ironic detachment, far from preventing emotional participation, has the effect of an even deeper emotional awareness of the tragic, and vice versa. The simultaneity and the mutual intensification of the comic and the tragic is fundamental to the tragicomic – the identity of opposites, laughing with one eye weeping (Guthke 46–7). Understood in this way, an awareness of the tragicomic genre serves as a valuable approach to *Der goldene Drache,* helping students to understand their inevitably ambivalent responses to this play, and ultimately yielding a more nuanced discussion. In turn, the play presents an interesting case study for modern drama's departure from the normative frameworks of tragedy and comedy and the metaphysical world order that these represent, towards *Zwischenspiele*, hybrid forms such as the tragicomic, shedding further light on the intellectual response to contemporary society.

Modern society as a *Zwischenspiel*

Among the many remarks about the prominence of tragicomedy in the modern era, the most frequently cited is from Thomas Mann's preface to the German translation (1925) of Joseph Conrad's novel *The Secret Agent*, in which he states that "the achievement of modern art is that it has ceased to recognize the categories of tragic and comic or the dramatic classifications, tragedy and comedy, and views life as a tragicomedy" (qtd. in Guthke 96). Writing shortly after the war, Christopher Fry no longer considers pure comedy conceivable when he writes in his essay "Comedy" (1950): "In a century less flayed and quivering we might reach it [comedy] more directly; but not now, unless every word we write is going to mock us" (qtd. in Guthke 119). Four years later, Friedrich Dürrenmatt offers a contrasting viewpoint in his *Theaterprobleme* (1954), while drawing similar conclusions. According to Dürrenmantt, tragedy is no longer able to cope with the modern world because it is devoid of tragic heroes; only comedy can do so, and only through comedy may the tragic emerge (59). For pure tragedy, Dürrenmatt argues,

> setzt Schuld, Not, Maß, Übersicht, Verantwortung voraus. In der Wurstelei unseres Jahrhunderts, in diesem Kehraus der weißen Rasse, gibt es keine Schuldigen und auch keine Verantwortlichen mehr ... Wir sind zu kollektiv schuldig, zu kollektiv gebettet in die Sünden unserer Väter und Vorväter (59).

Without guilt and responsibility, which has become lost amid the anonymous, bureaucratic, "faceless and nameless mass society" (Guthke 130), pure tragedy is inconceivable and comedy the precondition for the tragic. Furthermore, Dürrenmatt asserts that it is comedy that establishes the critical distance necessary for the audience to apprehend the reproaches, challenges, and criticisms addressed to them (see also ch. 3). In each case, neither comedy nor tragedy, traditionally conceived, is imaginable without recourse to the other. Thus, tragicomedy emerges as the quintessential modern drama and the only adequate expression of modern human existence, "das Gesicht einer gesichtslosen Welt" (Dürrenmatt 59).

An overview of drama since the early twentieth century – and not only of German-language theater – would seem to corroborate such views, even if most dramatists refrain from generic classification, preferring instead to designate each play simply a *Stück*. In postwar drama in particular, tragicomedy emerges as the predominant genre, the most notable among them being Franz Werfel's "comedy of a tragedy," *Jacobowsky und der Oberst* (1945); Dürrenmatt's *Der Besuch der alten Dame* (1956); Wolfgang Hildesheimer's *Die Verspätung* (1961); Karl Wittlinger's *Kennen Sie die Milchstraße* (1961); as well as numerous other plays not formally designated as tragicomedy, such as Dürrenmatt's *Die Physiker* (1961) and Max Frisch's *Biedermann und die Brandstifter* (1958). An overview of contemporary drama suggests that the tragicomic has lost none of the momentum gained in the preceding half century, even if it has lost its generic classification, with a number of plays operating in between genres and media in response to global crises as well as to the nuances of sexual and ethnic identity. From Jelinek's economic comedy, *Die Kontrakte des Kaufmanns,* Christoph Marthaler's economic tragicomedy, *Riesenbutzbach* (2009), to Dirk Laucke's tragicomic *Für alle reicht es nicht*

(2009) and *Bambule im Herbst* (2017), responses to global economic woes consistently infuse the comic with the tragic. Likewise, the global financial crisis forms the backdrop to Schimmelpfennig's tragic-comic drama, in which greed, exploitation and commodification appear to have pervaded every part and level of society in an invisible chain – from illegal and faceless Asian kitchen workers and the cricket/Asian migrant to the "Barbie" stewardess, at once exploitative and exploited. Schimmelpfennig's Golden Dragon restaurant thus presents a microcosmic "face of the faceless world," in which its representatives, to reformulate Dürrenmatt, are collectively enmeshed in the global web of exploitation, and where the line between perpetrator and victim – and producer and consumer – is not always clearly discernible. This obfuscation is underscored aesthetically by the continual exchange among roles, scenes, dialogue, and narrative, and across the conventional ethical and aesthetic boundaries of the tragic and comic.

Discerning the tragicomic: pre-reading exercises

To approach Schimmelpfennig's *Der goldene Drache* as a tragicomedy, then, it is necessary to sensitize students to fundamental characteristics of the genre, not with any specific normative intention, but rather a means to identify some generic techniques, test hypotheses, and generate a more nuanced discussion. Initial hypotheses are best explored in the context of tragicomic plots with which students are already familiar. One valuable exploratory exercise entails a discussion of contemporary popular culture, which has seen a proliferation of tragicomedies alongside myriad other hybrid sub-genres, such as the "dramedy," and the "sadcom" (Aroesti). This exploration begins with brief summaries of the basic plot of any number of recent or current TV series, including *Breaking Bad* (2008–13), *Transparent* (2014–19), *Orange is the New Black* (2013–20), *Dead to Me* (2019–20), or *Fleabag* (2016–19); or of a host of popular films, from *Four Weddings and a Funeral* (1994) or *Thelma and Louise* (1991) to Germany's *Good Bye, Lenin!* (2003), *A Coffee in Berlin!* (2012), or *Toni Erdmann* (2016).[2] Working together, and grouped according to common familiarity or interest, students summarize the basic plot or analyze a scene to determine the following: What is the theme? Who are the protagonists and how would you characterize them? How does it end? How did you respond to the ending? Think of a scene that provokes laughter! What kind of laughter is it? What do you think provokes this response? Find a scene that generates sadness! Can you find a scene that generates both responses? Is there a scene or a character that provokes ambivalent feelings – about which or whom you are unsure how to respond? A scene that simultaneously invites emotional involvement *and* detachment or alienation? What constitutes these ambivalent responses (for example: love *and* hate; admiration *and* envy; allure *and* aversion; empathy *and* antipathy; respect *and* shame (or perhaps *Fremdscham*)? Is the response provoked by a single character, or between characters in dialogue, or in the visual effects?

The vocabulary needed to complete this exploratory exercise, which should be prepared independently before the in-class group discussions, provides a starting point for further generalizations about the genre. In a second preparatory exercise, and for more advanced students of German, some excerpts from the German and non-German-language tradition may be introduced in order for students to test and further refine their initial hypotheses. In considering ambivalence as the co-existence of opposing feelings towards the same character or situation, it is worth probing Sigmund Freud's assertion that all feelings are necessarily ambivalent (Freud 26–92).

In the realm of art, Gotthold Ephraim Lessing similarly conceives of the tragicomic as a result of the simultaneity, rather than the succession, of the tragic and comic in art:

> Nur wenn eben dieselbe Begebenheit in ihrem Fortschritt alle Schattierungen des Interesses annimmt, und eine nicht bloß auf die andere folgt, sondern so notwendig aus der andern entspringt; *wenn der Ernst das Lachen, die Traurigkeit die Freude, oder umgekehrt, so unmittelbar erzeugt, daß uns die Abstraktion des einen oder des andern unmöglich fällt*: nur alsdenn verlangen wir sie auch in der Kunst nicht, und die Kunst weiß aus dieser Unmöglichkeit selbst Vorteil zu ziehen. (Lessing 357; emphasis mine)

Among the Romantics, E.T.A. Hoffmann posits the tragicomic as the quintessentially Romantic drama in *Die Sperapionsbrüder*: "Nur im wahrhaft Romantischen mischt sich das Komische mit dem Tragischen so gefügig, daß beides *zum Totaleffekt in eins verschmilzt* und das Gemüt des Zuhörers auf eine *eigne, wunderbare Weise ergreift* (Hoffmann 100; emphasis mine). This *serapiontisches Prinzip* would subsequently form the basis of twentieth-century magical realism.

Others, such as Friedrich Schelling and August Wilhelm Schlegel, posit that the tragicomic was the most genuine expression of the Romantic *Weltanschauung* and, for Schlegel, of the tensions and disharmonies of their time (Guthke 103–4). Taken together with the previous remarks of Thomas Mann and Friedrich Dürrenmatt, and notwithstanding the rather cursory nature of such an overview, it is possible to discern a continuous challenge to account for and justify art's ability to provoke responses of greater complexity than those of pure tragedy or comedy. It helps guide students, in turn, to articulate any ambivalence provoked by Schimmelpfennig's play and its ability to captivate the spectator in a distinctive, *wunderbare Weise*.

Staging the tragicomic: Drama workshops

To begin exploring such ambivalence in *Der goldene Drache,* perhaps the strongest illustration occurs in scenes 20 and 22, the most commonly cited scenes in performance reviews:

Szene 20

Der Mann, die Frau über sechzig, der junge Mann, die junge Frau, der Mann über sechzig.

DER MANN ÜBER SECHZIG

Im Thai-China-Vietnam-Restaurant DER GOLDENE DRACHE:

DER MANN

Der Alte setzt die Zange an.

DER MANN ÜBER SECHZIG

Ich setze die Zange an, das ist nicht so leicht, weil der Kleine den Kopf hin und her schmeißt, hin und her, pass auf, sonst haue ich dir aus Versehen noch einen Zahn raus, der in Ordnung ist, aber der Dünne hält den Kleinen, hält ihn fest, noch ein bisschen Schnaps.

Der Mann gießt Schnaps in den Mund des Chinesen.

DIE FRAU ÜBER SECHZIG

Nummer B2, Nun Cha Gio Chay, Reisnudeln, knusprig gebackene Frühlingsrollen, Salat, Sojasprossen, Gurke, geröstete Zwiebeln, Erdnüsse, vietnamesisches Basilikum und Koriander.

DER MANN

Ruhig, Kleiner, ruhig,

DIE JUNGE FRAU

Nicht, nicht

DER JUNGE MANN

Er setzt die Zange an,

DIE FRAU ÜBER SECHZIG

Nummer 82: Pat Thai Gai, Gebratene Reisbandnudeln.

DER MANN ÜBER SECHZIG

Ich setzte die Zange an,

DER MANN

Der Kleine schreit. Er sieht die Zange.

DIE FRAU ÜBER SECHZIG

Wir nennen ihn den Kleinen.

DIE JUNGE FRAU

Er bricht mir den Zahn aus dem Mund,

Lange Pause.

Er bricht ihn mir raus,

Kurze Pause.

Er bricht ihn mir raus –

DER JUNGE MANN

Und der Zahn fliegt durch die Luft.

Pause.

DER MANN ÜBER SECHZIG

Ich reiße ihm den Zahn aus dem Mund, den rechten Schneidezahn, und der blutige, halbverfaulte Zahn fliegt durch die Luft.

DIE FRAU ÜBER SECHZIG

Hoch durch die Luft –

DIE JUNGE FRAU
   Der Zahn
   Fliegt und fliegt und fliegt.
[…]

Szene 22:
Der Mann, die Frau über sechzig, der junge Mann, die junge Frau, der Mann über sechzig.
DIE JUNGE FRAU
   Der Zahn fliegt und fliegt –
DER JUNGE MANN
   Fliegt und fliegt –
DER MANN
   Und fliegt und fliegt durch die winzige Küche des GOLDENEN DRACHEN –
DER JUNGE MANN
   Der herausgerissene Zahn fliegt und fliegt
DIE FRAU ÜBER SECHZIG
   Fliegt und fliegt und landet im Wok.
   Nummer 82: Pat Thai Gai, Gebratene Reisbandnudeln, […]
   Weg mit dem Zahn aus dem Wok mit den gebratenen Reisbandnudeln Nummer 82, und ich will mit dem großen Löffel den Zahn aus der Pfanne holen
DER JUNGE MANN
   Nummer sechs, die Thai-Suppe mit Hühnerfleisch
DIE FRAU ÜBER SECHZIG
   Und dabei schießt der Zahn aus dem Wok,
   Fliegt, fliegt und landet in der Suppenschüssel,
   Nr 6, Thai-Suppe mit Hühnerfleisch, Kokosmilch, Thai-Ingwer, Tomaten, Champignons, Zitronengras und Zitronenblättern, (scharf)
   Die Nummer 6 geht gerade raus mit der schmalen, der Hübschen, 26, keine fünfzig Kilo, vom Golf von Tongking.
   Die Suppe Nummer 6 geht gerade raus, wird gerade rausgetragen, […]

This scene, in which the play's running gag culminates, illustrates a number of comic techniques to be explored in the classroom through a combination of dramatic reading and drama workshops. Indeed, one could argue that the play really only assumes meaning *through* performance, and partly because of the paucity of traditional stage directions, which are instead narrated by the characters themselves. As Affenzeller stated: "Der Autor Schimmelpfennig hat dem Regisseur Schimmelpfennig also einen Gefallen getan und ein Stück geschrieben, das erst auf der Bühne seine Geheimnisse preisgibt (und auch einige für sich behält)." Merely reading over and discussing the "plot" falls short of appreciating the central function of role-switching, the announced stage directions, the narrated events distributed among various characters in the third person that anticipate the action, and sometimes delivering others' lines. Moreover, the frequent interruptions of partial scenes (here, sc. 21) and the constant recitation of numbered Asian-fusion dishes disrupt the reader's sense of the whole and disorientate the second-language reader altogether. Assembling the disjointed parts collaboratively helps to make sense of the whole.

First, a dramatic reading quickly makes apparent the multiple roles that each of the five characters must adopt during the play, amounting to 17 roles altogether. Since the stage directions and narrative moments are not demarcated from the rest of the text, but rather delivered by each character, it is only possible to differentiate between these in dramatic readings. Narrative addresses to the audience ("Ich setze die Zange an ..."), dialogue ("pass auf, sonst haue ich dir aus Versehen noch einen Zahn raus, der in Ordnung ist"), a return to narrative ("aber der Dünne hält den Kleinen, hält ihn fest"), and another move to direct speech ("noch ein bisschen Schnaps"), intermingled as they are within one sentence, need to be clearly differentiated in intonation and tone. This, in turn, provides a valuable exercise requiring students to convey distinctions between narrated events and on-stage dialogue. A further advantage to this exercise is that the dramatic reading demands continuous active involvement and comprehension of all students, who, in their assigned roles, have to act out the narrated events. This is essentially an exercise in *Aus-der-Rolle-Fallen*, a common technique of comedy and a staple of Brecht's rehearsal techniques (see chs. 1 and 3). Such a combination of verbal and non-verbal interaction reinforces the vocabulary and serves as a starting point for creative and critical thinking.

One such opportunity for creative and critical thinking is presented in scenes 20 and 22, when the intermingling of the comic and tragic reaches a climax. In these scenes, the tooth, having previously landed in a cook's wok, is now propelled by the cook into a second flight, landing in the Number 6 soup that is making its way to its customer. The comic timing of this moment inevitably prompts raucous laughter, albeit an uncomfortably raucous laughter – with one eye weeping – given the tragic circumstance and outcome for the Asian worker. Indeed, such ambivalence presents a challenge for the audience, whose capacity for genuine involvement and empathy is evidently under critical scrutiny in this play. This particular moment in the play represents the culmination of comic and tragic ambivalence, requiring careful attention to staging, especially in the absence of stage directions. Such a challenge, however, can also turned into an opportunity: Students are animated to explore the simultaneity of the tragic and comic, of empathy and distance, through linguistic and physical means. Besides the initial challenge of determining who is doing and saying what when, other staging considerations include: How does the continuous on-stage recitation of food orders interact (if at all) with the tragedy unfolding in the same small kitchen space? How does their delivery alter the play's message? For example, should one continue to call these out with the same level of machine-like efficiency typical of a fast-food restaurant? This would underscore an implicit critique of the "facelessness" of a globalized food and service industry. Or should one rather draw attention to the unfolding tragedy of one's co-worker through distracted, distressed, interrupted delivery? This would underscore the empathy demanded by the victim's fate, otherwise faceless and ignored by the restaurant's customers and, by extension, the audience. Further, how should the other Asian cooks act out their response to the tooth's disappearance? It becomes apparent in subsequent scenes that none of the cooks, besides the one delivering the stage direction, is aware of the tooth's final landing in the soup. As they search for the missing tooth, the question arises as to whether the implied comedy (in the obsessive and continual search) detracts from or enhances the unfolding tragedy from the audience's perspective. A comedic performance might convey an implicit critique of the audience's complacency, on the one hand; it might, on the other, support the audience's complacency by providing nothing more than entertaining distraction.

Similarly, and in reference to the comic techniques of repetition, how can or should one deliver the line "Wir nennen ihn [the victim] den Kleinen," a phrase that has occurred repeatedly from the very beginning, and what is the effect of this repetition? Does it raise or lower our level of endearment to the victim? Does it gain or lose sincerity and how does this alter our response to the victim? Does this term of endearment develop irony with each repetition? If so, how does one deliver each repetition, and what is the effect? Investigating these nuances in performance, which must be carefully considered and handled, are essential to interpreting the play, for which ample time must be allowed.

However one might decide to stage the flight of the tooth, which unfolds over the course of several pages and which is interrupted by several other scenes, this improbable moment in the play seems to invite both wonder and prolonged reflection; the tragic and comic coalesce in a unique, *wunderbare[r] Weise*. Most productions have thus tended towards a slow-motion, magical moment, transporting the audience beyond the realistic realm of the restaurant, and protracting the audience's expectation. This "magical" moment is further underscored by a subsequent allusion to fairytales in which certain treasures – not teeth! – are discovered: "Andere Leute finden im Bauch eines Fisches einen goldenen Ring. Andere Leute finden Diamanten im hohen Gras" (sc. 26). When the tooth finally returns to the reality of the restaurant and is served with the stewardess's soup, a new series of questions and reactions is triggered in the audience: Will the tooth be discovered by the customer in time? How will the customer react to this discovery? How will the customer react to the waiter and the establishment itself?

The questions raised at the end of scenes 20 and 22 serve as a suitable moment to check students' comprehension as well as establish their *Erwartungshorizont*. The episodic, short-cut structure of the play, which builds on a series of cliff-hangers, provides plenty of opportunities for the instructor to introduce short reflective assignments for in-class discussion or take-home writing, depending on the structure of the course. Having read up to a certain point in the text (such as the end of scene 20), students are then asked to explore possible consequences in the ensuing scenes. This can be done in small groups as a discussion, or as a more extensive creative writing assignment that requires students to write the next scene involving the stewardesses and possibly also the waitress (see *Leitfragen*). Time permitting, these could in turn serve as role-playing activities.

As students will discover when they continue reading, its destination – the mouth of a stewardess, a regular customer – presents a turning point in the play insofar as it establishes the first physical contact between a kitchen worker (the "foreign") and the customer and, by association, the audience. On this point, Schimmelpfennig adds:

> Man kann sich ja über das Leben der Illegalen viel Wissen aneignen, die Informationen sind verfügbar, recherchierbar, aber was nützt mir das, wenn ich trotzdem keine wirkliche Verbindung dazu herstelle – zumindest für die Dauer eines Theaterabends. Das klingt konstruiert – aber im Fall des Stücks entsteht die Verbindung im Grunde erst durch den *fremden Zahn im eigenen Mund*. (Wille 2010)

Important in a dramatic reading or staging of this moment, then, is to negotiate a balance between the recipient's unexpected reaction to the tooth with one of disgust and outrage expressed by the other stewardess, forcing the audience – also implied customers – in turn to contemplate something that would normally repel it. The recipient's curiosity and decision to taste the tooth, rather than complain to the waitress, raises a number of interpretive questions that may be explored in a drama-based workshops: What is the function of the stewardess's curiosity in this context? By inviting the spectator to contemplate something that would normally repel it, does this implicitly force the spectator to connect with its foreign source? If so, how could one convey this curiosity physically? Is it detached curiosity or a grotesque or even pleasurable fetish, such that one might elaborate the tongue play ("Ihre Zunge fühlt nach dem Loch in dem fremden Zahn"; sc. 34). If the latter, this would implicate the audience voyeuristically in exotic fetishism. The disgusted and outraged reaction of the other stewardess, in contrast, represents the typical reaction. In this context, moreover, negative racial stereotypes concerning hygiene are potentially foregrounded, stereotypes that are further supported by the clichéd representation of the "Asianness": the generic name (*Golden Dragon*), the dishes approximating something vaguely and miscellaneously Asian, the "Asian" rug hanging on its wall – all constructions of Western imagination. Such considerations, which relate in part to the tragi*comic* of this play, also relate to the importance of maintaining a critical stance towards, rather than perpetuation of either of these stereotypical attitudes. By asking volunteer participants to explore these variations during a workshop, others serve as side-coaches, commenting on the action, gestures, and effect with each iteration, thereby also ensuring full participation.

It is necessary to build on such exploratory workshops with a discussion about the juxtaposition of the comic and the tragic. At this moment of the play, attention is directed towards the consumers (the two stewardesses), their fatigue after a long flight, their polite small talk, the fact that the best Asian soup is to be found in San Francisco – a less subtle commentary on the facelessness of globalized consumerism – and, finally, the discovery of and reactions to the rotten tooth in the soup. Meanwhile, the *junge Frau* admits an illicit affair to her husband, leading to their break-up, and the grandfather, hopeful that the young cricket/Asian worker-turned-prostitute will find ways to make him feel young again, loses control of his pent-up anger and lashes out violently. The juxtaposition of these tragic-comic scenes, and the apparent complacency of the stewardesses alongside the unfolding tragedies, deserves thorough exploration.

This point in the play triggers a series of connections, hitherto not palpable, among the various members of the household: the fact that they are all connected, in one way or another, to the Asian restaurant and its missing tooth. In order to guide students in establishing these connections amid the short-cut scenes, students fill out a table illustrating the entire building that houses the restaurant, and the small shop on the ground level, and the various levels of apartments above. By adding notes as they continue through the scenes, students may gather information about the characters' relations, situations, attitudes, and visualize their social standing. Starting with the lower level, where the restaurant and the shop are situated, the rising levels each represent a corresponding social level, which is further stratified ethnically by the illegal Asian workers, below, and the Western customers, above. Once all the characters have been introduced, such differences can be teased out during discussion and serve as a basis for improvisation exercises and possible staging solutions (see *Leitfragen*).

The connections among the cast of characters are more profound, however. As students will comment in the table provided for note-taking, each set of characters shares a deep existential dissatisfaction and the wish to become someone else, as suggested by the play's tagline on the title page, and repeated by each character throughout: "Wenn ich etwas anderes sein könnte, als ich bin. Wenn ich etwas ganz anderes sein könnte, als ich sein muss. Ein Mensch." Thus, the stewardess' polite small talk and the all-round smile, as though nothing were amiss ("alle drei lächeln"; sc. 26), is revealed as *performed* contentment. What becomes apparent in the ensuing scenes is that all relationships are susceptible to dissolution and alienation, whether they are aware of it or not. This becomes most apparent in the chain of violent abuse between the ant and the cricket, the young couple's break-up, the violence enacted by all male characters on the female cricket/Asian prostitute, who is left to perish, and in the fact that the stewardess has become accustomed to the Barbie-doll role she plays for her pilot-boyfriend. The key to the play's meaning is found precisely in these relationships: Not only those exploited, but also the exploiters long dolefully for better circumstances and alternative identities, underscored by the continuous transposition of roles.

The Brechtian overtone of this tagline – "Wenn ich etwas ganz anderes sein könnte, als ich sein muss. Ein Mensch" – is readily apparent to readers familiar with *Die Dreigroschenoper*: "Wir wären gut, anstatt so roh / Doch die Verhältnisse, sie sind nicht so!" (Brecht *Dreigroschenoper* 42–4). The critique of a capitalist society stripped of humanity underscoring Brecht's oeuvre is apparent in this play on every level and pursued to its tragic conclusion as the Asian victim, reduced to a mere skeleton, is carried by water to his homeland. For this reason, it is appropriate to precede this play with a reading of Brecht's *Der gute Mensch von Sezuan*, which encapsulates many of Brecht's typical approaches and is thematically highly relevant for Schimmelpfennig's *Der goldene Drache*. Even without familiarity with Brecht, it is possible to highlight the alienation and dehumanization apparent in the play by drawing attention to the nameless characters, who are reduced to a mere function, without distinctive characteristics and therefore generalizable and exchangeable, as well as the sparsity of physical descriptions more generally. The amorphousness enables each character and situation to transpire as emotional parallels, mutually illuminating and intensifying, such that the various social, gender, age and, most importantly, ethnic demarcations appear to be constructed so that they may be transgressed.

Furthermore, Schimmelpfennig adopts (epic) narrative and the principle of demonstrating rather than acting, of making theatrical means visible, defamiliarization techniques of commentary, interruption, role-switching, and constantly interrupted episodes rather than a continuous plot. *Der goldene Drache* serves as a textbook illustration of Brecht's rehearsal techniques designed to prevent identification between actor and role, such as requiring actors to speak in the third person; continual role-switching during rehearsal; *aus der Rolle fallen*, which involves a presentation of one's character, and speaking aloud the thoughts, feelings, and motivations of a character. Thus, an introduction to Brechtian defamiliarization and rehearsal techniques are well worth preliminary attention before introducing this play (see ch. 1). As we have seen, however, these techniques are not only reminiscent of Brecht in encouraging critical distance; they also provide the formal key to an understanding of the play's main theme, namely, the desire shared by all of the characters to become or play someone else. All the while, the actor is encouraged along Brechtian lines to maintain distance through demonstration, rather than identification with the part, as Schimmelpfennig points out: "Der Schauspieler wird zu einer Figur, aber er bleibt immer auch als Schauspieler präsent. Er kann nicht hinter der Figur verschwinden. Das macht die Sache transparenter, in gewisser weise auch menschlicher" (Wille 117). The transparent approach to each character eases the theatrical burden somewhat on non-native-speaking, non-professional participants as they negotiate the various roles; students are not expected to "become" realistic appropriations of these characters, but rather explore these identities as constructions. The play's tagline, which asks what it would be like to play someone else, can be taken up by students who imaginatively step into each different role to become co-constructors of these characters.

A valuable exercise involves asking students to prepare a series of gestures and movements that "embody" one of the characters. The rest of the class identifies the character and offers side-coaching on posture (and voice, if necessary): Which character is the student portraying? How is the character being portrayed? How might you alter the gestures, posture, or movements according to age, gender, occupation, or social status? What could be more exaggerated, and what should be more constrained, faster or slower, more upright or stooping? What do these gestures convey? With students at higher levels of proficiency, this may be done spontaneously; with groups whose level of proficiency is lower, or if participation is unequal, students are asked to jot down what they see and compare their comments. In this way, students explore the potential and perimeters of each character type, while recognizing points of intersection and contrast among them, all of which is valuable in a discussion about identity construction. At the same time, students begin to appreciate the play from an empathetic standpoint (see also Guenther 177–9).

In discussing the play's empathetic standpoint, numerous newspaper articles are available on the status of illegal workers in Europe and indeed worldwide. On the fate of workers from China and Vietnam in particular, a recent (2019) article in *The Guardian* may provide a valuable starting point for further reflection on the play (Aw). Reporting on the aftermath of a series of brutal attacks on Chinese migrants in and around Paris during 2015–2016 in a country with the largest ethnic-Chinese population in Europe, it describes the broader perception – and non-perception – of Chinese and Vietnamese who operate underground, forced to accept the lowest-paid work while remaining politely inaudible in national discourse and all but invisible in public life. The shame of being a "poor clandestine," of being an illegal immigrant, after having been displaced at least once (or twice in the case of Cambodians and Vietnamese) is very common:

> I sometimes think back to those days of poverty, when we were illegal and my family had no money, no possibility of earning money or of getting any social security. And I realise that a large part of the shame was what we were going to tell our family back in China. We had left to build better lives for ourselves in France, but here we were, worse off than before. We were trapped in a sort of double prison: by poverty in Europe, and by China and its expectations of us. (Aw)

These could be the very words of the young Asian worker as he reminisces in a lengthy monologue during his journey back to China wrapped in the fake Golden Dragon rug. Imagining his return, he remarks:

Hallo, Lieber ehrwürdiger Onkel, tut mir leid, das ganze Geld, die ganzen Scheine, die ihr damals zusammengelegt habt, seht ihr nie wieder... Nein, die Schwester habe ich nie gefunden... ich weiß nicht, bei wem sie ist, und was sie da tun muss für ihr Geld. (sc. 46)

Previous imaginary conversations with his family also indicate the shame he feels for not earning what is expected of him (sc. 32). Feelings of shame are important to consider in discussing character embodiment and empathy, as well as in final written reflections on the play, as suggested below. But as Schimmelpfennig remarks (above), as much as one is able to acquire plenty of information *about* illegal immigrants, it is of no real use without any real connection *to* them. Without empathy, there is no genuine reflection or call to action. For this reason, any critical reflection or cumulative analysis is best placed after a series of workshops or a full staging of this play; only then may empathy develop and authentic reflection begin.

Leitfragen

Preliminary in-class questions: These may be carried out in small groups as a text-scanning activity, or in full class discussion alongside a dramatic reading of the first scene (two pages). Once the initial setting is established, and before a dramatic reading, students mime what it looks like to work in a tiny kitchen in a fast-food restaurant, as the instructor (or other participants) calls out further suggestions based on the text. In general during a dramatic reading, students are asked to carry out the stage directions, as long as they have been introduced previously (using one of the techniques described in ch. 1).
Beschreiben Sie die Personen, den Ort, und die Zeit. Beschreiben Sie die Bühnenanweisungen? Was fällt Ihnen auf?

1. *Wer sind die Personen? Wie viele Personen gibt es? Wie viele Rollen werden jeweils gespielt? Wie heißen die jeweiligen Personen? Welcher Effekt wird Ihrer Meinung nach dadurch erzielt, dass die Personen keine Namen tragen? Und was bewirkt die karge Bühnenbeschreibung?*
2. *Wo spielt sich die erste Szene ab? Was für ein Restaurant ist das? Wie heißt dieses Restaurant? Liegt hier ein "typischer" Name für ein "asiatisches" Restaurant vor? Beschreiben Sie die Küche! Was wird hier gekocht? Wodurch zeichnet sich normalerweise ein Schnellrestaurant aus?*
3. *Wie sieht es in einer "winzigen Küche" eines Schnellrestaurants aus? Welchen Eindruck erweckt dieser Ausdruck? Was braucht man in einer solchen Küche? Gruppenarbeit: Versetzen Sie sich gedanklich in einen solchen Raum, und versuchen Sie die Probleme, die sich hierbei ergeben, in der Gruppe darstellerisch umsetzen. Vorschläge: Nehmen Sie Pfannen, Woks, rühren, umrühren, braten. Es ist eng, sehr eng! (Näher zusammenrücken!) Sie haben es eilig! Der Junge ist panisch vor Zahnschmerzen!*

4. *Lesen wir die erste Bestellung vor ("Nummer 83: Pat Thai Gai: gebratene Reisbandnudeln mit Ei, Gemüse, Hühnerfleisch und pikanter Erdnuss-Sauce, mittelscharf.") Was halten Sie von den servierten Essensgerichten? Inwiefern ist das "asiatisch"? Ist das eher thailändisch, chinesisch, oder vietnamesisch, oder eher eine Mischung aus allem?*
5. *Was ist das Hauptproblem in dieser Szene? Worin sehen Sie den hauptsächlichen Konflikt?*

As a reading guide, students complete the table (below), which represents the entire building that houses all the characters, modelled on the information provided for the first level (*Erdgeschoss*), and add information as they progress. This serves as a point of reference throughout the discussions and provide a useful point of reference for staging considerations: For most productions, the horizontal set is realized vertically on stage (see also Schulzová).

Im Zentrum steht das Restaurant: Der goldene Drache. Neben dem Restaurant befindet sich ein Laden. Über dem Restaurant sind Wohnungen. Alle Personen im Stück befinden sich in demselben Haus. Einige wohnen dort sogar.

- *Welche Figuren oder Konstellationen lernen wir kennen?*
- *Wer wohnt wo? In welcher Etage wohnen welche Personen? Fällt Ihnen etwas auf?*
- *Beschreiben Sie in Kürze die typischen Merkmale der Personen und die Situationen, in denen sie sich befinden. Was haben sie gemeinsam? Was fällt Ihnen auf? Sehen Sie Parallele? Welche Personen wirken komisch, welche wirken tragisch?*

Table 4.2 Reading Guide

In welcher Etage?	*Personen/Funktion*	*Situation/Handlungsstrang*
5. Etage (Dachgeschoss)		
4. Etage		
3. Etage		
2. Etage		
1. Etage (Erdgeschoss)	*Das Restaurant / die Küche- fünf Asiaten / illegale Arbeiter aus Asien … Lebensmittelgeschäft; neben dem Restaurant;Hans, der Lebensmittelhändler; Die junge Asiatin bzw. Prostituierte/Grille und Ameise*	*-Der junge Asiate hat Zahnschmerzen … -Hans verkauft "alles was man braucht." Er ist Kunde im Restaurant, wo er sich täglich das Essen holt. (Sz. 14)-Hans hält die junge Asiatin/Prostituierte in seiner Wohnung; die parallele Fabel der Ameise und die Grille*

Reading up to the end of scene 20 (about half of the play) for the next session, students begin considering what is tragic and what is comic before discussing their horizon of expectations as a group activity. In a follow-up writing exercise, students may write out the subsequent scene. (Due to the "cliffhanger" ending of each scene, this may be repeated at numerous other moments in the play.) The two creative writing exercises serve to anticipate the ensuing scenes, when the tooth's destination and the Asian victim's inner thoughts are dramatized:

> *Erwartungshorizont: Wie reagieren Sie auf diese Szene? (Finden Sie diese Situation komisch, schauderhaft, gruselig, tragisch, oder haben Sie gemischte Gefühle?) Versuchen Sie, Ihre Empfindungen in Worte zu fassen! Was passiert mit dem Zahn? Wohin scheint der Zahn zu fliegen? Was wäre am schlechtesten?*

Creative writing exercises

1. *Was könnte auf die Szene im Restaurant folgen? Schreiben Sie eine Szene und spielen Sie vor!*
2. *Der junge Chinese hat Zahnschmerzen. Lassen Sie seine Gefühle in einem inneren Monolog zu Wort kommen.*

Improvisation

Working in pairs, students summarize the main situation and conflict of each couple. Instead of presenting it to the class, however, students are "interviewed" by other members of the class about their situation (see also Guenther). Alternatively, bring one member of each couple (the two men or the two women, for example) into the restaurant and have them start up a conversation in which they have to get to know each other and reveal (or complain about) their current situation, and subsequently repeat with the other "half" of the couple. Other participants have to summarize the content of each couple's predicament.

Reflective writing exercises

1. *Erläutern Sie die Rolle der Fabel von der Ameise und der Grille in Schimmelpfennigs "Der goldene Drache." Wie wird die Botschaft der Fabel hier umgedeutet? Welche theatralen Mittel werden benutzt, um diese (neue) Botschaft (oder Lehre) zum Ausdruck zu bringen? Gehen Sie dabei sowohl auf den Inhalt als auch die Struktur bzw. theaterpraktische Aspekte ein.*
2. *Sie haben Artikel über die Erfahrungen illegaler Einwanderer in Europa gelesen. Welche vergleichbaren Probleme kommen in diesem Stück vor? Inwiefern werden die Probleme von "Anderssein" und von Vorurteilen –*

von der Fixierung einer Identität – in diesem Stück kritisch behandelt?.
Gehen Sie dabei sowohl auf den Inhalt als auch die Struktur bzw.
theaterpraktische Aspekte des Stücks ein.

Post-performance reflection paper

A post-performance reflective paper is based not only on the reading, discussions, and staging of the play (or substantial workshops), but also ideally after viewing recording of the production. The following suggestions are based on a guided reading of a critical review, in which students are required to identify each of the key aspects of the genre, from the title to the conclusion.

1. *Titel: Seien Sie kreativ!*
2. *Ort, Datum der Aufführungen (kurz angeben)*
3. *Ein Zitat, das Sie besonders treffend/wichtig finden, um die Rezension einzuführen.*
4. *Die Themen/das Genre: Warum soll das Publikum dieses Stück ansehen? Was ist das wichtigste Thema, und was ist die Botschaft des Stücks? Gibt es andere Handlungsstränge und Zusammenhänge? Wie wird das dargestellt? Welches Genre könnte das sein: Tragikomödie, Sozialdrama, globale Horrorkomödie, böses Märchen, Satire über Sklaverei, modernes Schauermärchen? Ist das ein besonders deutsch-europäisches Problem? Inwiefern ist das auch für die USA relevant und verständlich? Und welchen Aspekt fanden Sie persönlich am interessantesten?*
5. *Inszenierung: Das Ensemble, die Bühne, usw. Kritisieren Sie Ihre mitwirkenden Schauspieler bitte nicht! Aber Sie dürfen natürlich besonders gelungene/auffallende Aspekte oder Momente hervorheben!*
6. *Publikum: Beschreiben Sie das Publikum und die Reaktion des Publikums?*
7. *Fazit: Besonders wichtig ist Ihre Meinung zu Schimmelpfennigs Frage im Interview mit Franz Wille (unten). Inwiefern ist er diesem Thema gerecht geworden? Denken Sie dabei z.B. an Unterhaltung/Spannung, Leistung (performance), Anspruch (level of sophistication)!*

Interview mit Franz Wille, "Eine aufregende Zeit, um für das Theater zu schreiben." *Theater heute* (2010).

In diesem Interview (2010) mit dem Redakteur, Franz Wille, spricht Roland Schimmelpfennig über die Schwierigkeiten, etwas über das Thema illegaler Einwanderer in Deutschland zu schreiben. Außer den Schrecken der Abschiebegefängnissen kommen auch alltägliche Probleme draußen in der „scheinbaren Freiheit" vor, wie zum Beispiel das Problem illegaler Arbeiter, die auch keine medizinische Versorgung haben und dauernd Angst vor der Entdeckung haben.

Schimmelpfennig fragt sich: „Wie kann man als deutscher Theatermacher diesem Thema gerecht werden? Eine schwierige, aus meiner Sicht mit den normalen Theatermitteln so nicht zu lösende Aufgabe. [...] Wie kann man diese Menschen darstellen? Was gewinnt man, wenn man es auf dem naturalistischen Weg versucht, und was verliert man dabei? Die zunehmende Globalisierung und die Vernetzung der Welt wird das Theater in Zukunft noch oft mit dieser Aufgabe konfrontieren. [...] Mir ging es nie um Dokumentation. Das können Film und Fernsehen besser."

Frage: Wie hat Schimmelpfennig versucht, diesem komplexen Thema gerecht zu werden? Welche theatralen Mittel hat er benutzt? Ist es ihm Ihrer Meinung nach gut gelungen? Welche Mittel finden Sie wirkungsvoll, und welche finden Sie weniger wirkungsvoll?

Vocabulary

For all writing exercises, vocabulary and phrases specific to the task and each play are provided to help students articulate their arguments. In addition, students are asked to gather new vocabulary in their reading of articles and critical reviews. The following relate to this particular play and the particularities of its staging.

Theaterpraktisch, textbezogen:

eine Aussage (in indirekter Rede) wiedergeben – to recite, convey a statement
die Ansage – announcement
in Anlehnung an (+Akk.) – in reference to, based on
andeuten – to imply, suggest
filmische Schnitte – cinematic cuts
hindeuten; es deutet (auf etwas) hin – to indicate, point to
gelingen; es gelingt mir; es ist mir gelungen – to succeed
der Handlungsstrang, ("e) – plot line
der Leitfaden – main thread (running through piece), leitmotif
die Montagetechnik – montage technique
das Vorspielen – the acting, playing
unter (mehrere Figuren) geteilt – divided among (several characters)
verflechten, (mit einander) verflochten – to interweine, intertwined (with each other)

inhaltlich, thematisch:

sich mit etwas abfinden (können) – (to be able to) accept, come to terms with, reconcile oneself to sth.

erinnern an (+Akk.) – to remind (one) of
minderwertige Arbeit leisten – to do inferior work
verpfuscht (z.B. verpfuschte Zahnextraktion!) – botched

wertend:

schwer/leicht fallen; es fällt mir schwer; es fiel mir schwer – to find difficult/easy
wirksam, wirkungsvoll – effective
versehentlich, aus Versehen – by accident, inadvertently
anspruchsvoll/anspruchslos – sophisticated, ambitious/undemanding, lowbrow

Notes

1 The London premiere of Péter Eötvös' opera *The Golden Dragon*, based on Schimmelpfennig's play, was cancelled due to yellow-facing of an all-white cast in 2017, despite the production company's prior defense on grounds that the play was an example of "post-Brechtian storytelling" and that "quite deliberately, there is no realism." According to the Hackney Empire theater in East London, the Music Theater Wales' production "compromised the [Hackney] Empire's commitment and position as a champion of diversity and accessibility across the theatre industry, and therefore the decision has been taken to withdraw the forthcoming performance on 31 October" (Gayle).
2 On *Toni Erdmann* as a tragicomedy, see Glasenapp. For an overview of contemporary tragicomic films, see Zipfel, *Tragikomödien*.

Further reading and resources

Multiple recordings of productions in various languages worldwide are available on YouTube.
A post-performance discussion with Roland Schimmelpfennig (in English) after the English-language première by the Actors Touring Company directed by Ramin Gray, at the Arcola Theatre, Dalston, London, September 2011 in four parts:

1. http://www.youtube.com/watch?v=f12joji2fgk&feature=related
2. http://www.youtube.com/watch?v=-nBlewcSoEA&feature=related
3. http://www.youtube.com/watch?v=zmJwX-m6RxY&feature=related
4. http://www.youtube.com/watch?v=Sa-dFffQCGY&feature=related

Roland Schimmelpfennig discusses the American première of The Golden Dragon with Germany.info in Washington DC, November 2011. http://www.youtube.com/watch?v=8MgVfqZkZGw

References

Affenzeller, Margarete. "Wenn beim Asiaten die Zähne tief fliegen: 'Der goldene Drache.'" *Der Standard*, September 6, 2009. https://www.derstandard.at/story/1252036718395/akademietheater-wenn-beim-asiaten-die-zaehne-tief-fliegen-der-goldene--drache.

Amely, Joana Haag, et al. *Roland Schimmelpfennig: Der goldene Drache: Uraufführung.* Akademietheater, 2009.

Aroesti, Rachel. "No laughing matter: The rise of the TV 'sadcom.'" *The Guardian*, October 11, 2016. https://www.theguardian.com/tv-and-radio/2016/oct/11/bbc3-fleabag-louie-girls-transparent-master-of-none-sadcom

Aw, Tash. "Coming out of the shadows: what it means to be French and Chinese." *The Guardian*, November 26, 2019. https://www.theguardian.com/world/2019/nov/26/what-you-hear-about-chinese-people-in-france-feeling-scared-its-true

Berger, Peter L. *Erlösendes Lachen: Das Komische in der menschlichen Erfahrung.* Berlin: de Gruyter, 1998.

Blaser, Patric. "Eine Parabel über die Gleichgültigkeit." *Die Furche*, September 10, 2009. https://www.furche.at/autor/patric-blaser-2843

Brecht, B., Gay, J., Hauptmann, E., and Weill, K. *Die Dreigroschenoper: Nach John Gays 'The Beggar's opera.'* Frankfurt am Main: Suhrkamp, 1968.

Dössel, Christine. "Lang ist die Kunst, seicht das Leben." *Süddeutsche Zeitung*, September 7, 2009.

Dürrenmatt, Friedrich. *Theaterprobleme* (1954). In *Gesammelte Werke*, vol. 7: *Essays, Gedichte*. Zürich: Diogenes, 1996.

Freud, Sigmund. *Totem und Tabu* (1913). In *Gesammelte Werke*, vol. 9. Frankfurt am Main: Fischer, 1999.

Gayle, Damien. "Hackney Empire pulls out of Chinese takeaway opera over all-white cast." *The Guardian*, October 12, 2017. https://www.theguardian.com/uk-news/2017/oct/12/chinese-takeaway-opera-golden-dragon-hackney-empire-all--white-cast-music-theatre-wales

Glasenapp, Jörn. "Mixed Feelings: The Tragicomedy of Maren Ade's Toni Erdmann." *New German Critique*, vol. 46, no. 3, 2019, 35–51.

Guenther, Christina. "The Performance and Pedagogy of Migration in the Foreign Language Classroom: Staging Roland Schimmelpfennig's Der Goldene Drache." *Die Unterrichtspraxis*, vol. 50, no. 2, 2017, 171–183.

Guthke, Karl S. *Modern Tragicomedy: An Investigation into the Nature of the Genre.* Random House, 1966.

Hoffmann, Ernst Theodor Amadeus. *Poetische Werke*, vol. 5. Berlin: W. De Gruyter, 1957.

Isherwood, Charles. "Fried Rice and Noodles, and More Than a Dollop of Drama," *New York Times*, May 21, 2013. https://www.nytimes.com/2013/05/22/theater/reviews/the-golden-dragon-by-roland-schimmelpfennig.html

Jelinek, Elfriede. *Die Kontrakte des Kaufmanns; Rechnitz (Der Würgeengel); Über Tiere: Drei Theaterstücke.* Reinbek: Rowohlt, 2009.

Laucke, Dirk. *Für alle reicht es nicht.* Berlin: Kiepenheuer Bühnenvertrieb, 2009.

Lessing, Gotthold Ephraim. *Hamburgische Dramaturgie.* In *Werke in drei Bänden*, vol. 2: *Dramaturgie – Literaturkritik – Philologie und Allgemeines*. Munich: Deutscher Taschenbuch Verlag, 2003.

Marks, Peter. "'Golden Dragon' at Studio Theatre." *Washington Post*, November 8, 2011. https://www.washingtonpost.com/lifestyle/style/golden-dragon-at-studio-theatre/2011/11/08/gIQAAuna2M_story.html

Mayer, Hans. *Georg Büchner und Seine Zeit.* Wiesbaden: Limes-Verlag, 1946.

Mayer, Norbert. "Ein böses Märchen aus der Küche." *Die Presse*, 7.9.2009.

Mieder, Wolfgang. *"Entflügelte Worte": Modifizierte Zitate in Literatur, Medien Und Karikaturen: Mit 183 Abbildungen*. Kulturelle Motivstudien, vol. 16. Vienna: Praesens Verlag, 2016.

Obermueller, Nele. "Does German theater have a race problem?" *Exberliner*, May 30, 2012. https://www.exberliner.com/whats-on/stage/does-german-theatre-have-a-race-problem/

Peter, Anne. "Sieg der Artistik." *nachtkritik.cz* (online). April 6, 2010. http://www.nachtkritik-stuecke2010.de/preis/423-kommentar-zur-jurydebatte

Schulzová, Eva. "'Der goldene Drache': Roland Schimmelpfennigs Theaterstück nach einem bewährten Rezept." Ph.D. Diss. Masarykova U, 2012.

Sieg, Katrin. "Race, guilt and innocence: Facing blackfacing in contemporary German theater." *German Studies Review*, vol. 38, no. 1, 2015, 117–134.

Sieg, Katrin. "Refugees in German Documentary Theatre." *Critical Stages/Scènes critiques*. The International Association of Theatre Critics Journal, December 2016, No. 14. https://www.critical-stages.org/14/refugees-in-german-documentary-theatre/

Stadelmaier, Gerhard. "Was man den Zahn der Zeiten heißt." *Frankfurter Allgemeine Zeitung*, July 9, 2009. https://www.faz.net/aktuell/feuilleton/buehne-und-konzert/spielzeit-auftakt-in-wien-was-man-den-zahn-der-zeiten-heisst-1590911.html

Wille, Franz. "Eine Aufregende Zeit, Um Für das Theater Zu Schreiben." *Theater Heute*, 2010, 114–121.

Zipfel, Frank. *Tragikomödien: Kombinationsformen von Tragik und Komik im europäischen Drama des 19. und 20. Jahrhunderts*. Stuttgart: Metzler, 2017.

5   *Sprachspiel*: teaching *Kabarett*

Key considerations

Table 5.1

Arthur Schnitzler	*Zum großen Wurstel*
Premiere	Vienna, Lustspiel-Theater, 1906 (earlier version, Berlin, Überbrettl, 1901)
Performance Length	Approx. 75 minutes
Cast	30, plus additional on- and off-stage non-speaking roles.
Set	The setting is the theater comprising a main stage, a secondary stage for the marionette play, and the stalls for staged audience members.
Language	Some Austrian variation, register variation from colloquial to poetic, alternating between lengthy monologues, brisk dialogue, rhyming verse and song. Recommended at the advanced level (B2+).
Topic and Complexity	Sophisticated topic relating to questions of human and non-human agency, individuality, and authenticity.
Potential challenges	Some Austrian and somewhat antiquated, poetic language and monologues; large cast; space for three "stages."

Table 5.2

Yvan Goll	*Die Chapliniade*
Premiere	N.d. Published 1920.
Performance Length	Approx. 1/2 hour

DOI: 10.4324/9781003010289-5

Cast	1 principal character (Chaplin); 6 minor roles, and several crowd scenes.
Set	Part stage, part film.
Language	Little dialogue; some monologues in verse, somewhat antiquated. Recommended at advanced level.
Topic and Complexity	Chaplin, mass culture, mass media, technology; intertextual allusions.
Potential challenges	Mediating between stage and film; unequal role distribution; physicality of principal role.

Table 5.3

Erika Mann, Elisabeth Hartmann, Bertolt Brecht, Erich Kästner	*Kabarett* songs: "Hans im Glück," "Die Moritat von Mackie Messer," "Surabaya Johnny" I and II
Premiere	1934, 1928, 1929, 1930, respectively
Performance Length	5 minutes each
Cast	1 singer
Set	Cabaret
Language	Poetry, rhyme, wordplay
Topic and Complexity	Much wordplay and intertextual allusion
Potential challenges	Brechtian *Sprechgesang* is appropriate for all the songs, making it appropriate for non-trained participants.

Introduction

"This is a con job!" exclaims a member of the audience towards the end of Arthur Schnitzler's one-act burlesque, *Zum großen Wurstel* (1906). "Ein Schwindel! Darauf fall' ich nicht hinein! ... Das ist eines ernsten Theaters unwürdig! ..." (143).[1] Incensed at the sudden intrusion of characters borrowed from entirely different shows, the audience member refuses to go along with what he now realizes has been a desperate attempt to salvage the play. This is the latest in a series of similar disruptions from other audience members, rabble rousers, the Director, the Raisonneur, and even the Poet himself – all prearranged, he claims, to contrive a missing ending. Quarrelling with the Poet and Director, the audience member demands a proper ending and even challenges their authenticity, suspecting that they, too, are just part of the swindle. The Director returns the challenge, questioning whether the audience member – *im wirklichen Parkett* – is really a theatergoer, and invites him to join them on stage. Unsure whether any of this is part of the play or not (*Gehört das dazu?*; 145), the confusion causes unrest both on stage and in the stalls: audience members boo and stomp their feet; others leave, as do some members of the cast; and the marionettes, hearing the Poet announce the play's conclusion, extricate themselves from their puppet stage to take over the main stage, singing and dancing whatever they please: "Ei, nun tun wir, was wir wollen! / Reden, singen, tanzen, tollen!" (146). That is, until another unknown figure (*Der Unbekannte*) suddenly enters and, in an apparent act of authorial revenge, severs the marionettes' strings, who thereupon collapse to the ground. Order is apparently restored, and the Poet believes he is avenged: "Mein Rächer bist du" (146). When the Unknown Man turns to the rest of the cast, however, we discover that it is not only the puppets that have strings to be severed: "Dies Schwert hier aber macht es offenbar, / Wer eine Puppe, wer ein Mensch nur war. / Auch unsichtbaren Draht trennt diese Schneide / Zu manches stolzen Puppenspielers Leide!" (147). When everyone on stage – including the audience member *im wirklichen Parkett* and even the Poet – falls to the ground, we realize that the audience member was not only correct but also in on the whole act. In fact, we – along with Schnitzler's real audience *im wirklichen Parkett* – have all been conned.

Toying with the audience

The art of conning, meta-theatrical self-reflexivity, direct audience interaction, and audience mirroring on stage are hardly new to fin-de-siècle Viennese theater; such techniques recur throughout the course of theater history and the present book (see especially ch. 3, 6, 7). Reminiscent of Romantic comedy and *Volkstheater*, and prescient of Brechtian and post-Brechtian theater, techniques that blur the boundaries between fiction and reality are shared among many forms of socially and politically motivated modern theater. Nevertheless, these techniques are nowhere more pervasive or fundamental than in German *Kabarett*, in all its varieties and sub-genres. Schnitzler's *Zum großen Wurstel* is an illustrative case in point.

Before the conclusion of Schnitzler's play, even those cognizant of what a burlesque holds in store – a parody of a conventional literary work – would be hard pressed to recognize the various levels on which the "swindle" is constructed. Having fallen to the ground, the entire cast – including the marionettes, the Director, the Poet, and the intruding audience members – rise once more to repeat the whole performance from the beginning: "Meine Herren, hier ist zu sehen ... usw." (148). The repeated circular motion of the performance contributes to the *Schwindel*, implying not only a swindle but also the kind of dizziness caused by a spinning motion associated with the circus – *der reine Zirkus*, as *Der Bissige* ("The Biting Critic") remarks (144). Only when the actors rise to recommence the performance do the various levels of theatrical deception become discernible. Not only does it become clear that fictive audience members are situated on stage and planted in the real audience, but also that the puppets of the play within the play – the on-stage Wursteltheater – are themselves not real puppets, but rather real actors, and thus not manipulated by the visible strings: "die Drähte, an denen sie gelenkt zu werden *scheinen*, sind sichtbar" (104; emphasis mine). Nothing is quite what it seems, and even those without visible strings are eventually unmasked as mere puppets, whose puppeteer ultimately remains anonymous (*Der Unbekannte*): "Die Leute haben doch keine Ahnung," exclaims *Der Wohlwollende* ("The Well-Meaning Critic"). Whoever is in control and pulling the strings remains ambiguous. And the audience, in a state of dizzy confusion, is rendered powerless to distinguish fiction from reality, the stage from the stalls, actors from spectators – indeed the puppeteer from puppets, or even the human and non-human actors.

Rather than suspend disbelief, however, the audience is repeatedly compelled to *invoke* disbelief and critical skepticism throughout, all orchestrated by the play: fictitious audience members (*Skandalmacher, Ein Herr im Parkett*) and critics (*Der Wohlwollende, Der Bissige, Der Naïve*) are planted on and off stage to provoke the desired audience response – ranging from amusement to mistrust, disbelief and outcry – and to preempt criticism. If any strings are really being pulled, it is those of the real audience by the real author. Audience reactions are anticipated and predetermined on stage. Indeed, as the rather complex history of its composition makes clear,[2] the present published (1906) version of the play had already been adapted multiple times in response to audience reactions to earlier versions that had troubled Schnitzler (see also Neumann 167). Most troubling for Schitzler had been the insufficient reaction to the (third) version titled *Marionetten,* a puppet play performed in 1901 at Ernst von Wolzogen's Überbrettl cabaret in Berlin – the very first of such cabaret theaters to be established in Germany – and into which Schnitzler himself infiltrated the performance as an on-stage audience member (Neumann 168; *Kommentar*).[3] The spectators' lack of comprehension and interaction in 1901 is registered in the 1906 version, *Zum großen Wurstel,* in the lines of the Poet: "Das scheinen die Leute nicht zu begreifen!" (131). By incorporating additional characters as on-stage spectators of the puppet play within the play, and after further adaptation and revision, Schnitzler was eventually successful in provoking the desired response in 1912 at Vienna's Deutsches Volkstheater – a "veritable scandal." According to witness reports, real audience members interacted directly with on-stage actors (Neumann 178; *Kommentar*).[4]

Zum großen Wurstel as *Kabarett*

As one of the earliest performances (on March 8, 1901) at Ernst von Wolzogen's Überbrettl theater (established January 18, 1901), *Zum großen Wurstel* and its multiple adaptations offer insight into the workings of *Kabarett* on many levels. First, both its place of premiere and its setting are indicative of spaces where one could circumvent censorship, which was strictly enforced in Berlin around 1900. Its setting is the Wurstelprater in Leopoldstadt, a suburb of Vienna, which remained one of the few places where Josef Anton Stranitzky's cheeky, subversive *Hanswurst*, to whom the Wurstelprater owes its name, was still permitted to appear uncensored (see ch. 3). Schnitzler's play had been rejected at Berlin's Deutsches Theater by Otto Brahm, who deemed this *drollige[s] Stückchen* more suitable for Wolzogen's cabaret theater.

Wolzogen founded the Überbrettl theater to serve as a meeting place for both popular variety-show artforms, such as chansons and short skits, and more experimental literary art forms, with the goal of elevating (*Über*) the status of ordinary variety performance (*Brettl*) while attracting larger audiences. Invoking Friedrich Nietzsche – whose bust stood in the foyer of Wolzogen's theater in the Köpenicker Straße – the Überbrettl sought to achieve a kind of *Umwertung aller verbrauchter Werte* (Rösler 61). Wolzogen's added *verbraucht* underscored the urgency with which he and some of his contemporaries hoped to revitalize theater by subverting "obsolete" bourgeois social norms along with philistinism (Rösler 61–2; Chisholm 120–3). Hence the frequent parody of traditional theater, including the kind we witness at Schnitzler's Wursteltheater, in which hybrid puppets stage a conventional tragedy of misplaced jealousy among nobles, only to be deprived of its conventional ending. As Neumann has shown, Schnitzler's play works on many levels to subvert agency throughout (Neumann 173); the implicated audience, in turn, is invited to adopt a self-critical skepticism. Whether or not Schnitzler's play was considered theatrically too subversive or simply too farcical, one hears echoes of Brahm's reluctance in the incensed audience member's outcry: "Das ist eines ernsten Theaters unwürdig! ..." (143).

Theatrical parody and self-parody point to the second important aspect of *Kabarett* as a process of ongoing adaptation, anticipating audience reactions in order to provoke certain responses. Initially conceived as a *Konversationsstück* or *Salonkomödie* written in prose (1899), Schnitzler subsequently revised it as a pantomime and dream play (1900) before its adaptation into a puppet play in verse (1901), after which he adapted it as a musical with piano accompaniment (1903) and finally as a burlesque (1906) – the meta-theatrical adaptation to which only minor emendations were added (*Entstehungsgeschichte*). Each new adaptation builds on previous versions, and the fifth version alludes to other contemporary plays: The two intruding actors are borrowed from plays of Hugo von Hofmannsthal and Hermann Bahr (142; *Kommentar*). However, it is less the written text that claims Schnitzler's attention than the audience, whose reactions he dramatizes in the meta-theatrical version and to whom the play holds a mirror (see also Neumann 168). Not only the hybrid puppets visibly suspended by strings, but also those not visibly suspended are manipulated – an unsettling provocation to the audience to "suspend *belief*," to reflect critically and to probe behind appearances. Schnitzler's 1912 version, which effects the desired "scandalous" response through intertextual allusion to previous versions, is the outcome of such ongoing adaptation over more than a decade.

In similar fashion, *Kabarett* confronts its audience with established norms, stereotypes, and social and theatrical conventions in order to subject them to critique. This is achieved primarily through intertextual allusion. Like Schnitzler's play, *Kabarett* typically engages in a process of adaptation, from one genre or medium to another, from one audience to the next, tuned into a particular society and culture, and is therefore abundant in intertextual allusion. Such intertexts – established text types, familiar discursive patterns, and cultural allusions – are exploited in new contexts for critical, controversial, or ambiguous intent. This is already indicated by the names of countless *Kabarett* establishments that have adopted playfully allusive puns, from Wolzogen's Überbrettl (Nietzsche) and Max Reinhardt's *Schall und Rauch* (Goethe's *Faust*), to the critically biting titles of Klaus and Erika Mann's *Die Pfeffermühle*, West-Berlin's *Die Stachelschweine,* and East Berlin's counterpart *Die Distel* (later also *Die Distel im scharfen Kanal,* alluding to former GDR's highly dubious *Schwarzer Kanal*). Furthermore, an overview of over a century of cabaret repertoire reveals a predilection for overt political and cultural allusions, from lampooning Richard Wagner in the burlesque opera, *Die lustigen Nibelungen,* by Überbrettl's composer Oscar Straus in 1904 (Rösler 73–4), to confronting cultural stereotypes in playfully ethno-hybrid cabaret acts such as Serdar Semoncu's notorious *Hitler Kebab* or Bülent Ceylan's *Döner for one* (see Laurie Wylie's *Dinner for One*).[5]

While Schnitzler's *Zum großen Wurstel* points backwards to previous versions of itself and to its theatrical antecedents, it also paves many ways forward, especially for the innovative experiments of *Kabarett* and theater more generally through the twentieth century to the present. This includes the intermingling of various different forms of performance and perspectives (puppet theater, tragedy, comedy, song and dance); self-reflexivity, anti-illusionist intervention, inclusion of extra-aesthetic aspects (such as including the Director and the Poet on stage); the satirical challenge to convention, its use of hybrid puppets, its focus on text as process rather than as product; and in developing a mode of perception that probes critically behind the semblance of things. As such, *Zum großen Wurstel* opens up multiple avenues of exploration in the foreign-language and drama classroom. As one in a trio of *Marionettenspiele* among other similar cycles that employ hybrid puppets, this avant-garde play is a prototypical example of many subsequent experiments with physical forms of expression that push against the boundaries between fantasy and reality, dramatic and post-dramatic forms, humans and machines, the manipulator and the manipulated, human and non-human agency, and towards the post-human. Moreover, in anticipating contemporary concerns regarding human agency, individuality, and authenticity amid a media-saturated and technologically driven society in a "post-truth" era, it offers today's students of German a rich assembly of accessible entry points and valuable critical skills. The following sections outline such these points of entry, focusing first on hybrid forms of *Schau-Spiel*, in which language is almost upstaged by physical gesture, before moving to the second section, which considers subsequent approaches to *Kabarett* as *Sprach-Spiel.*

Towards the post-human

Schnitzler is by no means the first to engage human actors to impersonate puppets, or indeed to interrogate the limits of human agency – the core of Schnitzler's *Marionettenspiele* of 1906. Although no direct precursors are to be found on the Austrian or German stage, hybrid puppets do appear in the Symbolist plays of Maurice Maeterlink, Alfred Jarry, and others (*Kommentar*; Neumann 168). A less direct but perhaps more potent antecedent is found in Georg Büchner's *Dantons Tod* (1835), in which Danton views humans as puppets, "von unbekannten Gewalten am Draht gezogen" (Büchner 45; see also Lehmann 78). Similarly, in *Leonce und Lena* (1836), Valerio introduces the protagonists at a staged wedding as

> die zwei weltberühmten Automaten... Nichts als Kunst und Mechanismus ... Diese Personen sind so vollkommen gearbeitet, daß man sie von anderen Menschen gar nicht unterscheiden könnte, wenn man nicht wüßte, daß sie bloße Pappdeckel sind. (Büchner 143–4)

But when they discover each other's identity at the arranged royal wedding "in effigy," they (like Valerio) realize that their attempts to elude authority – the King's desire for a royal wedding – and act of their own volition have been futile. Like *Dantons Tod*, which was heavily censored, Büchner's *Leonce und Lena* was not performed until almost the turn of the next century (1895), at the *Intimes Theater,* a small open-air cabaret venue in Munich, under the direction of Ernst von Wolzogen – another instance of cabaret's facilitation of social-politically motivated and experimental art forms.[6]

The movement of puppets was regarded by some of Schnitzler's contemporaries, however, as an ideal towards which actors should aspire, as did his friend and playwright Hermann Bahr, and dramaturg Edward Gordon Craig (*Kommentar*). Following Heinrich von Kleist's *Über das Marionettentheater* a century earlier (1810), in which Kleist posits the unreflective marionette as the ideal performer (see ch. 1), Craig's fascination with puppets stems from his desire for complete control over the production, which was not achievable with a human actor "at the mercy of the winds of his emotions" (Craig 4). In his essay *The Actor and the Über-Marionette* (1907), Craig calls for the actor's departure from the stage to make room for the graceful, un-self-conscious inanimate figure – the *Über-Marionette* (11).

In challenging the central position of humans in theater and, by extension, in the world, these early manifestations of theatrical hybridity hold much potential for an exploration of post-humanism, which has gained increasing attention in the arts and performance throughout the twentieth and twenty-first centuries, albeit with varying valuative positions. The post-human fantasy of humanity "transformed, transcended, or eliminated ... by technological advances" (OED) has long inspired narratives of utopian promise and dystopian threat: The former promises enhancement and liberation from human limitations; the latter warns of technology's potential to imitate and surpass human capabilities. Such anxieties about the infiltration of emerging digital and cybernetic technology on the human will be familiar to students chiefly through recent science-fiction films and television series such as Michael Crichton's *Westworld* (1973; 2016), Stanley Kubrick's *Dr. Strangelove or: How I Learned to Stop Worrying and Love the Bomb* (1964), James Cameron's *Terminator* series and franchise (since 1984), Steven Spielberg's *A.I. Artificial Intelligence* (2001), *Minority Report* (2002), Alex Garland's *Ex Machina* (2014), to name but a few. Such debates were already being rehearsed on the European stage at the beginning of the twentieth century; their development may be best explored through a series of drama workshops, as outlined here.

Marionette workshops

Starting (for advanced students) with Kleist's essay *Über das Marionettentheater*, or (for less-advanced students) with Gordon Craig's *The Actor and the Über-Marionette*, a workshop introducing students to the physicality of the actor-as-marionette provides a suitable basis on which to build such an exploration. Using an exercise adapted from chapter 1, the actor-as-marionette may be interrogated alongside any number of artworks featuring hybrid marionettes, puppets, dolls, or robots[7] in order to determine the differing perspectives. Schnitzler's cycle of three *Marionettenspiele* (*Zum großen Wurstel, Der tapfere Cassian, Der Puppenspieler*), later complemented by two further one-act plays, *Die Verwandlung des Pierrot* (1908) and *Der Schleier der Pierette* (1910), all follow Büchner in likening human agency to the manipulated puppets that human actors purportedly control. As Neumann has already experienced while co-directing a performance of *Zum großen Wurstel* at Cambridge University in 2019 (Neumann 177), and as my own workshops and performances of these plays by Schnitzler and Büchner have made clear, such intricate boundary-crossings – between human and non-human actors, actors and audience – only become apparent during drama workshops and rehearsals. In the context of a foreign-language course, it provides an opportunity for students, rather than the instructor, to think independently through the blocking of a particular scene in order to arrive at such critical insights.

A distinctly positive, indeed increasingly idealistic view of the technology's permeation of the body develops in the Bauhaus movement, particularly in Oskar Schlemmer's *Triadisches Ballet* (1922), in which the aesthetically superior puppet serves as a harmonizing model of the organic and artificial, man and machine, conscious and unconscious, art and life. Motivated in part by his own injuries from World War I and by both the destruction and prosthetic reconstruction enabled by technological advancements, Schlemmer reconceptualized the performing body as capable of being altered and manipulated, such that aesthetics became subordinate and subservient to function, movement, and mechanics (see also Elswit 390–2). Technological advancement enabled Schlemmer to render Kleist's imagined hybrid puppets a reality.

The robotic body

If Schlemmer, Büchner, Kleist, and Schnitzler are positive in their assessment of the enhancing and liberating potential of mechanical construction for humans, they also ultimately draw attention to the limitations and frailties of humans and the potential threat of their total destruction, which became a reality during WWI. Following the failed revolutions of 1919, former optimism associated with technological gains gave way to pessimistic anxieties about the related losses – technology's potential to strip humans of all agency and reduce them to machines, or indeed eradicate them. The precarious place of the human in a technologically-driven and -consumed society becomes Yvan Goll's satirical nightmare vision in *Methusalem oder Der ewige Bürger* (1922), in which a tin machine (*Blechautomat*) that resembles a chocolate dispenser is able to impersonate a human. Whenever Methusalem feeds it coins, it moves with small steps and arm movements, telling jokes in a blaring (*plärrenden*) voice (Goll *Methusalem* 17), only to continue reciting jokes and laughing *ein unheimliches fernes Lachen* after Methusalem is shot dead and while his wife fusses about the goulash (72). The joke, it seems, is on the petty-minded bourgeois society that feeds the machinery of consumerism. This critique is underscored by the formal hybridity of the play, in which Methusalem's dreams and visions are filmed and projected on to the window of the room inhabited by Methusalem on stage – a nod to the emerging media innovation and its technical hand in the rise of mass consumerism.

The mass-cultural phenomenon of film informs both the aesthetics and the subject of Goll's *Die Chapliniade – Eine Filmdichtung* of the same period (1920), a short cinepoem written in German and subsequently translated by the bilingual poet into French (1923) and that served to introduce Charlie Chaplin via France to German audiences.

Yvan Goll's *Kino der Menschlichkeit: Die Chapliniade*

Boundaries are similarly pushed in this very short cinepoem, in which modern mass media (*Film*) and "high" art (*Dichtung*), art and technology, comedy and tragedy, fantasy and reality are embodied in the figure of Charlie Chaplin. Featured on many of the posters decorating the city, Chaplin's image suddenly comes to life: "Er sieht sich staunend die Passanten an, lächelt, steigt vorsichtig von seinem Postament herab, auf dem er als Herz-König abgebildet war, und legt ernsthaft Krone, Zepter, Reichsapfel auf einem Mülleimer nieder" (53). In six short episodes we follow Chaplin as he is pursued through the streets, subsequently departing by train for Mount Parnassus (the mythic site for divine poetic inspiration), murdering an infatuated co-passenger with his cane, digging through the desert to the center of the earth, begging for food, transporting himself to Marseilles and Hong Kong, and attempting to hang himself in a forest, only to return, finally, to the flat movie image from which he emerged. We witness Chaplin both as (cheerful) cinematic image and (cheerless) theater poet who is able to slip in and out of the imaginary realm and enchant the jaded masses, make even the grumpiest hunchback laugh (54), infuriate the poor billposter who tries to cash in on his fame (55), and charm women but not find mutual love. The many captivated passers-by pursue Chaplin through the streets, whereupon multitudinous replicas of Chaplin materialize from advertising columns, and which mutate just as fast back into a poster image. Along the way, his filmic self (*Plötzlich Film*, 60) even manages to inspire a revolution (61).

Weary of their monotonous working conditions, the workers place their hope for spiritual redemption in Chaplin, whom they regard as a divine savior: "Heil dem Befreier aus dem Jahrhundert der Arbeit! / Führ uns wieder zu uns zurück!… Erlöse uns von der Arbeit! … Befreie die Menschen aus ihrer Langerweile! / Bring uns die Revolution" (61). They kneel before him and make the sign of the Cross (57), until the billposter nails him back to his column, holding out his cap for tips: "Chaplin erscheint einen Augenblick als Christus mit Dornenkrone" (54). The Christ-like Chaplin registers the robotic regulation of the workers' monotonous existence: "Alles arbeitet… Magere Intellektuelle mit Brillen rammen Pflastersteine im Takt" – robbed of their individual mental faculties ("Schützt die Stirne! Tretet in den Denkerverein!"; 61). Digging into the earth's core, Chaplin perceives the results of their labor in gramophone recordings of the world's collected murmurings and linguistically impoverished soundbites: "Ist das alles, was die Menschen denken?" Chaplin wonders (60). "Im Mittelpunkt der Erde rauscht / Tumult der Lüge, Telefon der Dummheit, Wahnsinn der Radioprogramme. / Wie arm ist der Mensch" (60). Alienated from themselves and spiritually depleted, they implore Chaplin to release them from their labor, "return them to themselves," and bring them *einen Kommunismus der Seele!* (61).

Chaplin's appeal for the socially underprivileged is inextricable from the technological wonders of cinema – hence the original title, *Kino der Menschlichkeit* (Aping 56). His ability to transform himself and others back and forth – from a two-dimensional film star to a three-dimensional poet, cinema to theater, laughter to tears, even a doe into a human, and from place to place – beguiles both his cinematic audience and the literary avant-gardes, who similarly seek to transform their dull reality with their imagination: "Denn einzig wahr ist die Sehnsucht / Nach der unendlichen Illusion! / Die Wahrheit aber macht uns gähnen!" (60). And yet Chaplin, sobbing as he resigns himself to a lonesome fate, is ultimately forced back into his movie poster, to be immortalized in mass-produced art – "für die ganze Menschheit zu sterben!" (53). If art and technology, cinema and theater appear reconciled in the *Chapliniade*, then only to the extent that it reveals the spiritual impoverishment of a mechanized capitalist modern society. As Chaplin the Poet somberly witnesses, machine-like humans, drained of imagination and autonomy, have become as uniform and replicable as they are expendable. Chaplin remains, as Sabine Hake concludes, "a melancholic figure, a symbol of the losses rather than the gains associated with 'modern times'" (Hake 89).

The debate about "modern times" and the incursion of new media on traditional literary drama is one that began in the 1910s and continues in theater today. A striking example is Katie Mitchell's 2016 production of Elfriede Jelinek's *Schatten (Eurydike sagt)* (2012) at the Berlin Schaubühne, in which theater commingles with cinema. Presented from a dual perspective, the theatrical performance is filmed "on set" in real time and projected above the stage, allowing the spectator to witness the construction of film simultaneously in process and as final product. And by including "the real" (tech crew, cameras, large boom microphones, TV monitors, and a vintage Volkswagen Beetle) in the performance, Mitchell exposes the materiality of both the performance and the film and thus highlights the post-dramatic aesthetic for which Jelinek herself is well known. "The form is a synthesis of theatre and film which creates a third thing, which is like cubism in theater," Mitchell explains in an interview. "What the cameras do is they allow us to see all the sides of how something is constructed whilst looking at the constructed object" (Pearson).

All of this is foreshadowed in the avant-garde plays of Chaplin's contemporaries. In decentering human agency through hybrid puppets, automata, and robots, and in experimenting across drama, poetry, and new forms of media, many avant-garde artists anticipated current debates about post-humanism as well as what Hans-Thies Lehmann describes as the post-dramatic "dehierarchization" of the text itself (Lehmann 78). Although primarily "dramatic" – these plays still present a "mimesis of action" largely through dialogue on stage (Lehmann 36) – they do not all present a linear, cohesive totality associated with dramatic logic. Rather, as fragmented kaleidoscopes of hybrid forms that also move off stage and implicate the audience, these plays already reflect on the relation of conventional theater to the changing culture of media (here, silent film) and technology. For this reason, these plays are chiefly instructive in their re-thinking of the relationship of art to technology, art to society, gesture to speech, and most importantly as *Schau-Spiel.*

Performing the post-human

Such a reconfiguration of dramatic texts necessarily invites fresh production approaches, posing new challenges but also creative possibilities. On the one hand, their relative brevity makes them suitable either for individual performance or as part of a variety show. On the other hand, the convergence of theater, lyric poetry, cinema, dreams, the real and surreal, such as we have in both of Goll's texts, demands a collage-like blend of drama techniques, approaches, and technology. In terms of performance, *Zum großen Wurstel* requires marionette-like grace; *Methusalem* requires working out a robotic impersonation of a human in *Methusalem* – a Brechtian exercise in self-alienation (see ch. 1); and *Die Chapliniade* involves imagining the robotic body of alienated workers, the pantomimic acting style of Chaplin that also inspired Brecht, Valentin, and others (see ch. 3), as well as a fusion of traditional theater and film, of the three-dimensional and two-dimensional artforms. Moreover, by pushing the boundaries of the theatrically impossible in the visualized unconscious (dreams), short-cut scenes, and vast landscapes, Goll's texts, which are meant for both theater and cinema, invite critical reflection on the relationship among the media and genres.

In regard to performance, Goll's *Methusalem* and *Die Chapliniade* require an intermedial blending of theater and cinema, real and projected scenery, the complex interweaving of which demands an equal amount of attention to blocking and staging as Schnitzler's *Zum großen Wurstel*. Alternatively, a combination of theater and digital animation is feasible, along the lines suggested by Bettina Matthias in her innovative work on arts-based digital storytelling. Matthias employs digital technology as a lens through which to explore German Weimar culture, in which works of art provide "both the content and the medium with and through which students engaged in the period" (Matthias 38), and which students interpret imaginatively through digital animation, culminating in a curated exhibition. According to Matthias, such a "creative response to art allowed for a more complex engagement... [A]n interpretation of art that was in itself again open to interpretation," in contrast to the customary curatorial explanation (Matthias 45). Similarly, students may digitally animate Chaplin's poster image to create virtual actors and to realize what is impossible in theater alone.

In thinking through the technological and aesthetic underpinnings of these media, it is helpful to consider models by contemporary artists such as Fernand Léger, whose Cubist illustrations of the French version *La Chapliniade* draw attention to the fragmentation of the cinematic body as a series of accelerated still images creating the illusion of motion. Léger's *Charlot cubiste*[8] (1924), moreover, features a Chaplin puppet constructed from painted wooden blocks that also inspired scenes for a cutout animation film (Lista 5) and reappear in his 1924 film *Ballet mécanique,* which opens very briefly with a disarticulated mannequin of Chaplin (Townsend 186).[9] Like Goll, and like Katie Mitchell's "cubist" synthesis of film and theater in Jelinek's *Schatten*, Léger allows the viewer to see how the work is constructed. By analyzing the relations between the arts and the tensions these artworks draw out between man and machine, art and technology, students will be better prepared to approach the production self-reflexively. Digital media enables students to construct and modify virtual moving bodies, but in a way that "surpasses" the filmic technology that had once constructed Chaplin through its series of still images. In doing so, attention should be directed to the ways in which new digital technology transforms older cinematic technology. Physical "perfection" of the two-dimensional animation should be brought to bear on an interpretation of Goll's play, in which a melancholic three-dimensional Chaplin-as-Poet is outshone by his two-dimensional silent film star. Students, in turn, are animated to reflect on their own fragmented experience as both digitally mediated constructions and living bodies.

From *Schauspiel* to *Sprachspiel*

Chaplin captivated the European literary avant-gardes, filmmakers, and cabaret artists, resulting in a series of Chaplin imitators and followers (Aping 150–74), among them Karl Valentin, Liesl Karlstadt, and Bertolt Brecht (ch. 3). Many of these experimental artists shared an appetite for *Kabarett*, where the conventional division between "high" literary modernism and popular art was suspended, permitting a motley assembly of *Kleinkunst,* from film and theater, poetry, song, puppet theater, and dance, within one intimate space. *Kabarett* shares a spirit of social, political, and aesthetic reevaluation and some tendencies with the avant-gardes: a heavy reliance on intertexts for the purpose of adaptation, parody, and critique; crossing of social and aesthetic boundaries; implication of the audience; intentional misleading of the audience in order to expose its prejudices; and the complication or reversal of dramatic logic, all of which we have seen in Schnitzler and Goll. Beyond this, literary *Kabarett* also experiments with all forms of expression, and with language in particular. Thus, if the preceding attention to forms of *Schauspiel* might seem to obviate the need to study the language, the present section, which focuses on other examples of *Kabarett*, compensates in large measure due to *Kabarett's* heavy reliance on linguistic nuance. Puppet theater, shadow play, dance, pantomime, and silent film might have constituted one part of a cabaret evening; the remaining part included poetry, song, short plays, and skits complete the event.

Language play – the experimentation with its sounds, tones, rhythms, rhymes, as well as the poetics of alliteration, repetition, pun, metaphor – forms a key element of literary *Kabarett*, especially from the 1920s. The brevity and linguistic richness of these texts facilitate intensive language work (or play) for advanced language students. However, lower-level language learners have little room for such ambiguities and will find some of these texts too demanding. Nonetheless, by approaching these as adaptations of existing material, *Kabarett* can be motivating and productive on all levels, and especially for less confident students who benefit from such scaffolded support.

The practice of rendering one genre, style, or medium in another (which Richard Kern calls "transformed practice") helps students discern the relationships between "linguistic forms, and social contexts and purposes" (Kern 204) – by revealing the ritualized patterns of communications. When studying adaptations of one text to a new genre or medium, students need to consider their various formal markers and constraints before embarking on their own creative work. This includes discerning such differences as showing rather than telling a story, as is required in transforming a poem, song, or short story into a skit, and vice versa. In more advanced classes, students can be encouraged to recognize how established text types and discursive patterns are exploited in *Kabarett* in order to be controversial, ambiguous, subversive, deviant or incongruent. In doing so, students focus on discrete aspects of language, such as lexis, syntax, phonetic, and non-verbal features. *Kabarett* texts from the German-language tradition serve, in turn, as stimuli for students' own creative work as they also learn how to play with language, to appropriate, modify, repurpose, and work intertextually. And, by working within and across these communication conventions, we encourage students to think critically about how these texts are constructed.

I have described elsewhere an example of how to stage an engagement in *Kabarett* at all levels across the curriculum, one that prepares lower-level students as "primed" audience members for a performance of Brecht's 1920 adaptation of the fairytale *Hans im Glück* (Parkes). Other scholars have presented many various innovative approaches to teaching *Kabarett*, both as a course in cultural history (Bell); as a basis for "creative misbehaviour" and performance (McNally); and as an opportunity for a co-curricular performance event. McNally's comprehensive study provides a multitude of didactic models, including approaches that are determined by the form of the *Kabarett*-text itself. In a similar vein, the following brief examples mirror each text's construction by expanding on the common practices of adaptation and "conning the audience" already witnessed in Schnitzler's play. Rather than guiding students word for word through each text, this approach involves a series of problem-solving activities with the goal of making apparent the various layers of construction. To do so, it is necessary to establish certain expectations in order to "lead students astray," in order to then challenge these, as follows:

1. advanced organizer: setting the stage, establishing the theme, vocabulary, and genre, and expectations;
2. layer the information by withholding parts or elements of the piece in order to establish expectations and purposefully mislead;
3. highlight incongruence between student (audience) expectations and subversive element;
4. background information to fill gaps in cultural, historical, political, or literary allusions;
5. intensive reading, including a focus linguistic features and creativity, such as word play, lexis, register, irony, towards an interpretation;
6. exploiting given texts or using them as inspiration for own texts in creative writing exercise, in which an aspect of the language and/or genre gets "violated."

Erika Mann: "Hans im Glück"

To begin with a poem whose adapted source is widely familiar, and therefore accessible for foreign-language students, I recommend Erika Mann's poetic adaptation (1934) of a fairytale recorded by the Grimm brothers and published in the *Kinder- und Hausmärchen* in 1812. Familiarity with the fairytale and the genre helps alleviate the cognitive and linguistic burden, permitting more top-down reading strategies that in turn facilitate closer attention to the relationship of language to genre. Here, however, the fairytale departs from the conventional fairytale logic by inverting the traditional rags-to-riches narrative: Hans' "luck" or "happiness" resides in his seemingly unwitting loss of all material possessions, convinced as he is that every challenge or loss provides further proof of his good fortune.

The poetic transformation of this fairytale is guided by interactive reading exercises along the lines described by Swaffar and Arens (2005), which means, first of all, identifying the downward spiral of the narrative in a short, single-sentence précis for each paragraph (or episode), re-using language from the text itself in order to relate the cause and effect of Hans' misfortune: *Hans exchanges his earned gold for a passerby's horse, because...*; *a farmer offers Hans his cow in exchange for Hans' horse, because....* This somewhat mechanical approach nevertheless enables beginning learners to overcome linguistic deficiencies while creatively re-working more sophisticated language from the text, paying additional attention to discrete syntactic and morphological features (as is set up by the subordinating conjunction "*weil...*"). This is consistent with Kern's recommendation that a "systematic, patterned restructuring" of the narrative *forces* "the student to use different grammatical forms to paraphrase the same referential material" (Kern 208). And, as Claire Kramsch argues, "The very reconstruction of the text by the students makes apparent to them better than any analysis by a teacher some of its stylistic features" (363). This in turn can stimulate comparison and discussion in the ensuing class session.

Erika Mann's short satirical poem provides fertile groundwork for further creative reworking in dialogue with the original fairytale and the historical context to which it sardonically relates. In recasting Hans' concept of "fortune" (*Glück*) within the context of National Socialism, this is a biting resistance piece against National Socialism written for her ensemble, aptly named *Die Pfeffermühle* ("pepper mill"), and provides a rich source of creative adaptation for advanced language students.

An essentially dialogical approach to the text (within one class meeting) runs as follows:

1. Information about the author, year it was written, and context is withheld until students have been sensitized to the verbal irony ("Um mein Glück noch zu vollenden / Konfisziert' man meinen Pass... Die leidigen Rechte sind endlich dahin, / Was ich für ein Hans im Glück

immer bin!") and other rhetorical devices that complicate the surface reading of the text. These are subsequently related to the context in order to understand the critical content and to highlight the importance of historical-cultural context in the construction of meaning.

2. To complete the exercise, students are asked to adopt the same rhetorical devices, some of the phrases, and the refrain in order then to rework the text into a new context, preferably an equally controversial issue from their own cultural context. One simple example involves the vocabulary and morphological manipulation necessitated by each refrain "*Das leidige Geld/Die leidige Heimat/Die leidigen Rechte ist/sind* nun endlich dahin, / Was ich für ein Hans im Glück immer bin!"; emphasis mine) in order to conform to the new context.

3. As a follow-up in-class exercise, students may carry out an improvised dramatic reading (or pantomime) that not only helps them visualize and verbalize the narrative in an interactive format, but also begins focusing attention on the spoken dialogue and inner monologues that constitute the "drama" of the text.

4. As a final step, and one that should be carried out in small groups, students identify and work with the text's dialogues and transform these into new, more modern contexts, substituting Hans and Hans' gold, horse, pig, and goose for other characters, belongings, and situations. A condensed adaptation of the fairytale as a role-playing activity anticipates the loss of narrative cues in the dramatic form, reliant as drama is on dialogue and visualization.

In this way, students not only work with surface language forms by modifying vocabulary and manipulating forms, but also learn to work critically with language and reframe the content in a way that sheds light on the *Kabarett* poetry genre. Moreover, students are sensitized to rhetorical devices such as irony, which complicates the notion of the merely referential in language, and begin to understand both conventional and subjective ways of making meaning through language.

Bertolt Brecht and Kurt Weill: "Die Moritat von Mackie Messer"

One of the consequences of the evolution of *Kabarett*, with its cultivation of socially provocative and innovative small forms, is that a number of songs, extracted from larger works, would become so popular that they took on a life of their own, wholly independent of their original context. Such is the case with many of the songs of Bertolt Brecht, Elizabeth Hartmann and Kurt Weill, who collaborated on *Die Dreigroschenoper* (1928), *Aufstieg und Fall der Stadt Mahagonny* (1929), and *Happy End* (1929). Songs from each of these stage works have been adapted and readapted in a range of contexts, styles, media and languages, from cabaret and jazz to Broadway, pop, and rock and roll. To take the best-known example – although, in my experience, only rarely familiar to students – "Die Moritat von Mackie Messer" began with Lotte Lenya on the German stage before becoming the Broadway hit "Mack the Knife" in *The Threepenny Opera*, a jazz sensation (Louis Armstrong and Ella Fitzgerald), and further popularized by Bobby Darin and Sting, just to name a few.

In approaching the song, it is important to establish expectations first by getting a "feel" for the music before introducing the text. The music, which repeats the same strophic melody in simple duple time throughout, is structurally and harmonically straightforward and easily accessible. By playing an excerpt from the orchestral suite version – *Kleine Dreigroschenmusik*[10] – the instructor can play the song without the title, text, or visuals, so that students focus on the music alone. Some opening questions help students get a feel for the light, catchy tune, rhythm, delivery style, and prompt any associations students might have, emotional or other, with the music: *Welches Gefühl evoziert die Musik? Wie fühlen Sie sich, wenn Sie diese Musik hören?: fröhlich, traurig, amüsiert, ernst, entspannt, angespannt, irritiert, beängstigt …? Welche Instrumente hören Sie? Wo würde man diese Musik (und diese Instrumente) normalerweise hören? Können Sie leicht mitsingen?* Assuming that students will generally identify a light-hearted, upbeat, and catchy tune, these questions intentionally build up certain expectations about the kind of theme, context, and social setting.

If students are able to identify musical instruments such as the barrel organ, banjo, and saxophone in a wind and brass ensemble (noting the absence of stringed instruments) it will be possible to rule out conventional classical music genres and the associations with concert and opera halls and middle-class decorum. Its place within an "opera" will therefore come as a surprise, except that this is an adaptation of John Gay's *Beggar's Opera* – *eine Oper für Bettler*, subverting all middle-class expectations. The light, jazzy feel of the music establishes a light-hearted tone, and while it unlikely that students will be able to conjecture a specific theme, it is just as unlikely to for them to associate it with a murdering, raping criminal that is Mackie Messer.

As a next step, the text should be distributed. Working in groups, students determine the content of the song and then consider the effect of the music: *Wovon handelt der Text? Beschreiben Sie Mackie Messer! Finden Sie die Musik passend? Warum (nicht)?* The light-hearted, somewhat sentimental effect of the catchy tune seems incongruous with the genre of a murder ballad and the text, as though to celebrate and sentimentalize his criminal feats. This serves to introduce of Brecht's defamiliarization effect (*Verfremdungseffekt*), the technique of rendering the all-too familiar in a new, "strange" light so as to provoke critical attention. The music, then, plays an essential part in subverting audience expectation.

"Surabaya-Johnny" I and II

Alluding musically to "Mackie Messer," "Surabaya Johnny" from *Happy End* is another Brecht-Weill collaboration, and although it flopped on the

Berlin stage (1929), the songs took on a life of their own, especially in America. Like *Die Dreigroschenoper* and other works, Brecht's text is loosely based on a translation by Elisabeth Hartmann, this time of Rudyard Kipling's ballad "Mary, Pity Women." It was frequently performed by the popular cabaret artist Elfriede Katharina Nehrhaupt (stage name: Kate Kühl), who also played Lucy in the 1928 premiere of *Die Dreigroschenoper*. Furthermore, it would become subject to parody by Erich Kästner, in "Surabaya Johnny II" (1930). Kästner's version is interesting especially for its criticism of Brecht's borrowings from translations of Kipling that he also passed off as his own (Lyon 376) along with exotic colonial references from a position of relative provincial inexperience: "Du hast gelogen, Johnny, du bist nicht echt / Du bist nicht gereist, Johnny / Du bist nicht von Kipling, Johnny / Nimm die Pfeife raus. Du bist von Brecht... Ach, deine Kolonien / Johnny, sunny Johnny / Die lagen bei Berlin!"

Hauptmann and Brecht's version tells the story of a young woman who is seduced by Johnny, who quickly grows tired and abandons her once she shows signs of aging. Narrated in the first person, the refrain expresses her hopeless longing for the heartless Johnny, who, she surmises, wanted her not for love but for money. Rhythmically steady but harmonically more complex than "Mackie Messer," Weill's musical setting underscores the content, moving from the verse narrative to the longing expressed in the refrain, with diminished chords that convey a commensurately melancholic tone. For this reason, the Hauptmann-Brecht-Weill song may be approached in its complete form, rather than layered. When Brecht and Hauptmann's text is then replaced by Kästner's parody in "Surabaya Johnny II," however, the music adopts an entirely different function, amplifying Kästner's ironic overtones. A sardonic smirk is clearly audible in the sentimental refrain: "Surabaya-Johnny / Ach, deine Kolonien / Johnny, sunny Johnny / Die lagen bei Berlin! ... Du bist der geborene 'und Co.'"

The original song provides the scaffolding, and the parody provides inspiration for students' own creative adaptations, substituting key moments of the text with their own, with the goal of retaining the music, rhythm, and rhyme scheme:

1. Working with the text and music, students read the text aloud and underline where the stress falls in order to identify the meter (the quatrain, in which the first and third lines are in iambic tetrameter, the second and forth in trimeter) and the verse rhyme scheme (ABAB):

   Du kamst aus den Wäldern bei Pirna
   Du sagtest nicht Frau, sondern Weib
   Du warst tätowiert wie ein Seemann
   Du hattest nichts Warmes im Leib

2. Students repeat the exercise for the refrain (AAB):

    Surabaya-Johnny
    Surabaya-Johnny
    Kalkutta, Schanghai, Montreux
    Johnny, sunny Johnny
    Mein Gott, my god, mon dieu!

3. Students are asked to identify the overlapping theme of the "art of conning" in both versions of the song – the young woman in Brecht's text, and Brecht himself in Kästner's parody.
4. Students consider the political implications of the song in the context of Brecht and Weill's of *Happy End*, which is set in Chicago, and whose anti-capitalist sentiment is contained most succinctly in the famous line: "Was ist ein Einbruch in eine Bank gegen die Gründung einer Bank?"
5. To begin creating their own version based on Weill's setting, students reflect on instances of feigned authenticity – from personal experiences, to social media, post-truth politics, and corporate (or other) corruption – and begin drafting their own texts.

There are myriad opportunities for creative adaptation of all kinds, most of which were also introduced by Schnitzler in his reworking of *Zum großen Wurstel,* including adapting across genres and media; altering the point of view; inventing a new ending; recasting characters in new contexts; bringing characters from different texts into dialogue; and, most importantly, adapting a text to a new cultural or historical setting. Furthermore, *Kabarett* also enables instructors to tackle important social-political topics in short form: for example, nuclear energy in Friedrich Dürrenmatt's *Der Erfinder* (1961), an early *Kabarett* version of his longer tragicomedy, *Die Physiker*, or migration, ethnicity, cultural hybridity, and xenophobia, especially in more recent ethno-cultural cabaret (see especially Bower and Sieg). Time and resources permitting, a *Kabarett* performance for a live audience is a most productive and rewarding way to conclude this course of study, one that enables students to work cross-culturally and -medially, thematically, his-torically, and linguistically, and to put their own language play to work.

Notes

1   Arthur Schnitzler, *Marionetten*, ed. by Annja Neumann with Gregor Babelotzky, Judith Beniston, Julia Glunk, Kaltërina Latifi, Robert Vilain and Andrew Webber, in *Arthur Schnitzler digital, Historisch-kritische Edition (Werke 1905–1931)*, ed. by Wolfgang Lukas, Michael Scheffel, Andrew Webber and Judith Beniston, in collaboration with Thomas Burch, 2018–, reading text of "Zum großen Wurstel," p. 125, <https://www.schnitzler-edition.net/Lesetext/WUR/125>. All references are to this edition. This edition includes additional information based on materials from the archive in Cambridge University Library.

2 See "Entstehungsgeschichte zu 'Zum großen Wurstel,'" Arthur Schnitzler, *Marionetten*, https://www.schnitzler-edition.net/entstehungsgeschichtetext/10118.
3 This play, however, was not Schnitzler's first to be performed at the Überbrettl; in fact, "Episode," excerpted from his *Anatol*, was part of Überbrettl's program on opening night (Rösler 64–7).
4 See "Allgemeiner Kommentar *Marionetten*," https://www.schnitzler-edition.net/emendtext/10118.
5 Although generally unknown in the United States, and not well known in England, where it was first written for the theater, its German televised version has been a New Year's Eve tradition since 1962 in German-speaking countries and elsewhere in Europe. Its Turkish-German parody is also available on YouTube: https://www.youtube.com/watch?v=B-uEzblwUmI
6 For more information on the concept and context of the *intimes Theater*, see Delius.
7 I include "robots" here rather than "automata" to acknowledge the introduction of the word into English for the first time in Karel Capek's play *R.U.R.* (*Rossum's Universal Robots*) of 1921, the term "robot" deriving from Old Czech *robota* via Middle High German *robāt*, denoting "a central European system of serfdom, by which a tenant's rent was paid in forced labour or service" (OED). In Capek's dystopian satire, the factory-assembled robotic slaves gradually learn to think for themselves and revolt against their human manufacturers, leading to the latter's extinction.
8 Charlot was the name licensed in France.
9 Léger's film is accessible on YouTube: https://www.youtube.com/watch?v=wi53 TfeqgWM
10 This version is also readily available on YouTube: https://www.youtube.com/watch?v=I3R7RYwPsSg (Mackie Messer within the second number, beginning 01:53).

Further reading and resources

On puppets and acting

Craig, Edward Gordon. *The Actor and the Über-Marionette*. Florence: The Mask, 1908.
Kleist, Heinrich von. *Über das Marionettentheater*. In *Sämtliche Werke und Briefe*, vol. 2. Helmut Sembdner, ed. Munich: Deutscher Taschenbuch Verlag, 2001, 338–345.
Word Encyclopedia of Puppetry Arts: https://wepa.unima.org/en/

On the history of Kabarett

Jelavich, Peter. *Berlin Cabaret*. Cambridge: Harvard UP, 1993.

Anthologies of Kabarett approaches to teaching Kabarett

Bell, Michele R. "Exploring the Language–Culture Nexus through German 'Kabarett.'" *Die Unterrichtspraxis*, vol. 43, no. 2, 2010, 111–122.
McNally, Joanne Maria. *Creative Misbehaviour: The Use of German Kabarett within Advanced Foreign Language Learning Classrooms*. Oxford: P. Lang, 2000.

Recordings

Mann, Erika. *Erika Manns "Pfeffermühle"*– auf den Spuren des legendären Exilkabaretts 1933–1937. CD Berlin: Duo-Phon Records, 2005.

Kühn, Volker. "100 Jahre Kabarett: 1901-1933 : Texte Und Chansons." 2006.

Brecht, Bertolt. "Surabaya Johnny."   https://www.youtube.com/watch?v=aSLTvKC-P3Y

Kästner, Erich. "Surabaya Johnny II." *Erich Kästner: Die kleine Freiheit*. CD. Berlin: Duo-Phon, 2001.

On Charlie Chaplin's reception in Germany

Aping, Norbert. *Charlie Chaplin in Deutschland: 1915–1924: Der Tramp kommt ins Kino*. Marburg: Schüren, 2014.

References

Aping, Norbert. *Charlie Chaplin in Deutschland: 1915–1924: Der Tramp kommt ins Kino*. Marburg: Schüren, 2014.

Bell, Michele R. "Exploring the Language–Culture Nexus through German 'Kabarett.'" *Die Unterrichtspraxis*, vol. 43, no. 2, 2010, 111–122.

Bower, Kathrin. "Serdar Somuncu: Turkish German Comedy as Transnational Intervention." *Transit*, vol. 7, no. 1, 2011, 22.

Büchner, Georg. *Werke und Briefe: Gesamtausgabe*. Fritz Bergemann, ed. Wiesbaden: Insel, 1974.

Chisholm, David. "Early Literary Cabaret and Modernism in Berlin." In *Politics in German Literature*. Beth Bjorklund and Mark E. Corey, ed. Rochester: Camden House, 1998, 117–131.

Delius, Annette. *Intimes Theater. Untersuchungen zu Programmatik und Dramaturgie einer bevorzugten Theaterform der Jahrhundertwende*. Kronberg: Scriptor, 1976.

Elswit, Kate. "The Some of the Parts: Prosthesis and Function in Bertolt Brecht, Oskar Schlemmer, and Kurt Jooss." *Modern Drama*, vol. 51, no. 3, 2008, 389–410.

Mann, Erika. *Erika Mann und ihr politisches Kaberett 'Die Pfeffermühler' 1933 – 1937: Texte, Bilder, Hintergründe*. Helga Keiser-Hayne, ed. Hamburg: Rowohlt, 1995.

Goll, Yvan, and Goll, Claire. *Dichtungen: Lyrik, Prosa, Drama*. Darmstadt: Luchterhand, 1960.

Goll, Yvan, and Grosz, George. *Methusalem: Oder, Der ewige Bürger. Ein satirisches Drama*. Cologne: Kiepenheuer, 1922.

Hake, Sabine. "Chaplin Reception in Weimar Germany." *New German Critique*, vol. 51, no. 51, 1990, 87–111.

Kern, Richard. *Literacy and Language Teaching*. Oxford: Oxford UP, 2000.

Kleist, Heinrich von. *Über das Marionettentheater*. In *Sämtliche Werke und Briefe*, vol. 2. Helmut Sembdner, ed. Munich: Deutscher Taschenbuch Verlag, 2001, 338–345.

Kramsch, Claire. "The literary text in the classroom." *MLJ*, vol. 69, no. 4, 1985, 356–366.

Lehmann, Hans-Thies. *Postdramatic Theatre*. Jürs-Munby, Karen, trans. New York: Routledge, 2006.

Lista, Giovanni. "L'homme comme mesure de toute chose." *Ligeia*, vol. 33, no. 177-180, 2020, 3–5.

Lyon, James K. "Brecht's Use of Kipling's Intellectual Property: A New Source of Borrowing." *Monatshefte*, vol. 61, no. 4, 1969, 376–386.

McNally, Joanne Maria. *Creative Misbehaviour: The Use of German Kabarett within Advanced Foreign Language Learning Classrooms*. Oxford: P. Lang, 2000.

Neumann, Annja. "Wrestling with Marionettes: Entangled Embodiment and Posthuman Agency in Schnitzler's 'Zum Großen Wurstel'." *Austrian Studies*, vol. 27, 2019, 163–178.

2000 *Oxford English Dictionary*. Oxford UP, 2000.

Parkes, Lisa. "From Creative Adaptation to Critical Framing: Dramatic Transformations across the Foreign Language Curriculum." In *Integrating the Arts: Creative Thinking about Foreign Language Curricula and Language Program Direction*. Parkes, L. and Ryan, C., ed. Boston: Cengage, 2015, 43–60.

Pearson, Joseph. "Not Theatre, Not Film: Katie Mitchell's Third Art in the Shadow." *Schaubühne*, September 26, 2016. https://www.schaubuehne.de/en/blog/not-theatre-not-film-katie-mitchells-third-art-in-the-shadow.html. Retrieved January 10, 2021.

Rösler, Walter. *Das Chanson Im Deutschen Kabarett, 1901–1933*. Berlin: Henschelverlag Kunst und Gesellschaft 1980.

Schnitzler, Arthur. *Marionetten*, Annja Neumann with Gregor Babelotzky, Judith Beniston, Julia Glunk, Kaltërina Latifi, Robert Vilain and Andrew Webber, ed. In *Arthur Schnitzler digital, Historisch-kritische Edition (Werke 1905–1931)*, Wolfgang Lukas, Michael Scheffel, Andrew Webber and Judith Beniston, ed. in collaboration with Thomas Burch, 2018–, reading text of 'Zum großen Wurstel', p. 125, https://www.schnitzler-edition.net/Lesetext/WUR/125

Sieg, Katrin. *Ethnic Drag: Performing Race, Nation, Sexuality in West Germany*. Ann Arbor: University of Michigan Press, 2002.

Swaffar, Janet K., and Arens, Katherine. *Remapping the Foreign Language Curriculum*. Modern Language Association of America, 2005.

Townsend, Christopher. "Fernand Léger's Filmic Architecture." *Modernism/Modernity*, vol. 24, no. 1, 2017, 185–191.

6 *Hörspiel*: teaching radio plays

Introduction

On March 10, 1932, at 7:45 in the evening, Walter Benjamin invited his young audience of the Südwestdeutsche Rundfunk to join in a game. Listeners were asked to identify various sounds in a sequence of incomplete episodes, flesh them out imaginatively, and submit their responses to the radio station for the chance to win a prize (GS 7.2, 832; Schiller-Lerg 252–4). The fragments contained no verbal dialogue but rather a series of sounds depicting various scenes around the city, beginning with the general hubbub at a radio station (GS 7.2, 833), and occasionally punctuated by a hint to prompt the listener's imagination. Benjamin's objective was pedagogical: Listeners were to be attuned to the medium of the radio, the means of its production, and to the kinds of listening made possible by this new technology. His experiment aimed to encourage active, participatory listening and to stimulate listeners to co-construct the story. What Benjamin's young audience would hear on that evening's *Stunde der Jugend* was an early version his play *Radau um Kasperl* – a children's radio play about radio, sound, and the art of listening.

Originally broadcast under the title *Kasperl und der Rundfunk, eine Geschichte mit Lärm* and reproduced in summary form in the *Gesammelte Schriften* (GS 7.2, 832–6), this radio play recasts Kasperl, the popular comic hero of puppet-theater, in an unfamiliar world of invisible soundwaves. Just as children might learn certain values or models of behavior from Kasperl's past theatrical adventures, the present audience is invited to explore and learn from this new territory. Although we do not know how the audience responded to this listening exercise in 1932, we do know how Benjamin elaborated the remaining parts of the story in the published version, *Radau um Kasperl*, and that the listening experiment holds clues to approaching the complete version of the radio play.

Radau um Kasperl opens with the blaring sound of whistles and horns from a ship as the listener joins Kasperl on his way to the market to buy some flounder (GS 4.2, 674). Deafened by the noise and almost blinded by the fog, Kasperl collides with another customer, Herr Maulschmidt

DOI: 10.4324/9781003010289-6

(literally: snout-smith, muzzle-forger) – a radio announcer, it transpires, such as we have just heard in real time introducing this radio play. Thus, the opening foregrounds the invisibility of the medium of radio, which calls on both the real-time and story-time listener to envision the physical reality by acoustic means alone. Sight and sound are juxtaposed from the outset: "Können Sie denn nicht die Augen aufmachen," asks Maulschmidt; "Sperrens die Ohren doch auf!" Kasperl retorts (675). Kasperl immediately attunes his (invisible) audience to the value of listening over seeing, even during a routine errand in such an ordinary space as the market, thereby alerting us to the ubiquity of this invisible medium. Indeed, the medium of radio appears to be dubious: Its satirically named representative, Maulschmidt, craftily "forges" words with his "snout" and appears as if from nowhere. Hence Kasperl's frequent mockery and feigned naivety, as is typical of this figure in such perilous moments: "Seit wann werden denn Mäuler geschmiedet?" (675). The ambiguous tension between the potential of radio to be both instructive and menacingly dubious is what propels the remaining story.

The initial commotion caused by this sightless encounter is transformed into jubilation upon Maulschmidt's discovery of Kasperl's identity, which he is challenged to assemble from a few audible clues. The triumphant Maulschmidt, realizing the value of finally meeting this "experienced, famous friend of children," now tries to enlist Kasperl in a radio show (676). Uneasy about this prospect, however, Kasperl attempts to pun his way out of the situation by pointing to the danger of *Funken* (both "radio" and "sparks"), and to his fear *vor lauter Stille* (of "sheer" and "loud" silence) at the radio station, wittily underscoring the menacing ambiguity of radio. Once they reach the ominous-looking radio station – Maulschmidt's "radio palace" is Kasperl's "beastly box" (677) – Kasperl nevertheless seizes this opportunity to communicate with the entire world, just because he can. He does not do as he is told, however, cursing on the radio to level with his friend Seppl, who is likely listening. His prank causes much *Radau* (both "ado" and "hubbub") – and sparks (*Funken*) do indeed fly: "Haltet ihn! Tot oder lebendig ... Türenschlagen, Scheppern von Scherben. Neues Telefonläuten. Dazwischen Autohupen. Rufe: Da vorn! Um die Ecke!" as the radio representatives chase after him (679). With and through Kasperl, we discover the ominous and omnipresent threat of the radio, the invisible means of production, and its potential for manipulation and control, all of which Kasperl attempts to elude through his usual verbal wit and clever word play.

In tune with a typical comic structure (see ch. 3), the play ends with an inversion, albeit an unfortunate one. Maulschmidt's unrelenting pursuit of Kasperl leads us to the train station, the fairground, and the zoo. Along the way, Kasperl outwits, mocks, or insults various figures of authority, until he finally returns home to his wife, Puschi. Here, we witness him waking up in his bed, wounded yet confident in the belief of having shaken off

Maulschmidt and his radio team. He now tells Puschi of his plan to retaliate against the mighty Maulschmidt by breaking all twelve of his ribs with a cart and by singing a song about the entire episode in public (293). Unbeknown to Kasperl, however, Maulschmidt has already installed a microphone in his bedroom and recorded everything – including his planned revenge on Maulschmidt – for which Kasperl is compensated with a thousand marks. Even Kasperl, typically revered for his ability to outwit the authorities, as we have just seen, is now himself outwitted by the radio station – the ultimate negative inversion. Hence Maulschmidt's stinging riposte: "Wer zuletzt lacht, lacht am besten" (694).

As we accompany Kasperl on his escapade, we witness the interaction between the medium of radio (Maulschmidt) and the audience (Kasperl) that produces it. Audible throughout is the significance of listening: Kasperl remarks continuously on what he hears, rather than what he sees, in order to understand his surroundings. But what of this unfortunate ending, in which Kasperl's keen ears are now subjected to a secret recording of his own verbal rant? When he, who has attempted to escape from the radio station all along, becomes the unwitting producer of a recording about escaping the radio? What are we to learn from Kasperl, whose infamous childlike pranks would have typically helped him eluding the authorities? Whereas Kasperl's pranks would typically save him in the theater, it no longer guarantees his escape within the realm of this new acoustic medium.

At the very least, Kasperl's "hubbub" would appear to serve as a kind of cautionary tale, one associated less with the coarse disciplinary Kasperl of the early nineteenth century (such as the *Suppen-Kaspar* of Heinrich Hoffmann's *Struwwelpeter* stories) than with the more constructive role-model of the early twentieth century (Rothe 10–2). Understood in this way, the two versions of the radio play suggest two interpretive outcomes, both negative and positive. On the one hand, it serves to warn its audience of the potential dangers of this new mass media, portrayed as either a very dark or invisible power, capable of doing damage (*Funken*) and that invades every space, that manipulates – or "forges" (Maulschmidt) – words without consent, rendering even the most private conversation (in bed) publicly available (radio). In short, Kasperl introduces us to the technical reality of secret acoustic surveillance. On the other hand, it primes its audience in participatory, judicious, and creative listening and encourages all voices to be heard – and perhaps even rewarded, just like Benjamin's young listeners. The fact that Kasperl is also rewarded, albeit for his inadvertent contribution to radio, suggests nonetheless that one should remain mindful of the potential dangers of the medium's omnipresence.

Taken together, the initial experimental broadcast and the complete version offer a multitude of pedagogical implications, both in terms of effective listening strategies generally, and in approaching the radio play specifically. Both radio scripts, which represent just a small portion of Benjamin's engagement with the medium, are instructive and relevant for both the foreign-language student and the instructor. First, Benjamin's experiment counteracts the audience's "barbaric" tendency to surrender its creative and critical faculties, to hear passively rather than listen critically. By inviting the audience to co-construct Kasperl's story from acoustic signs, he envisions an alternative pedagogy, one that emerges dynamically through experiment and practice and in interaction with the recipient. While Benjamin is focusing on the specific technical conditions of the medium, his pedagogical proposals are consistent with listening strategies that promote second-language acquisition. Furthermore, the practical application of his radio and educational theory anticipates the kind of performative teaching and learning described by Manfred Schewe (see ch. 1).

Key in this educational perspective is Benjamin's rejection of a unidirectional practice of pedagogy and radio that turns its recipients into passive consumers. In his "Reflexionen zum Rundfunk" (GS 2, 1506–7), Benjamin calls upon radio to resist further advancement of the "consumer mentality" of the modern age, which has converted us into "dull, inarticulate masses ... that has neither a yardstick for its judgments nor a language for its feelings," and thus has become "quite helpless, quite inexpert in its critical reactions, and has seen itself more or less reduced to sabotage (switching off [*das Abschalten*])" (GS 2, 1506). Rather than mesmerizing (*fesseln*) listeners, Benjamin argues, radio must reverse the hypnotic tide by taking advantage of its own technology "to create in the public a new expertise" (GS 2, 1506). Radio must therefore fulfil its potential by enabling precisely the kind of interactivity – and creative listening – that his *Kasperl*-radio experiment invites. One hears echoes of Brecht, whose epic theater similarly aims to cultivate active rather than passive modes of spectatorship – hence his distinction between seeing (*sehen*) and gazing vacantly (*stieren*) (BFA 7, 112). Indeed, Brecht rejected the idea of radio as a one-sided form of mere distribution and sought instead to repurpose it as a communicative, interactive, and ultimately educative tool (see also Huwiler 47). Equally cautious regarding the "dubiousness" of radio as a one-sided, unidirectional and therefore "inconsequential" apparatus – "der Rundfunk [hat] eine Seite, wo er zwei haben müsste" – Brecht hopes to bring listeners out of their isolation and into a relationship with radio (BDA 24, 553). Moreover, his listeners should not only be trained (*belehrt werden*), but also trained to become teachers (*sondern auch belehren*) – in other words, to be transformed through the medium of radio into active agents for change (BDA 24, 555).

Tun ist besser als fühlen

In his explanation of *Der Flug der Lindberghs*, a *Radiolehrstück* for children and conceived as a practical application of his theory, Brecht outlines his pedagogical guidelines for the radio. His motto for this radio play, "doing is better than feeling," was placed visibly on the stage at the 1929 Baden-Baden Musikwoche, where a live theatrical performance of the radio play took place (*Versuche* 1, 17). For this pedagogical exercise, Brecht instructed the audience to adopt the role of the aviator – the part formerly reserved for Lindbergh alone, but later redacted by Brecht on account of Lindbergh's Nazi sympathies. Brecht had also retitled the radio play *Der Ozeanflug* and redacted any reference to Lindbergh altogether, converting any notion of individualistic heroism into a generalized function, and Lindbergh into "the pilots" [*die Flieger*], which were played by the audience in a collective performance.[1] In this way, Brecht proposed to democratize radio and transform the radio play from a form of entertainment into a participatory object of instruction. Like Benjamin, Brecht sought to exploit the possibilities of radio – at least theoretically – as an artistic medium in its own right, rather than merely a means for remediation, and to make transparent the means to its production. By arranging the orchestra, actors, titles, and technical apparatus visibly on stage, Brecht exposed the individual elements of its production in a way comparable to his epic theater: "ihre Trennung der Elemente, also des Bildes vom Wort und der Wörter von der Musik, besonders aber ihre belehrende Haltung, hätte für den Rundfunk eine Unmenge praktischer Winke" (BDA 24, 556).

The "practical hints" proposed by both Brecht and Benjamin are of significant pedagogical import for the foreign-language classroom. Both invite their listeners into a kind of "dialogical imagination" with the acoustic text, to discern distinct sounds – voices, sounds, noise, music – and to become part of the text; both propose an interactive approach, transforming listeners from passive recipients into active participants, collaborators, even teachers and producers; both democratize the radio, equalizing participation so that all voices may be heard; and both encourage critical listening skills capable of interrogating not only the text but also the medium itself. All of these practical hints resonate with strategies for developing listening proficiency as well as in critical interpretive skills. Indeed, both Benjamin's and Brecht's experimental radio plays have the twofold advantage of modelling listening strategies in active, critical listening and in approaching the radio play as a genre.

While not entirely neglected, the potential benefits of the *Hörspiel* for the foreign-language classroom have nevertheless remained underexploited, especially in recent years. A notable exception is Kita and Eley's ingenious treatment of Heinrich Böll's *Doktor Murkes gesammeltes Schweigen* in a module that ventures beyond surface-level comprehension to include a critical understanding of the role of radio in postwar *Vergangenheitsbewältigung* (Kita and Eley). Another exception, albeit not strictly an example of radio, is a collaborative performance of Brecht's *Ozeanflug* by the Departments of German and Theatre at Northwestern University (Lys et al.). One reason for the relative dearth in this area relates to the general neglect of listening skills until relatively recently, subordinated to speaking (Nunan 238) and decoupled from interactional competence altogether. Moreover, the transience of the medium has posed an obstacle of its own: Original broadcasts are often difficult to gain access to, even if they were recorded (which many were not), and not even all the typescripts are complete with extralinguistic directions. Benjamin's *Kasperl* typescripts, which were seized by the Gestapo shortly after Benjamin's suicide in 1940, but later rescued in 1945 and transported via the Soviet Union and East Germany to the literary archives of the Berlin Kunstakademie, are a case in point (Caselli 459). Of the numerous broadcasts from his broadcasting years (1927–1933), Benjamin's *Kasperl* radio play is the only one from which a recorded fragment has survived. Nevertheless, the play has been re-recorded in its entirety and made available on the Internet, where one has access to a multitude of contemporary radio plays and podcasts in any language.

Taking my cue from both Benjamin and Brecht, the following outlines a series of *Hörmodelle* – listening models – for approaching different radio plays in the spirit in which Benjamin and Brecht conceived them: as exercises in active, critical listening that transforms foreign-language learners into co-constructors and, ultimately, into producers of their own radio texts. In other words, I take the *Hörspiel* almost literally, as a "listening play" that makes room for play with listening. By exploiting listening in its myriad functions, learners develop critical and active listening skills that are also integral to a wide range of interactions, from general conversation and routine transactions to classroom instruction, interviews, games, and other negotiations – in other words, as a communicative act. These listening models may be taught independently or, in the larger context of a module or even an entire course on the *Hörspiel*, in conjunction with each other. The first of these serves two purposes: to attune students to the genre and to the technical apparatus of the *Hörspiel*, and to introduce the history of the radio play since its inception in Germany during the Weimar period and its (mis) use as a mass propaganda medium during the Third Reich and beyond – a danger anticipated by both Benjamin and Brecht, and upon which Böll consequently reflects (Kita and Eley 69–70). The second and third models focus on interactive and critical listening, and on discrete linguistic aspects as well as tone and register. Guided by Benjamin's and Brecht's proposals for participatory radio and "learning by doing," these models culminate in creative application.

Tuning into the Hörspiel

A brief introduction to the near-century-long history of German-language radio begins in 1924 with Hans Flesch's *Zauberei auf dem Sender* – a *Rundfunkspielgroteske*. Although the original broadcast was not recorded, a recording by the Hessischer Rudfunk from 1962 is readily available along with the script (see Resources). This 17-minute radio play serves to attune listeners to the first sound experiment in radio, to the magical aura as well as the fear surrounding this new, ethereal medium. First, students peruse the cast comprising all aspects of a live radio broadcast, from the Artistic Director

(Dr. Hans Flesch himself) and the Announcer to the technicians, and members of the orchestra. Anticipating both Brecht and Benjamin, Flesch makes audible the entire apparatus in a montage of different sounds and sources, dramatizing the distinct technical and organizational layers of the medium – its sounds, voices, transmission apparatus, and programming – as competing entities jostling for control. This is a radio play of and about the making (and unmaking) of a radio program: What begins as a routine programmed broadcast declines into pandemonium, not unlike Kasperl's hubbub. Various technical issues and uninvited guests interrupt the programmed music broadcast: the *Märchentante* who interrupts the artistic director to tell a fairy tale; the telephone that interrupts the *Märchentante*; the *Zauberer* who mysteriously emerges to conjure up chaos; extraneous noises, and so on. The cacophonous broadcasting station goes "crazy" (*ver-rückt*, further underscoring the medium's "dislocation" – its removal from a defined space). Flesch uses radio self-reflexively to tell the story and theory of an emerging medium, exemplifying both its technical (or magical) promise and the broader concerns that it raises: How does radio work? From where do these sounds originate? Who is authorized to speak? Who controls programming? What happens if we lose control, if it gets into the wrong hands, or perhaps worse still, if the technology assumes a life of its own? And, finally, is radio merely a medium of reproduction of extant artistic forms, or an artistic medium in its own right – *eine rundfunkeigentümliche Kunstgattung* (Flesch *Magic* 15)?

Visualizing acoustics

The opening two minutes of the radio play suffice to introduce core vocabulary of the radio, its transmission and reception technology, the station, the airwaves, and its operation: *Der Rundfunk, der Funk; der Sender, senden, die Welle, das Mikrophon einschalten, ausschalten; stören; der Schalter, abstellen; der Ansager, ansagen, einhängen.* Focusing as a next step on the formal aspects of the radio play – *Stimmen, Laute, Töne, Geräusche, Musik* – listeners determine the exact sources of each sound heard during the first six minutes of the play: whispered asides, radio announcements, orchestral music, telephone ringing, sirens, a kettledrum, a whistle, a distant but resounding voice, a fairytale, breaking news, a violin, a female singer with orchestral accompaniment, a drum roll, and pouring water.

Comprehension checks

"Was haben Sie gehört?" asks the Artistic Director, audibly unsettled by the constant interruptions and an unidentifiable voice during the programmed broadcast. This prompts a suitable opportunity to check comprehension. Pausing here (04:30), students have the opportunity to compare their notes with the summary provided in the ensuing dialogue, as well as to discuss extralinguistic details such as voice types (*reden, sprechen, rufen, flüstern, singen, schreien*), vocal volume, register, and timbre (*tief, hoh, laut, stark, machtvoll, leise, rauchig, volltönend, grell*) and affective tone (*ruhig, beruhigend, verwirrt, entnervt, entspannt, ungeduldig, irritiert, unheimlich*). Attention needs to be drawn to the function of the interruptions and to the question of radio broadcast control. One answer is suggested by an unidentified intruder, prompted by a kettledrum: "Jeder macht, was ihm gefällt. Der Sender ist verrückt geworden!," directly contradicting the Artistic Director and throwing the broadcast into further chaos. In struggling to identify and locate the unknown voice, we join contemporary listeners in wonder of the mysterious workings of radio. Hence the Artistic Director's growing unease about the inexplicable voices and sounds: "Wer hat denn den Leuten gesagt, dass sie spielen sollen?" (04:40). Various acoustic clues reveal physical symptoms of the Director's unease: his broken utterances, his sudden need for water, the breaking of the glass (06:16), which he drops when he is spooked by the mysterious music that nobody else can hear.

Filling the silence

Having established the central themes and conflicts, it is worth unpacking the chaos a little further. As a gap-filling task, students listen very carefully to the telephone call (beginning at 01:35) and work in pairs to imagine the other (inaudible) side of the conversation, presenting it as a brief dialogue. The telephone call comes from a member of the listening public who complains that he is not getting his money's worth in this disorderly broadcast. This detail points to the fact that listeners had to pay a monthly license fee of two Marks for radio service during the Weimar period (Flesch *Magic* 30), indicating the mutually dependent relationship between radio broadcasters and receivers, operators and consumers, innovation and regulation. Such a relationship introduces questions about the purpose of radio as a pleasant distraction from the burdens of everyday life, on the one hand, and as an intellectually stimulating, interactive artform, on the other – or as a combination of both. The former would essentially substitute (and remediate) already existing forms of entertainment such as the concert or theater; the latter would forge a new specifically radiophonic artistic form that acknowledges its mediating technology (Gilfillan 52–4). Complicating these considerations is the development of radio regulation within a complex history of competing forces and ideologies: Tensions emerged during the transition from its military control during WWI and the democratizing forces of the Weimar Republic, necessitating greater regulation, including a ban of private radio reception for a short period in 1922 – tensions that would continue through the Third Reich and the post-WWII period (Gilfillan 29–31).

As a brief but concrete illustration of the early stages and development of radio in Germany, these opening few minutes provide numerous points of entry for thinking about radio, the relationship between the genre and technology, and between public regulation and private listening. If the instructor chooses, these initial tensions may be further teased out in the remaining 12 minutes of the play, which may either be set for independent listening or completed in class: *Warum kehrt der Zauberer zurück? Was passiert, nachdem der Zauberer zurückkehrt? Welches Stück soll gespielt werden und was passiert? Was sind die Funktionen der Märchentante und des Zauberers? Wer oder was "gewinnt" schließlich im Radiospiel?* The remainder of the play centers on the role of the magician, who reenters to exact revenge on the radio station for not having entertained his magical powers previously: Under his spell, the performance of Johann Strauss' popular crowd-pleaser *An der schönen blauen Donau* is turned into a cacophonic funeral march. Disorder has prevailed – that is, until the Artistic Director manages to call on the general "will" in order to show who is stronger and reinstate order. As the recorded reading from a review summarizes: "Ernsthaftes Wollen hat den Spuk besiegt" (19:00). Thus, the role of the magician serves to highlight the tensions between order and disorder, control and chaos, conformity and innovation, reason and irrationality, location and dislocation. These are underscored by the literal and mental "derangement" (*gestört, verrückt*) of the radio station and the Artistic Director.

As a whole, the radio play invites listeners to explore radio innovation, its inner workings, its layers of acoustic montage, and the social-political background, while raising concerns about the control and purpose of the radio broadcast. Fears of control and interference, associated here with magic, are also grounded in a reality that would soon be handed to Reich Minister of Propaganda Joseph Goebbels, who reclaimed radio as a "Masseninstrument der Propaganda, das man in seiner Wirksamkeit heute noch gar nicht abschätzen kann" (Hagen 428). Its potency would ultimately be optimized and exploited by the National Socialists from 1933, when the *Volksempfänger* was made widely available and affordable for German-only stations. As an exploration in innovation, Flesch's play purposely interrupts the year-long tradition of broadcasting live classical concerts, ending with a performance by the Armed Forces Orchestra of "Deutschland, Deutschland über alles" (Koch and Glaser). In doing so, Flesch attempts to accomplish something entirely different from theater, the concert, or the cinema, and in a way that invites critical engagement of the audience.

This introduction to the genre and historical context may be developed further in conjunction with Benjamin's *Kasperl*-radio play, whose themes, theoretical concerns and approach are consonant with those of Hans Flesch. Another suitable pairing is Orson Welles' radio production of *War of the Worlds* (1939), with which many students will already be familiar. This production also staged an interruption of a broadcast but, quite in contrast to Benjamin and Flesch's critical listening, in such a way as to dupe its audience into falling for the fake newsflash of an alien landing. One possible approach involves pairing Flesch's radio play with Benjamin's completed

Radau um Kasperl for further listening and analysis, using the original script (the listening game) to prepare students for the listening. Another approach for more advanced learners involves exploiting the original listening game, *Kasperl und der Rundfunk, eine Geschichte mit Lärm,* taking students to the next level in co-constructing a text.

Sonic storytelling

Because the original broadcast was not recorded, the following exercise is based on the script of Benjamin's original broadcast of *Kasperl und der Rundfunk, eine Geschichte mit Lärm* (GS 7, 832–5). Its brevity (four pages), relative simplicity (as a game suitable for German children), and ready-made listening instructions for an authentic text make it a suitable exercise for foreign-language learners.

Anyone who has already used the *Hörspiel* in the classroom will have already noted the practicality of a narrative point of departure for student scripts, both for foreign and native speakers. Some have already proposed using short stories, fairytales, or theater plays as a basis for student transformations from prose to drama, or vice versa (Deubel; Kita and Eley; Koepke; Thomas). This enables students to focus entirely on spoken expression, which must carry the weight of meaning for the plot, character, social standing and relationships. Special attention needs to be paid to aspects of register (vocabulary, syntax, grammar) and tone, and is therefore more suited to intermediate-high and advanced language courses.

To begin, it is helpful to introduce the character of Kasperl stories in his various incarnations. Many students will already be familiar with Heinrich Hoffmann's *Struwwelpeter* stories, but less so with other versions. A brief introduction to Kasperl as a popular puppet figure who generally outwits the authorities, along with other characters such as his wife Puschi, his friend Seppl, and incarnations of the Devil, would suffice to establish expectations: the lessons in overcoming evil forces with the kinds of virtues commonly promoted in the children's fairytales.

As a next step, the instructor reads the original radio announcement that includes the offer of a prize for the best version submitted by a listener. If further motivation is desired, one potential prize is a full class performance and recording of best version by student vote. Depending on the size of the group, students may work in pairs or in small groups to complete the announced task of co-constructing the radio play.

Conceived primarily for children, but also with an older audience in mind, the childlike creativity, humor, and relative linguistic simplicity make it a productive basis for creative exploration. During class, students can begin to flesh out the opening narrative as a dialogue:

> Kasperl ist von seiner Frau Puschi auf den Markt geschickt worden, um einen Fisch einzukaufen. Er tritt auf, die Weisungen seiner Frau, damit er sie

nicht vergißt, immerzu vor sich hinsprechend: Wie lang der Fisch sein soll, wie schwer, wieviel er kosten soll, vor allem aber, daß er sich unterwegs nicht aufhalten darf, da sie ihn schnell braucht; daß er sich sputen muß. Während Kasperl noch so vor sich hin memoriert, kommen nacheinander: eine Frau, die ihn bittet, ihr den Marktkorb zu tragen, natürlich will sie was dafür bezahlen; ein junges Mädchen, das ihn bittet, ihr ihren Hund zu halten; ein Soldat, der ihm einen Brief geben will, den er in den Postkasten werfen soll – Kasperl aber bleibt standhaft, lehnt alles ab, denkt immer nur an den Fisch. Wie er nun gerade mit dem Fischweib verhandelt, kommt der SPRECHER dazu. Beide wollen denselben Fisch kaufen, kommen so miteinander in Streit. Wie sie aber währenddessen voneinander erfahren, wer sie sind, wird der Sprecher auf einmal sehr liebenswürdig.... (GS 7.2, 833)

Even though all the narrative cues are provided, students still need to decide what and how to realize acoustically, and what kind of expression and tone can be gleaned from the text. Focusing first on this short passage, students discuss the many possibilities in small groups and share them in full class. To follow up, students may listen to the opening of the available recording of the full radio play, though this might pose a challenge for those unfamiliar with the southern Bavarian dialect. As with all listening exercises, it is necessary to listen to the text at least twice.

In transforming the remaining text into a radio play, it suffices to select some (but preferably not all) parts of the ensuing *Radau* – the episodes of hubbub unleashed by Kasperl on and around the radio. Referring back to the preparatory listening exercises (Flesch's *Zauberei*), students need to consider how they will realize audibly any changes in place, time, character, and situation, marking these up in their own scripts. (Further practical guidelines for a collaborative *Hörspiel* project are outlined in Appendix A.)

Critical framing and creative adaptation

While Benjamin's *Kasperl* play exists both as incomplete experiment and finished version, many other radio plays are conceived for the radio as well as for other media. For example, Brecht's *Der Ozeanflug* has survived primarily as a theater play; Borchert's *Draußen vor der Tür* was first conceived as a theater play, then a radio play, rewritten for theater, and then for cinema (see ch. 4); Vicki Baum's *Menschen im Hotel* appeared as a novel (1929), as films (1932 and 1959) and as a radio play (1958); Böll's *Dr. Murkes gesammeltes Schweigen* (1955) was first written as a short story (see also Kita and Eley); and Jelinek's *Am Königsweg* is conceived both as a theater play and as a radio play – among many more that are accessible in their various forms today. A side-by-side comparison has the advantage of cultivating critical insight into the different ways in which meaning is created and re-created. While each adaptation generally aims to preserve the meaning and spirit of the original, each medium and genre works within a certain set of communication conventions that become transparent when juxtaposed with another genre. Recognizing different symbolic and linguistic modes of expression across different genres and media provides a "critical framing" (Kern 204) for students to engage in the creative process themselves (see also ch. 5). Kita and Eley have described such a model for working with Böll's *Dr. Murkes gesammeltes Schweigen* both as a short story and a radio play, and in preparation for undertaking their own adaptation of a short story (Kita and Eley 75). By providing such a narrative scaffold, students are relieved of an additional cognitive and linguistic burden to indulge more freely in creative language play while further developing their communicative competence.

Sounding out the *Hörspiel*

One of the positive outcomes of the early radio and sound experiments of Benjamin, Brecht, Flesch – among many others – has been their further development and realization in postwar Germany. Building on these cutting-edge foundations, the *Hörspiel* has continued to flourish, especially in Germany, where both regional and national radio stations continue to broadcast new radio plays. Many of these plays are broadcast on the radio and made available via radio websites and podcasts for download. Several sub-genres have meanwhile developed, especially through the experiments of the 1960s' *Neues Hörspiel*, ranging from narrative to post-dramatic radio productions and sound-art. An estimated 300 radio plays are produced every year – in other words, one almost every day – in what Stefan Fischer calls "the biggest radio-play scene in the world." Since 2019, when Germany marked 95 years of radio history, *Berliner Hörspielnächte* have been celebrating a radio revival online and as communal outdoor events. During the pandemic of 2020–21, as live performance events remained on hold and theater companies turned to radio to reach their audience, radio plays, podcasts, and other forms of streaming-media entertainment saw audience growth (OECD), becoming "comfort food" of spatial and social isolation. The feasibility of overcoming "spatial isolation" (*räumliche Isoliertheit*) was already recognized by media theorist Rudolf Arnheim in 1930 as the "great miracle [*Wunder*] of radio" (Arnheim 11). A different kind of spatial and social isolation forms the motive for Mariana Leky's *Der Aufzug* (2013), a more recent and relatively straightforward narrative radio play that serves in what follows as a basis for intensive listening and for creative story completion.

Mariana Leky: *Der Aufzug*

The premise of Leky's *Der Aufzug* is relatively straightforward: Astrid, a young hypochondriac who suffers from claustrophobia, among many other things, decides to try to visit her doctor before the weekend. As she tries to compose herself on the way up to the doctor's office, she gets stranded in the lift with an irritated, rather aggressive doctor, who is equally harried due to impending appointments. The uncomfortable situation is exacerbated by their clashing personalities and escalates further as their repeated attempts to escape from the lift fail: The emergency button (*Notfallknopf*) does not work properly, and her mobile phone is not getting a signal. Once the play has divulged everything the listener needs to know about the characters, their personalities, and the conflict (09:27), the instructor prompts the students to resolve the conflict. The resolution, however, is much less straightforward than the premise: How does their personality conflict develop? Do they get out of the lift and, if so, how?

The introductory lesson is dedicated to the play's first 25 seconds only, which establishes the main character and motivation. This involves intensive and recursive listening, as the main character's rapid speech, which underscores her general anxiety, is at times difficult to decipher. Students begin by focusing on determining the place and situation, and thus on what is heard rather than what is said: *Wo spielt sich die Szene ab? Wie wissen wir das? Was hören Sie (Stimme, Geräusche, Töne, Klänge)?* The instructor helps students fill in their vocabulary gaps during the ensuing discussion of the identified sounds: *das Klirren (der Schlüssel), Tappen, Fußtritte, Telefonklingel, Anrufbeantworter, Türenschließen.*

Next, we focus on the characterization of the protagonist – on what is said and how as she prepares to leave her apartment, listening for the acoustic clues to her nervous energy: her rapid, broken utterances, her frustration about a misplaced bag, the dropping of keys, double-checking for her keys and medical card before she leaves. In a third (and possibly a fourth) repetition, students should try to discern the message left on the answering machine, in which she explains that Holger – presumably her partner – is away on business and that she is most likely visiting the doctor. These details suffice to summarize character and theme: *Was wissen wir über die Hauptfigur (Lebenssituation, Persönlichkeit)? Wie wissen wir das? Fassen Sie die Situation kurz zusammen!*

Following the introductory lesson, students listen to the next nine minutes (00:38 to 9:27) individually at home, paying attention to the following:

1. *Was lernen wir über die Frau? Welchen Eindruck macht sie und warum? Worüber redet sie in ihrem Selbstgespräch? Was scheint ihr Problem zu sein? Schreiben Sie wichtige Wörter und Phrasen auf!*
2. *Wem begegnet sie im Aufzug? Was wissen wir über diese Person? Was für einen Eindruck macht sie? Wie geht sie mit der Frau um? Wie drückt sie sich aus? (Schreiben Sie Beispiele auf!)*
3. *Was passiert im Aufzug? Fassen Sie die Konfliktsituation zusammen!*
4. *Wo befindet sich der Aufzug?*
5. *Wie versuchen die Figuren, sich aus dieser Situation herauszuretten? Was*

macht die Situation noch schwieriger? Was funktioniert nicht und aus welchem Grund?

6.   *Beschreiben Sie den Konflikt, der zwischen den zwei Personen im Aufzug entsteht!*

Answers to these questions supply essential information for the continuation of the story. Not only the central problem of being stuck in the lift, but also the personal conflict that develops between the two personalities needs to be resolved. Time should be reserved to broach individual comprehension difficulties, such as the occasional indecipherable phrase or word, before continuing to discuss details of expression, diction, tone, and intonation.

Fine tuning

The following presumes that students are at least somewhat familiar with stylistic features of spoken discourse in German. The relative syntactical simplicity of natural spoken discourse (in German, *Verbalstil*) is counterbalanced somewhat by other features that pose their own challenges: dialect, elisions and ellipses, contractions, idioms and colloquialisms, varying stress and intonation, and, perhaps most importantly, modal (or flavoring) particles (*Abtönungspartikeln*). As *planned* speech that resembles spoken discourse, and with the option of repeated listening, however, the radio play mitigates some of the greater challenges of natural everyday oral speech. Nevertheless, because modal particles are as significant as intonation in expressing subject position, emotion, and attitude towards the addressee, these deserve additional attention. Presuming that the next class follows more than one day later, students would preferably prepare the following exercise before class discussion; otherwise, the instructor should reserve ample time to do so during the next class:

Pragmatische Untersuchungen:

Komm schon!
… ist schon gut.
… doch eben gerade …
… vielleicht doch mal …
Also gut.
Das haben wir ja!
Hör'n Sie mal!
Das gibt's doch nicht, das ist doch, ich meine …
Haben Sie denn keine?
Irgendwie eben.

1.   *Welche Phrasen hören Sie? Wer sagt sie? In welchen Situationen kommen diese Phrasen mit Abtönungspartikeln vor?*

2.   *Was wird durch die Partikeln an den Ton der jeweiligen Sätze geändert?
     Was drücken sie möglicherweise aus? (interessiert, ungeduldig,
     überrascht, freundlich, unfreundlich, resigniert, bedrohlich, ermunternd,
     verärgert, entrüstet, kritisch, warnend, bejahend, widerspruchsvoll?)*
3.   *Hören Sie sich den Text noch mal an und unterstreichen Sie die betonten
     Wörter!*

In-class discussion is dedicated to expressive nuances. Students compare
and correct their answers with each other, and exchange ideas about how
stress and intonation modify the meaning or tone – for example, from an
unstressed but impatient or imploring *doch* to a stressed and therefore
contradictory *doch!* Although such details are challenging for most students
and can be time-consuming, it is well worth the additional attention if they
are to fine-tune their understanding of the characters' interactions. Just as
her *schon* flavors the *komm (schon)* with impatience, so does the doctor's use
of *doch eben gerade* add exasperation to an otherwise neutral request to be
more cautious: "Ich habe Sie [doch eben gerade] gebeten..." followed by a
brief *also gut* to indicate eventual conciliation. Students should listen to
these utterances at least once more in class, marking and imitating intonation and stress in preparation for an exercise that puts these into practice.
They then select some of these phrases and incorporate them, with stresses
underlined, into short *Streitgespräche* of their own to check
comprehension. More attention to stress is valuable due to the common
tendency of learners to emphasize the particles rather than the verb, which,
except in the case of a contradictory *doch*, generally occurs infrequently.

As a final stage, students work in pairs or threes to deliberate possible
endings for the story. They are prompted to consider all the points of
conflict and character details, paying special attention to their expressive
features, and draft a plot outline for the ensuing class session. This should be
submitted in a short paragraph before they begin drafting the dialogue. This
exercise, for which further guidelines are suggested in Appendix A, requires
sufficient time for additional recursive listening and writing, incorporation
of appropriate particles, sound effects, and fine-tuning before rehearsals
begin in preparation for a recording.

The interactive *Hörspiel*

Radio plays are to be heard, and thus the final product, written and
produced in collaboration, is ideally presented to the rest of the class.
To resume the role of passive recipient, however, would tempt students
to tune out, but more importantly, would defeat the purpose of active,
critical listening cultivated in the *Hörspiel* exercise. "Der Rundfunk
muss den Austausch ermöglichen," Brecht reminds us (Brecht BDA 24,
554). Heeding Brecht's and Benjamin's theoretical aspirations for participatory radio, which remained only theoretical during their time
(Huwiler 47), it is possible to exploit today's technology for the

purposes of transforming the medium into an interactive tool and student listening into a communicative exercise. Students are prompted to note what they hear and identify characters, place, and plot, building on the preparatory listening exercises (see Appendix B). Additional evaluative comments may be incorporated and, using one of the many technological resources available through course content managements systems (or other platforms such as VoiceThread and YouTube), students may annotate specific moments of the audio as they would in a social-media platform. In this way, students react and interact with their peers while also pointing out moments that might need further refinement – or indeed further room for *Hör-Spiel*.

Note

1 These redactions are included in the version reprinted in Brecht's *Versuche*, vol. 1–4.

Further reading and resources

Recordings of Hörspiel

Benjamin, Walter. *Radau um Kasperl. Gesammelte Schriften*. Rolf Tiedemann and Hermann Schweppenhäuser, eds. Suhrkamp, 1972, 677–678.
Benjamin, Walter. *Radau um Kasperl*. SWR2/MDR Hörspiel, 2018. Retrieved from https://www.podchaser.com/podcasts/swr2-horspiel-465439/episodes/radau-um-kasperl-walter-benjam-35205097
Brecht, Bertolt. "Der Ozeanflug. Radiolehrstück für Knaben und Mädchen." *Versuche*, vol. 1–4. Berlin: G. Kiepenheuer, 1930.
Flesch, Hans. *Zauberei auf dem Sender*. New recording of the Hessischer Rundfunk, 1962, reproduced by the Landesmedienzentrum Baden-Württemberg: https://www.lmz-bw.de/medien-und-bildung/medienwissen/audio/hoerspiel/zauberei-auf-dem-sender/

Current Hörspiel broadcasting and resources

Deutschlandfunk: https://www.deutschlandfunkkultur.de/dlf-hoerspiel.3047.de.html
Österreichische Mediathek: https://www.mediathek.at
Radio stations: http://www.hoerspiel.com/radio-sender-hoerspiel/
Schweizer Radio und Fernsehen: https://www.srf.ch/sendungen/hoerspiel/uebersicht

On the history of the German-language Hörspiel

Flesch, Hans, et al. "Magic on the Air: Attempt at a Radio Grotesque." *Cultural Critique*, vol. 91, no. 91, 2015, 14–31.
For a succinct introduction, visit the Landesmedienzentrum Baden-Württemberg: https://www.lmz-bw.de/medien-und-bildung/medienwissen/audio/hoerspiel/hoer-spielgeschichte/

For more detail, visit the Deutsches Rundfunkarchiv: https://www.dra.de/
Gilfillan, Daniel. *Pieces of Sound: German Experimental Radio*. Minneapolis: Minnesota UP, 2009.

On radio theory

Arnheim, Rudolf. *Rundfunk als Hörkunst*. Hanser, 1979.
Brecht, Bertolt. "Der Rundfunk als Kommunikationsapparat. Rede über die Funktion des Rundfunks." *Werke*. Große kommentierte Berliner und Frankfurter Ausgabe, vol. 21, Frankfurt am Main, 1992, 552–557.
Brecht, Bertolt. "Erläuterungen zum "Ozeanflug." *Werke*. Große kommentierte Berliner und Frankfurter Ausgabe, vol. 24, Frankfurt am Main, 1992, 87–89.

References

Arnheim, Rudolf. *Rundfunk als Hörkunst*. Munich: Hanser, 1979.
Benjamin, Walter. *Gesammelte Schriften*, 7 vols. Rolf Tiedemann and Hermann Schweppenhäuser, ed. Suhrkamp, 1972–1989.
Bertolt Brecht. *Große kommentierte Berliner und Frankfurter Ausgabe*, 30 vols. Werner Hecht et al., ed. Frankfurt am Main: Suhrkamp, 1988–2000.
Buck-Morss, Susan. "'Verehrte Unsichtbare!': Walter Benjamins Radiovorträge." *Walter Benjamin und die Kinderliteratur: Aspekte der Kinderkultur in den Zwanziger Jahren mit dem Katalog der Kinderbuchsammlung*. Klaus Doderer, ed. Frankfurt am Main: Juventa, 1988, 93–101.
Caselli, Daniela. "Attack of the Easter Bunnies: Walter Benjamin's *Youth Hour*." *Parallax*, vol. 22, no. 4, 2016, 459–479.
Deubel, Hildegard. "Produktion von Hoerspielen im Literaturunterricht." *Deutschunterricht*, vol. 45, no. 10, 1992, 460–465.
Fischer, Stefan. "Art of the Radio Play in Germany: Look Who's Talking!" Paul McCarthy, trans. Goethe-Institut e.V., Internet-Redaktion, May 2016. https://www.goethe.de/en/kul/med/20746648.html
Flesch, Hans. "Magic on the Air: Attempt at a Radio Grotesque." *Cultural Critique*, vol. 91, no. 91, 2015, 14–31.
Flesch, Hans. "Zauberei auf dem Sender: Ein Versuch einer Rundfunkgroteske." *Zauberei auf dem Sender und andere Hörspiele*. Ulrich Lauterbach and Günther Rühle, ed. Frankfurt am Main: Verlag Waldemar Kramer, 1962.
Gilfillan, Daniel. *Pieces of Sound: German Experimental Radio*. Minneapolis: Minnesota UP, 2009.
Hagen, Wolfgang. "Akustische Medienwirkung und Medienreflexion: Invasion of Mars und Zauberei auf dem Sender." In *Handbuch Literatur & Audiokultur* Natalie Binczek and Uwe Wirth, ed. Berlin: de Gruyter, 2020, 421–433.
Huwiler, Elke. "Storytelling by Sound: A Theoretical Frame for Radio Drama Analysis." *The Radio Journal – International Studies in Broadcast and Audio Media*, vol. 3, no. 1, 2005, 45–59.
Kern, Richard. *Literacy and language teaching*. Oxford: Oxford UP, 2000.
Kita, Caroline A and Eley, Michelle R. "Cultivating Critical Listening: Hörspiele in the German Classroom." *Die Unterrichtspraxis*, vol. 52, no. 1, 2019, 69–81.

Koch, Hans J. and Glaser, Hermann. *Ganz Ohr: eine Kulturgeschichte des Radios in Deutschland.* Cologne: Böhlau, 2005.

Koepke, Wulf. "Das Hörspiel im Sprachunterricht für Fortgeschrittene." *Die Unterrichtspraxis*, vol. 2, no. 2, 1969, 1.

Lys, Franziska. "Performing Brecht: From Theory to Practice." *Body and Language: Intercultural Learning through Drama.* Gerd Bräuer, ed. Ablex, 2002, 207–231.

Nunan, David. "Listening in Language Learning." *Methodology in Language Teaching.* Jack C. Richards and Willy A. Renandya, ed. Cambridge: Cambridge UP, 2002, 238–241.

OECD. "Culture shock: COVID-19 and the cultural and creative sectors." OECD Policy Responses to Coronavirus (COVID-19). Paris: OECD Publishing. September 7, 2020. Retrieved from: https://www.oecd.org/coronavirus/policy-responses/culture-shock-covid-19-and-the-cultural-and-creative-sectors-08da9e0e/

Rothe, Katja. "Die Schule des Entzugs. Walter Benjamins Radio-Kasper." *Sinnhaft. Strategien des Entzugs*, vol. 22, no. 1, 2009, 74–89.

Schiller-Lerg, Sabine. *Walter Benjamin und der Rundfunk: Programmarbeit zwischen Theorie und Praxis.* Munich: Saur, 1984.

Thomas, Emma Lewis. "Das Märchen als Hörspiel: An Exercise in Conversation, Recitation, and Writing." *Die Unterrichtspraxis*, vol. 6, no. 1, 1973, 29–32.

Appendix A.

As with theater productions, the varying levels of ability and commitment among students makes collaborative work more challenging to assess. Should the *Hörspiel* project require a form of assessment, some practical guidelines are necessary for both the instructor and the students. The following provides some suggestions:

1. *Length*: The suggested time limit is a maximum of 8–10 minutes, especially considering the intended (peer) audience. Length also depends on the number of participants; too many participants will inevitably result in overlong scripts and unequal workload.

2. *Number of participants*: A recommended two to three collaborators on the drafting of the script. This helps not only to minimize confusion and unequal effort but also the overall length of the script. For double-spaced 12-point font scripts, the anticipated reading time amounts to approximately two minutes per page, though this may vary. Therefore, the entire script will amount to approximately 4–6 pages in total. More students may be involved in the performance and/or recording if necessary.

3. *Equal distribution of workload*: To ensure equal workload and effort, each student is responsible for one part of the script, each contributing approximately two double-spaced pages. Each will also assume responsibility for a technical aspect, from making or identifying suitable sound effects, to editing the final version.

4. *Writing tips*: Students should avoid introducing too many additional characters so as to avoid confusing plotlines that also contribute further to the length. During drafting stages, it is also advantageous to remind students of helpful clues for the listener, such as naming a person's name, including appropriate sound effects to indicate location or situation.

5. *Assessment*: Because this is an exercise in both writing and speaking, both deserve assessment, and because the recording is free from additional pressure and distractions associated with live stage performance (including nerves, line-learning, or other disruptions), room can be made for an assessment of the students' intonation, stress, and level of comprehensibility (pronunciation). However, the greater weighting of the assessment should fall on the written portion of the final product.

6. Free open-source editing software that work on all operating systems include Audacity, Ocenaudio, or Audiotool; for Mac users, Garageband.

Appendix B.

Interactive listening: Questions to prompt peer reflections and interactions:

Welche Charaktere kommen in dieser Szene vor?

Woran sind die verschiedenen Charaktere zu erkennen? (Ton, Ausdrucksweise, Dialekt?)

Ist die Szene gut verständlich?

Wie werden die Geschehnisse verdeutlicht? (Welche Stimmen, Geräusche oder Töne hören Sie?)

Beschreiben Sie die Stimmung! Wie wird diese Stimmung geschafft? (Stimme, Geräusche, Musik?)

Wie endet die Geschichte? Was haben Sie nicht verstanden? Wie könnte man die Geschehnisse deutlicher darstellen?

7 *Endspiel*: teaching contemporary transcultural and post-migrant theater

Table 7.1

Premiere	Duisberg, 2. December, 2010; since 2010, small black-box space, primarily in the Ballhaus Naunynstraße, Berlin-Kreuzberg
Pages	65
Performance Length	Approx. 1 hour
Cast	3 females, 5 males; all but one with a migrant background
Set	Set entirely in a classroom
Language	Mostly current colloquial German and teenage slang with profuse vulgarities; simple syntax, short sentences or phrases and much repetition; some literary language from Schiller; some code-switching with Turkish and Arabic.
Topic and Complexity	Politics of migration, integration, racism, stereotypes; post-migrant theater; transculturality; stereotypes, deconstruction of identity; German educational system; Enlightenment, *Sturm und Drang*, Friedrich Schiller; Christianity, Islam; drama pedagogy as theme.
Potential challenges	Obscene language and some gestures might be offensive and might require editing in certain educational contexts; not suitable for high schools; references to dramas by Schiller require additional time for explanation and/or additional reading, as does the important political background. Potential resistance to cross-ethnic casting.

Introduction

Nurkan Erpulat and Jens Hillje's contemporary and highly provocative play, *Verrücktes Blut* (2010)[1], culminates in a trans-linguistic *anagnorisis*. Sonia Kelich, the teacher of an unruly school class made up of various ethnicities, attempts to inculcate in her pupils the virtues of German language and culture by staging some scenes from the German literary canon. Amid a cacophony of spitting, snorting, crotch-scratching, cell-phone

DOI: 10.4324/9781003010289-7

chatter, and general verbal and physical abuse, Kelich announces the goals of her lesson, which is to be dedicated to the drama of Friedrich Schiller. Her unstated goal is to assign roles from Schiller's *Die Räuber* and *Kabale und Liebe* in the hope of reforming her disruptive pupils, following Schiller's "aesthetic education," by cultivating their *Spieltrieb*: Through role-playing the youths might learn to appreciate an affinity with Schiller's characters, which would thereby invite them to rescue themselves from their real-life problems and become full participants in "German" culture and society. After all, as Kelich later remarks, the play's focus on themes of oppression, violence, freedom, power, money, love, and poor communication are highly relevant for today. Such assurances of relevance, however, fall on deaf ears, as her cavorting pupils reject her rescue mission with vulgar taunts. Desperate to take control, Kelich seizes a gun brought to class by one of the pupils, forcing the entire class at gunpoint into various roles from Schiller's plays and pummeling their faulty pronunciation in the process. She emerges from her almost catastrophic class resigned to failure, at which point she switches to her native Turkish, thereby also revealing her own identity as a Turkish migrant. Her pupils, the audience, and by extension, the college students reading this drama at the conclusion of a third-year course on German drama and theater have all been completely outwitted.[2]

The significance of this discovery far exceeds its linguistic hoodwinking. Not only does Kelich's code-switch reveal her identity as a migrant, rendering everything she apparently stood for, along with her entire pedagogical enterprise, highly dubious. It also serves the even more critical function of exposing her pupils' identity as far less authentic or stable than previously assumed. Having been operating under the false presumption that Kelich – who has adopted the surname, it transpires, from her German spouse – propounds "German" values from a position of "native" authority, the pupils now indicate that they, too, might have acted differently had they made this critical discovery earlier: "Krass, wenn Sie das früher gesagt hätten," exclaims Hakim (Erpulat 62). Whether they would have been more eager recipients of Kelich's pedagogical strategy, and whether this moment of *anagnorisis* signals a better or worse destiny, however, remains uncertain. As one member of the class, Hasan, remarks towards the conclusion: "Aber was wird aus mir, wenn das [Theater] hier zu Ende ist? Oberstudienrat, wie Sie Frau Kelich? Ein echter Erfolgskanake?" (65). What is clear is that all participants have evidently performed a role, possibly projected onto them, either as the stereotypically self-hating immigrant pupil (*Kanakenselbsthassnummer*; 63) or as the model immigrant German teacher (*Erfolgskanake*; 65), and that their identities are unstable, unreliable, and in a stage of transition.

Sonia Kelich's linguistic code-switching is thus of highest dramatic consequence in this play. It interrogates the very notion of a stable identity and fixed stereotypes, thereby deconstructing the purported opposition of migrant/non-migrant, on the basis of which such stereotypes are founded and reenacted. Even the role assumed by the audience is forced from a position of sympathy to one of complicity: Initial compassion for Kelich's "enlightened" integration project is discredited by the violence to which she resorts; the assumed conflict between Muslim and German culture is rendered spurious at the moment of *anagnorisis*; and when Hasan, at the very end, aims the gun at the audience, the latter becomes just as socially responsible as it is theatrically implicated. Hasan's final gesture, then, may be variously interpreted as an indictment for typecasting migrants as the roguish, despicable Other (see also Layne and Landry), or as a plea to renegotiate of the very notion of "Germanness" and "German culture."

In view of globalization, especially amid the current so-called migration crisis, previous monolithic conceptions of national cultural and linguistic identity are being contested, and particularly fervently in Germany, which has not been considered an immigrant country until relatively recently. The landscape of German theaters, also witness to a transition from "migrant" to "post-migrant" theater, reflects this transition in Germany's political landscape. "Post-migrant" theater distinguishes itself from "migrant" theater primarily on the basis of its critical interrogation of existing narratives of migrants in Germany that have generally betrayed fixed associations with first-generation migrants (Sharifi 2017). As the first broadly successful example of post-migrant theater and set entirely in a predominantly post-migrant classroom, *Verrücktes Blut* is thus highly instructive on a number of political and pedagogical levels. Politically, the play engages the transitional political stage (from a non-immigrant to immigrant nation) as well as the associated educational reforms. Pedagogically, the play probes the use of drama as an approach to teaching German language and culture in the twenty-first-century global context. In particular, it showcases theater as a transitional space where linguistic and cultural identities may be negotiated and where social and linguistic agency are manifestly interdependent. As a result, the play may encourage our students to connect their transitioning language acquisition to their own discursive identity formation as multilingual subjects in a global community (*Standards*). How to sensitize students to the political complexities and aesthetic and discursive nuances at play in a drama such as *Verrücktes Blut* forms the key challenge – and opportunity – that I outline in what follows.

Ius Sanguinis / *Verrücktes Blut*

"Der selbstbewusste Umgang mit dem Fremden setzt den selbstbewussten Umgang mit dem Eigenen voraus."[3]

Before reading the play, it is vital to situate it in its cultural-political context by sketching some of the important turning points in immigration politics, the most significant of which predates the premiere of *Verrücktes Blut* (2010) by only a decade. On January 1, 2000, a new citizenship law came into effect that dramatically re-conceptualized Germany as a nation of immigration. As such, the new legislation signaled Germany's departure from the long-standing hereditary citizenship law (*ius sanguinis*) towards a vastly more liberalized and inclusive territorial definition of citizenship (*ius soli*). Thus, whereas previous generations of migrants were unable to acquire citizenship based on the territorial principle, existing merely as *ausländische Mitbürger* – "foreign fellow citizens" without citizenship – new generations born in Germany to foreign parents could now acquire citizenship.

This greater liberalization, however, was accompanied by new "assimilationist" policies that are often understood as a unidirectional, normative process of "making similar." Thus, while generally more accommodating and sensitive to rights of migrants, new public policies reflected a reluctance to fully embrace the pluralistic and multilingual reality that this entailed, as the debates about *Leitkultur* of the early 2000s also indicated. Moreover, and as Gramling convincingly shows, the resultant reemphasis on the German language and language acquisition played a decisive part in this process of acculturation. The effect, he argues, is that while implicitly acknowledging "the plurality of languages spoken among a given populace," certain "segregative strategies" were in place "in order to minimize the effect of multilingualism on public life" (Gramling 131). Most significantly, legal residence became dependent on sufficient language and cultural competency.

The coincidental "PISA-Shock" of 2000 and 2003, which shook the German educational system out of its self-assured complacency, complicated these issues further. When the Organization for Economic and Cooperative Development (OECD) published the results the first Program for International Student Assessment (PISA) in 2001, schoolchildren in Germany – presumed to be *das Land der Dichter und Denker*[4] – were ranked below average on the international scale. Significantly, the results also correlated with the socio-economic background of the schoolchildren, as well as the inadequate language proficiency of migrants: "Gerade die Leseschwäche ist nach Ansicht zahlreicher Experten das Ergebnis einer seit Jahren verfehlten Integrationspolitik," reports *Der Spiegel*:

> "Eine deutschsprachige Erzieherin kann nicht viel ausrichten, wenn die Kinder beim Spielen untereinander türkisch oder arabisch reden" [...]. Viele Pädagogen fordern schon lange, den Schülern fremder Zunge das Deutsche besser beizubringen, damit das Niveau in den Klassen nicht noch weiter sinkt. (*Spiegel*, 2001)

The PISA-Shock would dominate the media for many years, giving rise to such popular programs as the six-part series, *S.O.S.-Schule,* televised by ZDF in 2006 (and since made available on YouTube),[5] which documented the "cry for help" to reform a failing *Hauptschule* in Berlin. The concerning achievement gap between the academically orientated *Gymnasien* and poorer-performing *Haupt-* and *Realschulen* prompted a transformation of education policy. Since the majority of migrants attended these failing schools, it only followed that PISA would not only become a "significant event in educational policy-making" with particular regard to migrants (Tillmann et al.) but would also alter the public discourse on immigration in general. Most importantly, greater support for migrant children, including special programs for early language training did help to bridge the achievement gap with discernible success, at least according to the most recently published PISA results (OECD-PISA, 2015). As a result, standardized assessment of language proficiency would comprise a significant part of Germany's first Immigration Law (*Zuwanderungsgesetz*) of 2005.

Such apparently promising developments notwithstanding, the renewed focus on "integration" through *Bildung* and improved language competency could also be couched in less favorable terms as a means to control and limit immigration, as is suggested by the full title of the immigration law: "Gesetz zur Steuerung und *Begrenzung* der Zuwanderung und zur *Regelung* des Aufenthalts und der Integration von Unionsbürgern und Ausländern" (emphasis mine). Indeed, the PISA-shock, compounded by concurrent immigration reforms, no doubt fueled niggling suspicions among certain right-wing conservatives that *Überfremdung* is accountable for Germany's tarnished image as an educational leader and *Kulturnation*. Precisely these perceived connections are exploited, for example, in the 2010 highly controversial bestseller, *Deutschland schafft sich ab,* by former social democratic politician Thilo Sarrazin. According to Sarrazin, migrants from Muslim countries (especially Turkey) are responsible for the drastic drop in Germany's educational standards, as evidenced in the PISA results – reason enough, for Sarrazin, to appeal for a radical restriction on immigration in order to stem the allegedly *feindliche Übernahme* of Islam in Germany.

The fact that Sarrazin's controversial book appeared in the same year (2010) that Erpulat and Hillje's *Verrücktes Blut* was first performed (in Duisburg and subsequently in Berlin) may well have contributed to the huge success of the play, which was selected as "best play of the year" in 2011 by *Theater heute* alongside Elfriede Jelinek's *Winterreise*. The controversy sparked by the book did not escape the attention of those involved in the play's production either, and has assumed a prominent place as a "critical intertext" that the play critically confronts (see Landry). Not that Sarrazin would be required reading in order to appreciate the social-political context, as an interview with the actors and director makes clear: Sarrazin's voice, while louder than others – for some claimed that he was speaking for the "silent majority" – sounded all too familiar: "Das alles sind Themen, mit denen wir groß geworden sind. Dafür habe ich keinen Thilo Sarrazin gebraucht," remarks Sesede Tersiyan, the actor who played the teacher, Sonia Kelich (*Tagesspiegel*, 2011). But such voices seemed to form a clearly audible chorus around 2010, when, as Landry points out, both Chancellor Angela Merkel and Bavaria's CSU leader, Horst Seehofer, famously pronounced the imperative of successful integration over parallel existences: "Der Ansatz für Multikulti ist gescheitert," claims Merkel, reemphasizing what Seehofer had previously driven home in his *Sieben-Punkte-Plan* for integration: "Deutschland ist kein Einwanderungsland," insists Seehofer, and integration ought not be

> nebeneinander, sondern miteinander leben auf dem gemeinsamen Fundament der Werteordnung unseres Grundgesetzes und unserer deutschen Leitkultur, die von den christlich-jüdischen Wurzeln und von Christentum, *Humanismus* und *Aufklärung* geprägt ist. (*Spiegel*, 2010, emphasis mine)

Among Seehofer's list of imperatives, and as a guarantee against punitive restrictions, is the "ability" and "willingness" to integrate, demonstrated most clearly by early acquisition of sufficient language skills. Similarly, Merkel insists that migrants not only be encouraged (*gefördert*) but also challenged (*gefordert*), while also remaining welcoming to migrants and acknowledging the integral part that Islam plays in German society: "Er [der Islam] ist ein Teil Deutschlands - das sieht man nicht nur am Fußballspieler [Mesut] Özil" (*Spiegel*, 2010). In *Verrücktes Blut*, Hasan might not be inclined to agree, since Özil would represent what Hasan dubs an *Erfolgskanake* – reserved for those immigrants, like Kelich, whose assimilation into German culture is viewed as successful but for whom there is little room left. Only eight years on (2018), Özil's controversial resignation from the national football team over racism claims only adds to the many critical questions raised by *Verrücktes Blut* in 2010.

As the preceding account reveals, materials on the immigration and education debate in Germany are in no short supply. Besides news sources cited previously, introductory materials suitable for upper-intermediate and advanced levels include short texts such as Wladimir Kaminer's "Der Sprachtest" from *Russendisko* (Kaminer, 2000), which offers a satiric account of the linguistic hurdles of citizenship, and episodes of *Was guckst du* by the Turkish-German satirist Kaya Yanar, which provides a mordantly self-ironic take on Turkish-German experiences. Finally, news coverage of the *Kopftuchdebatte*, which came to a head in 2002 when Fereshta Ludin, a teacher of Afghan descent, lost her appeal to the German courts for permission to wear her headscarf during class, provides an essential introduction to the dual and conflicting principles of religious freedom and state neutrality in matters of the civil service. The importance of this background preparation cannot be underestimated, as it helps bridge the inevitable cultural gap that poses an additional obstacle to reading comprehension; it also partly helped students circumvent some linguistic (primarily vocabulary) difficulties.

Taken together, this background forms the essential political backdrop to Erpulat and Hillje's *Verrücktes Blut*, which adopts a thought-provoking, critical stance towards these public discourses, without, however, offering any solutions. Even the title seems to express ambivalence towards discourses on immigration: While supposedly a translation of a Turkish phrase meaning "wild young man" (Layne 55), *Verrücktes Blut* – translated into English as "Crazy Blood" – is as provocative as it is elusive for its target (German) audience. Neither its alleged original Turkish origin, which is most certainly inaccessible, nor its translation are particularly enlightening. However, by understanding *verrückt* not only as an adjective to mean "crazy" but also in its verbal form (*verrücken*) to mean "to displace," "to dislocate" and "to move out of place," we may interpret the phrase *verrücktes Blut* as a playful turn on the shift from the concept of "being" German (*ius sanguinis*) to "becoming" German *(ius soli),* as reflected in the amended 2000 citizenship law. Despite the more inclusive citizenship laws, "blood" has essentially been displaced, dislocated, and feels out of place, as does the title itself. No matter how one interprets it, the title enacts the kind of linguistic displacement that seems to reaffirm rather than open borders (Apter), thereby denying the audience full access to the meaning of the play.

Attention to the title thus provides a productive point of entry to this play because it not only highlights a crucial question about the role of language in integration, but also establishes the first instance of "alienation" that performs a critical function throughout the play. First, the German language forms a crucial part of Kelich's pedagogical approach, as she ruthlessly corrects her pupils' pronunciation at gun point, turning -*isch* to -*ICH,* and *Friedrisch* to *FriedrICH,* and so forth. While providing a potentially amusing moment of recognition for foreign-language students, correct pronunciation is, for Kelich, an imperative for proper execution of Schiller's roles and, by extension, for successful acculturation to German culture. Her pupils are at best "bad copies" of the native speaker, an ideal to which they can only aspire, and one that Claire Kramsch has repeatedly criticized as unrealistic and unnecessary in the context of today's global and multilingual language classroom. For Kelich, however, the primacy of language is tantamount to successful education and integration, as are the ability and willingness to embody the roles assigned to the pupils. By coercing them linguistically and physically into "native"-like performances of "Germanness" through Schiller, Kelich ultimately effaces part of their cultural identity, while claiming to liberate them from the presumably oppressive traditions that have prevented them from enjoying the full benefits of German culture. Here, students should make careful notes on details of Hasan's and Mariam's character and compare them to those from Schiller's characters, whom they are supposed to emulate. Paying attention to Kelich's interspersed commentary as her pupils read their parts aloud is very instructive for understanding these role assignments: Hasan is assigned the role of the cunning and power-hungry Franz Moor[6] from Schiller's *Die Räuber* in order to combat the timidity that has resulted from years of bullying and sexual abuse; and Mariam is assigned female roles that successfully overcome patriarchal oppression ("Mariam will rebellieren lernen"; 46), which Kelich associates with Mariam's headscarf, in order to become empowered by Western values ("Kopftuch weg. Spür der Amalia nach"; 50). Thus, many aspects of the polemical integration debate – from Seehofer's emphasis on the Christian, Humanist and Enlightenment foundations of German culture to the primacy of the German language – are clearly discernible in Kelich's lesson on Schiller. The humiliation tactics to which she resorts – such as forcing male pupils to drop their trousers – cast serious doubt on such coercive measures of Kelich's "Enlightenment" project.

The irony of teaching migrant pupils the humanistic virtues of Schiller's aesthetic education at gunpoint is surely not lost on the audience, whose uneasy sympathy with her character begins to shift towards the disruptive, wholly unappealing group that appears to confirm every negative stereotype of migrants in Germany today. Kelich's dogged determination to pound out multiple reiterations of *VERNUNFT* and Schiller's maxim, "Er ist nur da Mensch, wo er spielt," to the point of absurdity (20–1) can by now only arouse great discomfort, if not alarm. The grave implications of this irony, however, may be overlooked by students if they are not also properly primed with contemporary integration politics and critical possibilities of the play's aesthetic form. Without careful attention to details of form, the play will most likely be mistaken as a mere affirmation of these negative stereotypes. Thus, the second important aspect introduced by the title of the play – its "alienating" effect – is equally important in its interpretation. It is therefore important to devote some time to the opening moments of the play, when the actors enter the stage as actors before performing the exaggerated act of adopting their roles as migrant schoolchildren. Careful attention must be drawn to this opening moment in order to establish the critical gap between the actors and their roles, which is subsequently taken one level further when the acting migrants are forced into their roles from Schiller's plays.

As a play (Schiller) within a play (the migrant classroom) within a play (actors appearing as themselves), the audience is supposed to remain removed – thrice – from the unfolding action and thereby maintain a kind of Brechtian critical attitude. Understanding the significance of these different levels of role-playing, moreover, is essential to our understanding of the play's critical take on the politics of migration. However, maintaining detachment established at the outset can pose a challenge, as it apparently did for some audiences, as Erpulat noted, despite techniques designed to intervene when gaps begin to close and the audience succumbs to realism.

Embodied interrogation

To approach techniques of detachment and defamiliarization, it is helpful to familiarize students with Bertolt Brecht's theory and practice of theater beforehand, or in the context of other dramas that exploit Brechtian techniques. Particularly useful here are the salient characteristics of *Verfremdungseffekte* and *Gestus*, excerpted from his rehearsal notes for *Mutter Courage*, the *Kurze Beschreibung einer neuen Technik der Schauspielkunst, die einen Verfremdungseffekt hervorbringt*, and on his delineation of "epic" and "dramatic" theater in his "Anmerkungen zur Oper *Aufstieg und Fall der Stadt Mahagonny.*" Brecht's break with naturalistic depictions of character and plot deserves special attention here precisely because it motivates a shift in narratives about "being" (*der unveränderliche Mensch*) towards "becoming" (*der veränderliche und verändernde Mensch*). By reconsidering theater as a space where identities do not exist unproblematically but rather where they demand critique, Brecht's theories provide a critical lens through which to consider the shift in naturalization discourses in Germany from "being" German to "becoming" German.

In this regard, it is perhaps no surprise that such Brechtian techniques have also been adopted by other contemporary playwrights in critical explorations of current immigration and identity politics. Brechtian rehearsal techniques are explicitly employed, for example, in Roland Schimmelpfennig's *Der goldene Drache* (2008), a tragicomedy about the shadowy aspects of a globalized world – of greed, exploitation, human trafficking, and the lack of human rights for illegal immigrants, and in which not only the exploited, but also the exploiters long dolefully for better circumstances and alternative identities. Schimmelpfennig directs each actor to slip in and out of various roles without regard for race, gender, age, or indeed species, thereby maintaining distance between the actor and his or her role: Women adopt male roles, young adopt older roles, Germans play Chinese immigrants, and vice versa; deliver their lines in the third person, often as monologues directed to the audience rather than as a response to their interlocutors; and occasionally interrupt the play with the phrase *kurze Pause*. In this way, supposedly naturalized identities are destabilized, and meaningful communication often fails, with the effect of problematizing the damaging, occasionally violent discrimination based on gender, age, class, and ethnicity. Despite the tragic ending, Schimmelpfennig establishes a connection among all the characters in their common fundamental desire to become *ein anderer Mensch* (see also ch. 4).

A series of one or two workshops based on excerpts from Brecht's theoretical texts help facilitate a more critical interrogation of the opening of the play. This is especially important because an interpretation lies precisely in one's perception of the distance between actor and role. Without this critical embodied interrogation, the reader is easily tempted to understand the linguistic signs at face-value, as a perplexing affront of negative migrant stereotypes, possibly triggering a negative reaction to the text (and to the instructor!). The following outlines a series of exercises and workshops designed to help prime students in the critical potential of distancing techniques of anti-realistic theater and in the adoption of a critical stance in *Verrücktes Blut*. Ideally, these teaching suggestions, taught over two and a half weeks, build on a week's introduction to Brechtian techniques and an introduction to the political context, as suggested here:

Day 1: Political backdrop (preferably two days of introduction)
Day 2: *Verrücktes Blut*, pp. 2–11 (Workshop)
Day 3: *Verrücktes Blut*, pp. 12–19 (end of prologue)

Day 4: *Verrücktes Blut*, Akt 1, Szene 1–3, pp. 20–44
Day 5: *Verrücktes Blut,* Akt 1, Szene 4 – Akt II (End)
Day 6: Workshop and discussion, *Verrücktes Blut,* Akt II, Sz. 1

Day 2: *Verrücktes Blut, Prologue* (2–11)

From the very opening scene, it is essential to scrutinize the verbal and non-verbal choices – the choice of gesture, vocabulary, register, tone, and in this case, even the choice of language – to better understand the power dynamics between the characters as they struggle to negotiate their subject position. This is particularly important in a play such as *Verrücktes Blut*, in which language and code-choice are intimately related to the dynamics of social, ethnic, gender, and sexual identity. Critical language awareness in this case also relates directly to the play's aesthetic dimension. An understanding of the linguistic signs and political context is insufficient to fully understand the nuances of this play; perception of the play's aesthetic dimension forms a crucial part in our understanding of the relation of performance to identity construction. And embodied performance prompts deeper reflection and a more precise, nuanced interpretation – adding, in turn, an additional level of play acting to this play within a play.

Leitfragen

Prolog (2–5)

1. *Geben Sie eine knappe Beschreibung von Ort, Zeit, Personen, und Situation zusammen! Wo spielt sich das Stück ab?*
2. *Was fällt Ihnen an der Sprache auf? Wie gehen die Schüler miteinander um? Beschreiben Sie den Ton! Welche Wörter oder Phrasen werden wiederholt? Welche Fluchwörter erkennen Sie?*
3. *Welche Gesten und Wörter wirken aggressiv, bedrohlich, vulgär, oder brutal? Unterstreichen Sie Ihre Beispiele!*
4. *Gibt es im Prolog auch einige despektierliche Ausdrücke.? Was soll hier unter "Kanakengesten" verstanden werden? Und wie könnte eine "übertriebene Ghettobegrüßung" aussehen?*
5. Lesen Sie die Regieanweisungen auf Seite 3. Was fällt Ihnen auf? Warum heißt es "anscheinend zufällig"?

Prolog (5–11)

The most important intertext for *Verrücktes Blut* is Schiller's *Die Räuber*. It is not vital to read the full text of Schiller's *Die Räuber*, or the other intertexts – *Kabale und Liebe* and his treatise – "Über die ästhetische Erziehung des Menschen in einer Reihe von Briefen" in order to understand *Verrücktes Blut*. It is possible to read the many references alongside a summary of the play and central ideas of his *Ästhetische Briefe*, particularly in relation to characters in *Verrücktes Blut*. However, if time permits and students' language level is sufficiently advanced, a full reading of *Die Räuber* and parts of the *Ästhetische Briefe* will greatly enrich their understanding and make for a more nuanced and highly rewarding discussion of *Verrücktes Blut*.

1. *Beschreiben Sie kurz Sonia Kelichs Unterrichtsplan: Was ist ihr Hauptziel (5–6)?*
2. *Fassen Sie Sonias Beschreibung von Dichtung und Epoche des Sturm und Drang kurz zusammen.*
3. *Welche Aspekte von Schillers "Die Räuber" möchte Kelich hervorheben? Wie versucht Kelich, Schiller für ihre Schüler zugänglich und relevant zu machen? Was halten Sie davon?*
4. *Beschreiben Sie, aus Sonjas Perspektive, die Figurenkonstellation von Schillers "Die Räuber." Welche Tugenden bzw. Laster schreibt Sonja den Figuren jeweils zu?*
5. *Wie lässt sich Sonjas Lehrsatz bewerten? Wie reagieren die Schüler darauf? Wie gehen sie mit ihrer Lehrerin um?*
6. *Wer scheint/scheinen die "Aufrührer" der Klasse zu sein? Begründen Sie Ihre Überlegungen!*
7. *Beschreiben Sie Hasan: Wie wird er von den anderen behandelt? Was hat Hasan, und welche Gründe könnte das haben? Unterstreichen Sie relevante Textstellen!*

In-class discussion and workshop (1–5)

1. **Warm-up**: *Verrücktes Blut* stage directions for vocabulary building:

   a. The instructor reads (and if necessary also demonstrates) 4–5 stage directions at a time for students to carry out, adding additional directions in groups of 4–5, mixing and combining them as they build their vocabulary. The directorial responsibility is handed over gradually to the students as they practice in pairs (using the informal singular "du" form) and subsequently in small groups or in full class (using the informal plural "ihr" form).

Table 7.2 Bühnenanweisungen

an den vorderen Bühnenrand kommen	to step to the front of the stage
sich dem Publikum zuwenden	to face the audience
sich (von etwas/jdm.) abwenden	to turn away (from something, someone)
auf jdn. zugehen	to go up to someone
einen Schritt auf jdn. zugehen	to step towards someone
jdn. anfassen	to grab, touch someone

jdn. nachäffen	to ape, mimic someone
jdm. die Brille abnehmen	to take someone's glasses off
jdn. packen	to seize, grab someone
jdn. schubsen	to shove, push someone
sich kloppen	to fight with someone
das Kopftuch binden, Halstuch binden	to tie a headscarf, scarf
Stühle in eine Reihe stellen	to place chairs in a row
spucken	to spit
rotzen (Schleim geräuschvoll rausspucken)	to snort and spit
flirten, anmachen	to flirt, hit on
streiten	to argue, quarrel
Haare korrigieren	to fix one's hair
anpöbeln	to verbally abuse
Handy einstecken	to put away, pocket one's cell phone

b. Students repeat the exercise, this time exaggeratedly (*übertrieben*).

c. Discussion of reading questions (*Leitfragen*) and collection of initial impressions of the opening four pages.

d. Read-through and workshop on play's opening and gestures (3–4; see below).

e. Have students embody and exaggerate what they might consider a *Ghettobegrüßung* ("ghetto greeting").

2. *Embodied interrogation*

Appearing "on stage" as "actors" preparing for their roles in real time, the actors are directed to chat among themselves (as actors), and crucially, become aware of the audience before placing their chairs "seemingly randomly" around the stage. After preparing their roles as migrant schoolchildren (putting on a headscarf, jackets and caps, kerchiefs, and putting away a cell phone) on stage, each actor then steps forward one at a time "als Privatperson an den vorderen Bühnenrand und wird dort zum Kanaken" (3), at which point, they confront the audience with various so-called *Kanakengesten* or, at least, a selection of those gestures with which students feel sufficiently comfortable: *rotzen, spucken, Haare korrigieren* (3). After one actor leaves to change into her role as teacher – "geht sich umziehen, wird zu Sonia [Kelich]" (3) – she returns *mit einem Stapel Reclameheft durch die Tür*, and her pupils greet her with an *übertriebene Ghettobegrüßung* (4). Most important here is a proper discussion of the significance of *Kanake* as a concept that has been more positively repurposed more recently (following Turkish-German author Feridun Zaimoglu's lead in his book *Kanaak Sprak*) than its earlier exclusively derogatory designation of first-generation *Gastarbeiter* (Layne 55). Although used in contemporary language among youths and self-identifying Turkish-Germans, it nevertheless remains a loaded term (see also Landry 113). It is important to practice the Brechtian technique of actors visibly stepping in and out of their roles, rather than having already disappeared into them. Per Erpulat's stage directions, exaggerated and repeated performance of such gestures breaks any illusion that these are natural or stable, but rather parodistic mimicry, and by acting these out, students should establish the critical distance between the actor and role, between being and mimicking. Attention to these opening stage directions enable students to establish the critical distance between the actor and role, between being and mimicking. It soon becomes clear through the repeated stage directions that this is in fact a play *about* mimicry, as various characters are directed in the text to mimic one another (*nachäffen*).

After teasing out the implications of this initial setup, it is worth viewing a performance of the opening scene by the Ballhaus Naunynstraße in Kreuzberg, Berlin, readily available on DVD. This helps clarify any remaining doubts about how these so-called *Kanakengesten* might be performed, and about the diverse makeup of the cast, as well as witness this particular audience's reactions to this scene, which are primarily laughter. Whether the laughter stems from recognition or from unease, it serves to confirm the critical distance setup by the actors, and which Erpulat and Hillje attempt to maintain throughout the play through various techniques that students connected to those of Bertolt Brecht.

Excerpt 1

   Prolog (3–4)
   Die Darsteller kommen auf die Bühne, unterhalten sich, bemerken das Publikum und setzen sich anscheinend zufällig auf die Stühle: v.l.n.r.: Erol, Rahel, Gregor, Altan, Musa, Nora, Tamer, Sesede. Sie unterhalten sich.
   Ruhe.
   Nora bindet ihr Kopftuch, alle ziehen die Jacken an, binden Halstücher um, Käppis auf, stecken Handys ein etc.
   Sie nehmen ihre Stühle und gehen durch die "Tür" an der rechten Seite auf die "Bühne," stellen die Stühle in einer Reihe auf und setzen sich, v.l.n.r.: Hasan, Sonia, Latifa, Bastian, Mariam, Musa, Ferit, Hakim.
   Kanakengesten zum Publikum:
   (Signal von Nora, langsam anfangen) Rotzen
   Spucken,
   Ruhe,
   (Signal von Gregor) Schwanz korrigieren,
   (Signal von Gregor) "Fick dich"-Anpöbeln,
   kurz Haare korrigieren,
   mackerig Jacke korrigieren,

(Signal von Nora) Halbschritt vor und zurück) Ruhe,
(Signal von Nora) Guck mal-Tussi,
(Signal von Nora) über Sex reden,
(Signal von Nora) Schwanz korrigieren,
Anpöbeln.
Übergang zur Gruppe. Ab jetzt passiert alles untereinander; alle Signale von Altan.
Sesede geht sich umziehen, wird zu Sonia.
Rotzen, Spucken, Fick dich Anpöbeln, Handy telefonieren mit Tussi-Stimme, Schwanz, Spucken, Flirten, Streit.
Ruhe.
Sonia tritt mit einem Stapel Reclamehefte durch die Tür.
SONIA: Guten Morgen! *(Sie wiederholt es mehrfach.)*
Übertriebene Ghettobegrüßung.

After dealing with the shock value of the obscenities that depict the migrant classroom setting, we turn our attention to the opening stage directions. It is worth discussing the significance of the opening stage directions to check the students' understanding. It is particularly important that they understand how the play adopts a critical stance, lest they be lured into the play's apparent realism.

a. Discussion of the function or effect of repetition and exaggeration (as opposed to naturalistic appearance on stage)
b. Discussion about the difference between appearing on stage in character and appearing on stage to change into character. Focus on vocabulary and gestures that make clear that they theatrically "show" rather than naturally "be" the character, which requires prior familiarization with Brecht's "epic theater" (see also ch. 1).

Post-discussion creative writing: Select one of the following characters and write an inner monologue relating to a specific point in the first ten pages: Kelich, Hasan, or Mariam. Feel free to include any idiosyncratic language you have noticed so far.

Improvisation

In order to probe students' understanding of the text further, we may take our cue from Brecht by staging our own interruptions. A variation on "hot-seating" (Even; Guenther), one such interruption requires that students adopt roles from the play and be interrogated to explain the current situation and justify motivations. This exercise not only transforms the discussion by putting the students in the hot-seat, but also requires thorough preparation and a good level of textual understanding and recall, including their characters' vernacular speech and body language. For *Verrücktes Blut*, the whole class may be interrogated by imagined external visitors – a school inspector, another teacher – who investigates the situation in the classroom at a point of high tension, such as when the pupils manage to retrieve the gun from Kelich (Act II, Sc. 1). Because certain characters tend to exhibit certain idiosyncrasies (repeating the same words, phrases, and gestures), students may be encouraged to incorporate some of these creatively in their improvisations. Depending on the level and ability of a particular class, some individual preparation before this in-class activity is recommended. Such an exercise facilitates precisely the kind of critical reflection on the underlying social tensions that Brecht intended in his "interrupting" techniques.

Approaching the songs

Similar to Brecht's use of songs in his plays, the insertion of songs between scenes interrupts the action and invites critical reflection and provides a much-appreciated momentary relief from the mounting tension (see Appendix A). However, whereas Brecht's songs aim to interrupt, undercut, ironize, or comment on rather than underscore the theatrical illusion, Erpulat's folksongs have the reverse effect of enacting a kind of illusory belonging, albeit with the same ironizing result. Students need additional prompting on the function of these particular songs within the specific context of this text. Erpulat inserts a series of well-known eighteenth- and nineteenth-century folksongs and patriotic songs – "Wenn ich ein Vöglein wär," "Herbstlied," "Nun ade, du mein lieb Heimatland" "Gelübde," "Schlaflied" – which all the characters step forward to sing, in "perfect" German and in harmony. In particular, the patriotic sentiment of Hans Ferdinand Maßmann's "Gelübde," which begins "Ich hab mich ergeben mit Herz und mit Hand / dir Land voll Lieb und Leben, mein deutsches Vaterland," prompts reflection on the implied acquiescence on the part of the migrants in Kelich's German class, as Layne points out. Thus, the songs preserve their ironizing function. However, quite in contrast to Brecht, these songs also have a pseudo-harmonizing – rather than a centrifugal – effect, as if to reinstate order and harmony in the cacophonic lesson, making homogenous the otherwise disunited, multiethnic class and, by extension, theater. By temporarily relieving the mounting tensions, the music summons the characters into a sense of imagined harmonic belonging, enacting a kind of *Zugehörigkeit* rooted in one's ability to listen (*hören*) and obey (*gehorchen*). In *Verrücktes Blut*, the songs seem to conjure up an aura of unity that is often associated with singing the national anthem today – just as the refusal to sing the national anthem has the opposite effect of disunity. As we have frequently witnessed in recent years, such refusal among members of the German national football team, including Mesut Özil, has sparked much political furor. Here, characters of various migrant backgrounds demonstrate an illusory, momentary union and "successful" linguistic integration through song. Put another way, they are linguistically coerced into singing folksongs that serve to underscore an ideology of German national identity.

But nothing is quite as straightforward as it might seem in *Verrücktes Blut*, which resists any definitive or stable meaning. By breaking down the fourth wall at the meta-theatrical level and unifying the characters on and off stage, the songs amplify the artificiality of such constructions of difference and distance, revealing them as theater. Thus, the songs also serve to diminish precisely those notions of difference that the play aims to deconstruct. By the second half of the play, none of the characters' gendered or ethnic identities remains stable, as they gradually negotiate their identity through dramatic readings of Schiller. It is worth devoting additional time to specific moments in this act, allowing students time to prepare dramatic readings or in-class performances. Performance encourages students to read between the linguistic signs and actually embody the text, stimulating a much more nuanced understanding that raises many more questions than answers. And learning to ask critical questions is precisely what *Verrücktes Blut* demands – perhaps the richest of lessons to be learned from an embodied interrogation of this text.

Akt II

In the second act, Mariam, having refused Kelich's increasing insistence that she rid herself of her headscarf (45, 50, 51), adopts Schiller's version of a female role and eventually even abandons her headscarf (Sc. 1); Kelich reveals herself linguistically to be of Turkish descent and finally takes off her wig (Sc. 3); both Mariam and Hasan redirect some of the reprimanding one-liners against the teacher who previously delivered them; and Hasan, the previously timid victim of abuse, fully adopts the role of Schiller's Franz Moor, turning the tables by seizing the gun and forcing the show to go on (Sc. 4). These moments each deserve careful consideration.

Excerpt 2

Akt II, Szene 1 *(56–7)*
[...]
HAKIM: Bete, du weißt, dass du gleich stirbst. Bete, denn ich bring dich um. Du Sohn einer Hure. *(Tritt ihn)*
MUSA: Lass mich los.
MARIAM: *(zieht ihn zurück)* Lass ihn los, Hakim. Das bringt es nicht. Eh, das bringt es echt nicht. Fessel' seine Hände.
HAKIM: Wie? Ich hab' nichts zu fesseln.

MARIAM: Hier. Fessel ihn mit dem Tuch. *Mariam nimmt sehr langsam das Tuch ab und wirft es auf den Boden. Schocksekunde. Zittern. Ausbruch von Miriam.*

MIRIAM: *(Urschrei)* Grroughoääääää.

LATIFA: Mariam, was ist los? Was ist denn los?

MARIAM: Cool, cool, cool, ich bin cool. *(Sie berührt ihr Haar, erschrickt davor.) Hakim nimmt schnell das Tuch vom Boden. Mariam gibt die Pistole Hakim. Körpertanz.*

HAKIM: Alles in Ordnung?

FERIT: Mariam, was bist du jetzt? *Mariam tanzt mit Latifa. Ausbruch von Hakim – Hose runter, kurzer Ausbruch. Hakim gibt die Pistole Ferit. Hakim fesselt Musa die Hände. Latifa tanzt. Parallel entdeckt Mariam das Handy.*

Focusing in particular on a performance of Act II, Sc. 1, a series of questions emerge and become ever more urgent in the staging of their actions, movements, and gestures, including:

1. What is the motivation for Mariam's role reversal? What does it really mean when Mariam takes off her headscarf? Is it a result of a long-suppressed urge to liberate herself, inspired by Schiller's version of female power and resistance, as Kelich would like to believe? Or does it simply serve the practical end of tying up another classmate?
2. What does her sudden burst of emotion mean – *(Urschrei) Grroughoäääääää* – and why does she suddenly start dancing? What kind of dance is it and what did it express? Does it express authentic liberation, or is it rather to satisfy the audience's desire to see her "liberated" from oppression?

As mentioned earlier, one's interpretation of this play rests precisely on the perception or non-perception of the gap between actor and role, and by invoking Brecht once more, students may better appreciate the importance of the play's aesthetic form. For, without this critical distance, Mariam's seemingly ecstatic reaction upon abandoning the headscarf would confirm a sense of liberation. With the critical distance, however, Mariam's abandonment of the headscarf might instead be interpreted as a kind of striptease (Stewart 64), and her ensuing reaction a performance to gratify the audience, rather than a genuine physical release. In other words, the characters on stage may be consciously performing stereotypically imagined, rather than real cultural differences.

What Mariam subsequently discovers on her cell phone is a video of Hasan, presumably being abused – the reason for Hasan's apparent cowardice throughout. Focusing on Hasan at the end of the play further raises the question as to the extent to which such stereotypes are possibly only projections and thus performances.

Akt II, Szene 3–4

After Kelich slips into Turkish and reveals her heritage (Sc. 3), Hasan now fully embraces the role of Schiller's cunning and callous Franz Moor, refusing to end the show. The following summarizes key discussion questions raised by these final two scenes:

1.   Why does Kelich violently coerce schoolchildren if she, too, is also a migrant herself? Why can she not relate better to her pupils? And what does this mean for her own "integration"? Is integration only truly "successful" at the point when one's foreign heritage is all but erased, and seemingly brutally in this instance? What, then, does this imply for those who have gained citizenship (*ius soli*) to become Turkish-Germans or another hybrid, hyphenated German identity?
2.   Why does Sonia Kelich introduce Schiller's *Die Räuber* in order to try to impart German "Enlightenment" values, when the roles selected seem to be such poor role-models, exhibiting precisely those negative traits that Kelich claims to counter?
3.   Are their values (especially honor and freedom) really any different, in the end? And how could one even assume to represent any kind of singular – and by implication superior – "German" culture?
4.   And why does Hasan wish to continue playing his role after the play has ended and after everyone else has switched to Turkish? Why does he shoot at the audience at the very end?

In discussing each of these interrelated questions, refer students again to Kelich's introduction of Schiller and to the citations from Schiller interspersed throughout. As Kelich emphatically announces at the beginning of her class, Schiller's dramas – staples of every schoolchild's educational diet – promise to elevate these troubled youths to new cultural and social heights. Moreover, Schillers' texts are within her pupils' grasp, if only they can appreciate their own affinity to the *junge[n] Wilden* of Schiller's *Sturm and Drang* period (6), as Kelich presents it: "Das Stück *Die Räuber* hat auch heute noch Aktualität, da die Themenbereiche, z.B Unterdrückung, Gewalt, Wunsch nach Freiheit, Macht, Geld, Liebe und Kommunikationsarmut, noch nicht veraltet sind" (6, 10). By recalling the details of Kelich's lesson plan, it is possible to interrogate the dubious motives she repeatedly presents up to the moment when she seizes the gun, when she forces them to respond to Schiller's "aesthetic education" – which by now seems all the more absurd: "Wie kann der Mensch dazu gebracht werden, mit seiner Freiheit verantwortlich umzugehen – [...] Durch die Kunst, durch Spiel, durch Selbstbildung im Spiel!" (20). Her turn to violence appears to be motivated by sheer frustration with a class that refuses to share her belief in the educational value of German literature, and that refuses to embrace Schiller by perfecting a performance that completely erases their ethnicity. If Kelich is able to perform this to perfection, such that her ethnic heritage is imperceptible, then she is the "success" story of aggressively assimilationist policies in an exclusive, homogenous society. And because her violently authoritarian approach finds further correlation in violent actions of Schiller's characters, then her pupils' outright rejection of Schiller until now seems justified.

Even if Schiller's *Die Räuber* and *Kabale und Liebe* are central to the German canon, the plays' central characters fail to provide role models; rather, they serve to deconstruct the alleged differences between "German" and "non-German" identities, thereby undercutting any claim to cultural superiority, or *Leitkultur*. By deconstructing identities and presumed cultural differences in this play, Erpulat and Hillje seem instead to gesture towards a transcultural understanding of culture and identity. And if both their audience and the students understand it in this way, then both the dramatists and instructor have achieved their goal.

In a final twist, however, Hasan announces that he would rather remain in this German drama class and continue playing Franz Moor – himself an outcast in appearance and in character and hardly worthy of emulation – than to return to a world that remains deaf to his concerns: "Das Einzige was in dieser Schule funktioniert, ist die Bühne. Theaterbühne. Wir spielen Theater. Aber was wird aus mir, wenn das [Theater] hier zu Ende ist?" (61). What counts is that Hasan at least gets to "play a role" that is different from the role into which he is otherwise continually typecast. As Hasan points out, and as the furor surrounding Özil further illustrates, it is already difficult to maintain this kind of performance of the so-called *Erfolgskanake*, and Germany's capacity is limited: "Tja, tut uns Leid, aber Erfolgskanakenkapazität ist gerade zu Ende" (65). Most significantly, it is important to note that Hasan no longer responds to Kelich's menacingly relentless stage directions; rather, he, like Mariam before him, seems at the very end to have fully adopted the role of Franz Moor.

Excerpt 3

Akt II, Szene 4 (64–5)

HASAN: (*hat die Waffe*) Keiner geht hier raus.

SCHUSS.

BASTIAN: Was ist denn jetzt mit dir?
MARIAM: Was soll das denn?
MUSA: Es ist vorbei, komm runter …
HASAN: Halt die Klappe, Musa …
MUSA: Ich bin kein Musa mehr …
HASAN: Doch, bist du … Bist du! Du bist Musa.
MUSA: Oh Mann komm…
SONIA: Erol, Erol, tu das mal weg, es ist vorbei jetzt …

FERIT: Mann, ist doch fertig, wir können Döner essen gehen …
HASAN: Ihr legt euch jetzt hin alle. Alle hinlegen.
BASTIAN: Das ist jetzt doch nicht dein Ernst.
LATIFA: Tu die Pistole weg, Mann …
HASAN: Geb ich die Waffe nicht zurück. Geb nicht zurück. Gehen wir
              hier raus, und was dann? Was passiert dann? Ändert sich gar
              nichts. Also will ich, dass das hier mein Leben lang weitergeht.
HAKIM: Bitte …
HASAN: Haltet die Schnauze. Wir spielen weiter. "Räuber."

SCHUSS.

HASAN: Und ich werde Franz spielen. Ich bin Franz und ich bleibe Franz
              … Ich habe große Rechte über die Natur ungehalten zu sein …
              Warum musste sie mir diese Hässlichkeit aufladen? Gerade mir
              diese Hottentottenaugen? Was seht ihr in mir? Einen
              Schauspieler oder einen Kanaken? Immer noch? Frisch also!
              Muthig ans Werk! – Ich will Alles um mich her ausrotten, was
              mich einschränkt, daß ich nicht Herr bin.

If the play's opening employed techniques to emphasize the artificiality and theatricality of the performance, then the play's closing obfuscates any clear demarcation between Erpulat's and Schiller's roles. Towards the end, both Hasan and Mariam slip imperceptibly in and out of their assigned roles, and in and out of Turkish, adopting willingly their characters' lines, which become interspersed with and indistinguishable from their own. Hasan is not only playing Franz at the end; he has effectively *become* Franz Moor: "Solang wir spielen geht's klar. Einziger Ort, der funktioniert. Und er ist schalldicht. Schalldicht! Hört uns jemand? Herr muß ich sein, daß ich das mit Gewalt ertrotze, wozu mir die Liebenswürdigkeit gebricht" (65). The absence of any textual disjuncture allows Hasan to slip undetected behind Franz Moor and thereby challenge the audience's spectatorial assumptions about German identity. But if Hasan seems resigned to a world that remains deaf to his theatrical protest, fully absorbed by the soundproof theater (*schalldicht*; 18, 65), then it is important to note that Hasan's actor, Erol, is called out by Kelich when he threatens to shoot at his peers (64). By calling on the real-time actor, the "soundproof" fourth wall is broken, letting the play's complex internal tensions resonate with the external social-political reality. Such a metatheatrical maneuver reorients our spectatorial attention away from the stage and towards the audience itself. And when Kelich then announces the conclusion of her lesson ("Der Unterricht ist zu Ende"; 65), she no longer addresses her class, but rather the audience directly, as does Hasan when he shoots into the audience at the end. Both Kelich's and Hasan's final gestures suggest that the play's lesson, finally, is intended to instruct the audience. But what is the audience supposed to learn from a play that resists simple answers to the many questions it raises?

From colorblind casting to a post-ethnic vision

Of all the questions raised by this play, Hasan's concluding question is perhaps most crucial: "Was seht ihr in mir? Einen Schauspieler oder einen Kanaken? Immer noch?" (64). In Brechtian manner, these answers are to be actively sought by the audience. By asking the audience what they *see*, Hasan challenges notions of a German identity visibly marked by race, and his parting shot critically implicates the audience as co-conspirators in the social ills presented on stage. Crucially, it also implicates theater – specifically canonical German theater – in the construction of German identity and the representation of racial stereotypes. His plea for a response from the audience articulates a desire for a more inclusive, post-ethnic vision of German society generally and of the theater landscape in particular, one that rectifies the paucity of opportunities for artists of color in German theater, whose largely exclusive casting practices betray ongoing blindness to the increasingly diverse demographic reality.

As Hasan's performance makes clear, a "person with migration background" is quite capable of playing Franz Moor, yet the scarce opportunities in German state-funded theater ensembles are at best limited mostly to the role of the illegal immigrant,[7] the exotic foreigner, the refugee,[8] the prostitute, criminal, or the ominous intruder.[9] Such roles serve to reinforce the general political discourse of national cultural integration. But even these socially marginal roles are frequently assigned to non-migrant actors – an ongoing problem that has been highlighted by recent blackfacing controversies (Obermueller; Sieg). Whoever gets to play these roles is still up for debate. Dea Loher and Roland Schimmelpfennig, who share a Brechtian approach to non-naturalistic representation, represent two sides of this debate. For Dea Loher (*Unschuld*, 2012), the "artificiality of theatrical means" outweighs any "dubious authenticity" of migrant actors playing "illegale schwarze Immigranten" (Loher 47). This gave director Michael Thalheimer license, controversially, to stress artificiality through black face paint that would fade during the performance to reveal white actors in an apparent attempt to invite the audience to "see through" race (Sieg 128). For Schimmelpfennig (*Der goldene Drache,* 2008), by contrast, the artificiality of representation is stipulated in the fluidity of role assignments: No actor is limited to one role, but rather plays multiple different roles across ethnicity, gender, age, and even species. Though different in effect, Loher and Schimmelpfennig share a similar approach to challenging the spectator's view of identity (no matter how successful) as fluid, and not indelibly marked by race. But neither solves the issue that

Erpulat and Hillje raise, namely, of dramatic content or exclusive casting practices. As is clear by the end of *Verrücktes Blut*, both Hasan and Mariam would in fact prefer to have roles in a play by Schiller. Their plea is for transcultural theater in a post-racial society, one that is colorblind in the more positive sense. This requires a transformation not only in casting practices but also in dramatic content, not only challenging traditional narratives of migrants but also renegotiating traditional notions of national identity. A similar plea is echoed in Elfriede Jelinek's *Die Schutzbefohlenen* (2013), in which contemporary refugees form the chorus in Europe's oldest refugee drama, Aeschylus' *The Suppliants,* giving them a "legitimate" voice to be heard, rather than a problem to be silenced and potentially deported. Such a reimagination of contemporary German society constitutes the primary objective of post-migrant theater.

Such questions of representational practice and content have special import for anyone considering a performance of *Verrücktes Blut*, and even more so outside Germany, where these issues have the potential to become particularly thorny. In the context of a foreign-language course that is also culturally removed once more, questions regarding who may or may not embody the roles of migrants are particularly sensitive. Even playing migrants "as these young people are seen," rather than "as they are," as Erpulat insists (*Tagesspiegel*, 2011), still involves re-creating a racialized stereotype. However casting decisions are made, we run the risk of either reinforcing stereotypes or simply mocking these (by having, say, a color-blind casting of white students in the United States play non-white Germans). Such a discussion is especially important in the U.S. context, where such cross-ethnic casting practices have been more sensitively handled than in Europe, and student discomfort about potential unintended stereotyping (or even blackfacing) must be addressed. Ultimately, it comes down to whether the urgency of Erpulat and Hillje's critique of contemporary society outweighs the potential for misunderstanding, either with the students or with the (non-German-speaking) audience. Addressing this question must be integral to the discussion of the text, through thorough historical background, embodied workshops and critique, whether as a full production or as an in-class performance.

Post-performance reflections

Whether one decides to mount a full production, or whether one opts for a smaller, in-class performance of a single scene, a performative approach to this text emphasizes the importance of gesture and movement as well as language. It motivates students to embody a position in their interpretation of a scene or character, enabling students to achieve a far more sensitive and nuanced interpretation of the play's complexities and, ultimately, a deeper transcultural understanding. Together, these activities serve as pre-writing exercises, which require further reflection and synthesis of their embodied interrogations. The sample essays (Appendix B) encourage students to reflect further on the trans-cultural gesture – that Schiller served not to reinforce but rather deconstruct some of the presumed cultural differences – and indeed to help develop their transcultural competence. In the process, moreover, students may take their cue from Hasan by negotiating their own identity through dramatic readings.

This kind of awareness is particularly relevant for intercultural understanding and tolerance, where theater allows identity to be negotiated, developed, and challenged. Furthermore, it is even more pertinent in a play about the role of language proficiency in identity formation, and where language and code-choice are intimately related to the notion of social identity and a sense of self. On the one hand, a willingness to "play" with the language of others affords them increased agency; by acting upon reality, they thereby wield symbolic power, in the performative sense described by Judith Butler and Alexei Yurchak (Kramsch 8–9). In this respect, students can certainly take something away from Schiller's concept of the *Spieltrieb* and begin to develop their own symbolic competence and identity. On the other hand, the play demonstrates the affective challenge of being forced to assume the language and culture of others – especially of those from ethnically different backgrounds. The fact that the migrant pupils initially resist their Schillerian roles because they perceive their assignment as coercive could serve as a gentle warning for our own students, with implications that are not entirely unrealistic, as anecdotal evidence sug-gests.[10] Indeed, *Verrücktes Blut* provides a fascinating test case for the uses and abuses, the benefits and potential pitfalls, of foreign-language drama pedagogy.

Given such potential pitfalls, it is important, first of all, not to follow Kelich by compelling students into undesired roles. Furthermore, sufficient and well-scaffolded self-reflective groundwork on the historical, political, theoretical, and aesthetic background cannot be overstated if we are to preclude potential misunderstanding and resistance among students. Recurring reflection on embodied performance in drama workshops helps to sensitize students to the significance of theater in the development of their own linguistic agency, transcultural competence, and critical language awareness. Just as Kelich is able to perform a linguistic turn on the classical device of *anagnorisis*, so, too, may students become critically cognizant of its theatrical significance and likewise be encouraged towards greater linguistic agency and creative language use.

Notes

1 An earlier version of this chapter appeared in *Unterrichtspraxis*, , vol 53., no. 1 (2020), 66–81.
2 The moment of linguistic code-switching is especially significant and effective because it triggers *anagnorisis* precisely at the moment of reversal [*peripeteia*].
3 Deutscher Bundestag, 2007, cited in Sharifi, 2011, 205.
4 Although its origin remains somewhat unclear, this designation took root in

early-nineteenth-century Germany and has been commonly used ever since – either in earnest or in jest – in reference to Germany's alleged academic and spiritual superiority. For its use with particular reference to the PISA-Shock, see Wolfgang Mieder (428).

5 For more information, see https://www.presseportal.de/pm/7840/825639.

6 "Moor" is also a term of identity for a Muslim (e.g., *Othello*), from Latin *maurus*, describing someone from North Africa. In Hellenistic Greek, *mauros* appears as an adjective denoting "black."

7 Roland Schimmelpfennig, *Der goldene Drache* (see ch. 4).

8 For example, Lutz Hübner, *Willkommen* (2016); Dea Loher's *Unschuld;* Elfriede Jelinek, *Die Schutzbefohlenen* (2013); Julya Rabinowich, *Fluchtarien: Monolog für drei Stimmen mit Tastatur* (2009); *Auftauchen: Eine Bestandaufnahme* (2010); *Tagfinsternis: Ein Drama in 4 Akten* (2014); Juli Zeh and Charlotte Roos, *Yellow Line* (2012); Feridun Zaimoglu and Günter Senkel, *Schattenstimmen* (2008). A history of post-migrant productions made possible by the independent theater company Ballhaus Naunynstraß is available here: http://www.ballhausnaunynstrasse.de/archiv. Its founder, Shermin Langhoff, has since become artistic director, alongside Jens Hillje, of the Maxim Gorki Theater Berlin, a company that has recently established "Exile Ensemble" for professional actors forced from war-torn nations exile, and whose recent focus on intercultural topics and contemporary social and political conflicts can be traced here: https://gorki.de/en/programme/2019/12/all

9 For example, Dea Loher's *Unschuld* (2003), in which illegal immigrants Fadoul and Elisio are presented as already guilty of letting a woman drown herself upon their arrival.

10 One report from a colleague on a full performance of this play alerted me to the potential problem of resistance from students who felt similarly coerced into to playing roles assigned to them; another experienced outright rejection of the play due to the presence of stereotypes and of a gun in a classroom setting.

References

Apter, Emily. *Against World Literature: On the Politics of Untranslatability*. London; New York: Verso, 2013.

Brecht, Bertolt. *Anmerkungen zur Oper Aufstieg und Fall der Stadt Mahagonny*. In *Gesammelte Werke*, vol. 17, Frankfurt am Main: Suhrkamp, 1967.

Brecht, Bertolt. *Kurze Beschreibung einer neuen Technik der Schauspielkunst, die einen Verfremdungseffekt hervorbringt*. In *Gesammelte Werke*, vol. 22.2, Frankfurt am Main: Suhrkamp, 1967, 641–659.

Brecht, Bertolt. *Werke: Große kommentierte Berliner und Frankfurter Ausgabe* (BFA). Werner Hecht, Jan Knopf, Werner Mittenzwei and Klaus-Detlef Müller, ed. Frankfurt am Main: Suhrkamp, 1998–2000.

Geißler, Rainer. "Sozialer Wandel in Deutschland." *Informationen zur politischen Bildung*, vol. 4, no. 324, 2014, 4–83.

Der Spiegel. "Integration: Merkel erklärt Multikulti für gescheitert." *Der Spiegel*, October 16, 2010. Retrieved Dec. 28, 2018 from http://www.spiegel.de/politik/deutschland/integration-merkel-erklaert-multikulti-fuer-gescheitert-a-723532.html

Der Spiegel. "PISA-Analyse: Sind die deutschen Schüler doof?" *Der Spiegel*, December 13, 2001. https://www.spiegel.de/lebenundlernen/schule/die-pisa-analyse-sind-deutsche-schueler-doof-a-172357.html

Erpulat, Nurkan and Hillje, Jens. *Verrücktes Blut*, nach dem Film "La Journée de la Jupe". von Jean-Paul Lilienfeld. Reinbek: Rowohlt, 2010.

Even, Susanne. "Multiple Hotseating." *Scenario*, vol. 5, no. 2, 2011, 106–107.

Gramling, David. "The New Cosmopolitan Monolingualism: On Linguistic Citizenship in Twenty-First Century Germany." *Die Unterrichtspraxis/Teaching German*, vol. 42, no. 2, 2009, 130–140.

Kaminer, Wladimir. *Russendisko*. Munich: Manhattan, 2000.

Kömürcü, Onur. *Postmigrant Theatre and Cultural Diversity in the Arts: Race, Precarity and Artistic Labour in Berlin*. Doctoral thesis, Goldsmiths, U of London, 2016.

Kramsch, Claire. *The Multilingual Subject: What Foreign Language Learners Say about their Experience and Why it matters*. Oxford: Oxford UP, 2009.

Landry, Olivia. "German youth against Sarrazin: Nurkan Eruplat's *Verrücktes Blut* and *Clash* as political theater of experience." *51 Jahre der Gastarbeitermigration in Deutschland*. Seyda Ozil, Michael Hofmann and Yasemin Dayıolu-Yücel, ed. Göttingen: Vandenhoeck & Ruprecht, 2012, 105–122.

Langhoff, Shermin and Ohr, Kristina. "Theater kann eine Identitätsmaschine sein": Interview mit Shermin Langhoff." In *nah & fern: Das Kulturmagazin für Migration und Partizipation*, vol. 43, 2010, 18–23.

Layne, Priscilla. "Between play and mimicry: the limits of humanism in *Verrücktes Blut*." *Colloquia Germanica*, vol. 47, no. 1/2, 2014, 31–57.

Loher, Dea. *Unschuld. Das Leben auf der Praca Roosevelt*. In *Theater heute*, vol. 44, no. 10, 2003, 47–59.

Mieder, Wolfgang. "'Entflügelte Worte.' Modifizierte Zitate in Literatur, Medien und Karikaturen." *Kulturelle Motivstudien*, vol. 16. Vienna, 2016.

Obermueller, Nele. "Does German theater have a race problem?" *Exberliner*, May 30, 2012. http://www.exberliner.com/culture/stage/does-german-theatre-have-a-race-problem/

OECD-PISA. Programme for International Student Assessment. PISA 2015 Results. Paris: Organisation for Economic Co-operation and Development (OECD)., 2015. https://www.oecd.org/pisa/PISA-2015-Germany-DEU.pdf

Sharifi, Azadeh. "Postmigrantisches Theater. Eine neue Agenda für die deutschen Bühnen." *Theater und Migration: Herausforderungen für Kulturpolitik und Theaterpraxis*. Wolfgang Schneider, ed. Bielefeld: Transcript, 2011.

Sharifi, Azadeh. "Theatre and Migration. Documentation, Influences and Perspectives in European Theatre". *Independent Theatre in Contemporary Europe*. Bielefeld: Transcript Verlag, 2017, 321–416.

Sieg, Katrin. "Race, guilt and innocence: Facing blackfacing in contemporary German theater." *German Studies Review*, vol. 8, no. 1, 117–134.

Tagesspiegel. "*Verrücktes Blut* im Ballhaus Naunynstraße: 'Mensch, das ist ja besser als Hollywood!' *Tagesspiegel*, December 5, 2011. https://www.tagesspiegel.de/kultur/verruecktes-blut-im-ballhaus-naunynstrasse-mensch-das-ist-ja-besser-als-hollywood/4157030.html.

The National Standards Collaborative Board. World-Readiness Standards for Learning Languages. 4th ed. Alexandria, VA: ACTFL, 2015. https://www.actfl.org/sites/default/files/publications/ standards/World-ReadinessStandardsforLearningLanguages.pdf

Tillmann, K., Dedering, K., Kneuper, D., Kuhlmann, C., and Nessel, I. *PISA als bildungspolitisches Ereignis: Fallstudien in vier Bundesländern* (Vol. 43). Wiesbaden: VS Verlag für Sozialwissenschaften, 2008.

Appendix A. Approaching the folksongs

Discussing Brecht's use of music and songs as *Verfremdungseffekte* is an effective way to approach the use of folksong in *Verrücktes Blut*. Taking as an example Brecht and Kurt Weill's use of song in *Die Dreigroschenoper*, the songs themselves serve to interrupt, rather than underscore, the dramatic action. This is also marked by the appearance of actor-singers at the front of the stage; special lighting to illuminate the singers and the accompanying instruments; and projected song titles. A brief review of the most famous of Kurt Weill's songs, "Die Ballade von Mackie Messer" from *Die Dreigroschenoper* suffices to convey the alienating effect of the music itself (outlined in ch. 5).

Introduction of folksongs in *Verrücktes Blut*: it is important to highlight the Brechtian technique of interrupting the dramatic action by stepping forward to sing. In order to consider the potentially harmonizing aspect of these folk songs, it is useful to consider the role of the national anthem, and the German national anthem in particular. *Wann singt man normalerweise die Nationalhymne? Zu welchen Anlässen? Welche Gefühle evoziert das Singen einer Nationalhymne?* Then we discuss images of the national team singing the anthem from the last two World Cups: *Wer singt? Wer singt nicht? Warum (nicht)*?

To press the issue further, introduce some quotations from the press expressing outrage at their refusal to sing. Ask students to consider the relevance of singing for community, and the specific etymological relation in German of singing and music to the notion of belonging by brainstorming: *Was assoziieren Sie mit den Verben "hören"? Welche anderen Verben oder Nomen leiten sich davon ab?* At the very least, spontaneous responses may include verbs such as *gehören, zuhören and anhören*, and with additional prodding might also recall *angehören, zugehören* and the nominal forms *Angehörige, Staatsangehörigkeit*, and *Zugehörigkeit*.

With this in mind, it is instructive to view the DVD in order to consider the songs' placement and effect – how "well" the cast sing together (in this recorded performance), with perfect pronunciation and perfectly in tune. Lines of inquiry include: do you think the songs effect a momentary relief from the growing tensions? Do you get a sense of "being together"? Or rather, given the recent furor surrounding the refusal of certain members of Germany's *Nationalelf* (national soccer team) to sing, is it possible to reconsider the function of the songs in terms of their potential for coercion.

Appendix B

Analytical and reflective writing

1. *In* "Verrücktes Blut" *werden Vorurteile und Klischeevorstellungen über Jugendliche mit Migrationshintergrund reflektiert. Welche Klischees scheinen eher kritisch dargestellt oder sogar demontiert zu werden, und welche Techniken werden hierfür eingesetzt (z.B. Parodie, Übertreibung)?*

2. *Erläutern Sie Hasans Monolog am Ende des Dramas* Verrücktes Blut. *Wie ist sein Monolog – der auch aus Schiller zitiert – zu interpretieren und was bedeutet dieser Monolog für seinen Charakter und für Drama als Ganzes?*

3. Verrücktes Blut *spielt sich in einem Klassenzimmer – also in einer Lehreinrichtung – ab. Erläutern Sie die Funktion von Schiller für den Unterricht sowie für das ganze "Spiel im Spiel." Was will die Lehrerin mit der Lektüre von Schiller erreichen, und inwiefern gelingt es ihr? Inwiefern Was soll der Zuschauer daraus lernen?*

Index

Lightning Source UK Ltd.
Milton Keynes UK
UKHW022349210622
404777UK00003B/32